RECLAIMED

A Memoir

ANTONIA WILLIAMS-GARY

ISBN: 978-1-943563-19-7

Published by MLStimpson Enterprises

P.O. Box 1592

Cedar Hill, TX 75106

Cover art by Anthony Harris, 42 ZOOM PHOTOGRAPHY

Cover design by K and T Graphic Designs

Author photo by Chrystal Garrett, Beauty is...

CONTENTS

ACKNOWLEDGMENTS

First, I want to recognize and honor my sons, Kito and Issa Gary, who blessed me with their support and encouragement by telling me, "Mom, this is your story, and you need to tell it." They still hug me even after reading all the 'bad' parts.

Thank you for the support from my loving daughters in law, Stephanie Darty-Gary and Erica Davis-Gary.

This book was read, edited, and commented on by several wonderful women- all of whom I call "friend": Gwen Armstrong Johnson; Sandy Howard, PhD.; Kaaren Johnson Street; Lynette Williams-Austin; Kerry McGlynn, Ruth Williams, and Dianne Saulney Gaines (read in part).

Thanks also to all who served on my cheering squad until this work was completed: Bobby Klein; Rene Higgenbotham Brooks; Collette Grimes; Toni Randolph; Carol Hall; Rosanne Gordon; Sandra Bontemps; Alicia Casity; Elizabeth Chapman; and, never last or least, Robbie Bell.

There are also a few good men to thank: Anthony H., David W., O. Maxwell, "New York John", Mr. Broadway, Willie G. and Richard Williams. Thank you all for caring enough.

FOREWORD

Ms. Antonia Williams-Gary has written an outstanding memoir which has an enduring quality that will accompany it.

As an applied sociologist, I would recommend this book to anyone interested in women's issues, the black family, the social construction of race and gender, and identity theories.

While reading it, I laughed. I cried. At times my jaw dropped and my eyebrows raised in surprise by Ms. Gary's fiercely candid, insightful and unapologetic story. She shares her triumphs and disappointments in a way that allows the reader to identify with her.

In many ways this is a story about identity. It reflects the social problems, concerns and triumphs that gender, race/ethnicity, status and family articulate. It entails the dual nuance of social life; on one hand, of the individual having experiences, and on the other hand, the same individual sharing how she experienced being observed. The story also reflects how one's society constructs meaning from a peripheral point of view and how that peripheral view affects the way a person experiences social life.

I was also taken with the reverence that Antonia has for family history and culture which she juxtaposed against a segregated America. She describes how her African American-Bahamian background shaped, informed and contradicted her sense of self while being enthralled in a tumultuous marriage with an African American man who held a high profile public office.

The historic and contemporary social value of this story jumped off the page.

Antonia and her husband were both determined and driven; culturally and socially informed by their status as people of color. However, both responded to their historic similarities from different ends of the social continuum. Thus, making Antonia's story an important addition to the literature on contemporary, African-descended women, and expands the known, yet often missed reality that minority (race/ethnicity and gender) populations have a broad range of experiences.

Ms. Gary's narrative illustrates how social constructs (social collective arrangements) such as patriarchy and race influenced the autonomy of her and her husband, denoting many nuances at the intersections of race/ethnicity and gender; social constructs which often overshadowed their public image and their private lives. On numerous instances, Antonia perceived herself as 'other', such that her real experiences became secondary to the story created under public scrutiny and public demands.

However, Ms. Gary's narrative is also a story of capitulation and triumph against social labeling that often acts to silence women's voices in an attempt to make them invisible.

Ms. Gary is willful, compassionate and passionate about life. She is also confident and demanding. And while our American society has become more multicultural, many of the historic social problems discussed in this book are still prevalent.

-Sandra L. Howard, PhD

INTRODUCTION

This is a story about how I survived an emotionally abusive marriage.

Much of my story takes place in Miami, Florida, my birthplace, and during a period (1970s-1990s) when the City was undergoing a turbulent transition from being a small, near southern town, to becoming a major international center of tourism and commerce.

My husband, Howard Gary was a municipal administrator; an expert in public finance, when he was appointed City Manager of Miami (1981-1984). He was engaged in the vagaries of police-sparked riots, Haitian and Mariel (Cuba) refugees, booming economic growth, white flight, and the stench of third world politics.

I was his helpmate.

His style was that of a bully. At times, at the office, that served him well. But not so much at home.

I remained caught in the tender trap of that marriage far too long- twenty three years.

It took me a long time to realize that emotional abuse is real. After all, he never hit me and I had no external scars to show. I have since learned that I am not alone and that many women in this country, regardless of station and standing, have suffered similarly from being under the power and control of men; especially men in lofty positions.

So, this story is for all the survivors; particularly those who cannot get off the never- ending spin of the Power and Control Wheel which encompasses a wide range of abuse: physical, sexual, as well as emotional.

Women of color are uniquely vulnerable to emotional abuse. Too often in hiding, like me, they may resort to drugs, alcohol, and/or food addictions, and/or turn to the church for comfort.

My story tells about my path to freedom from harmful attachments; starting with my divorce and followed by a decade-long journey toward peace and serenity.

I hope everyone who reads this Memoir will take away some lesson; for their own personal use, or to help another woman who may still be trapped.

DEDICATION

*To my sons, Kito and Issa, and my grandchildren Issa Jr., Peyton, Isaiah,
Eriss, Sydney, Enzo and Corinne. I love you.*

"If God said, pay homage to everything that has helped you enter my arms,
there would not be one experience of my life, not one thought,
not one feeling, not any act, I would not bow to."
Rumi

BOOK ONE

ON BEING MRS. GARY

LOVE AND LOATHING UNDER PUBLIC FIRE

MIAMI, FLORIDA JANUARY, 1984, AROUND MIDNIGHT.

The shrill of the telephone ring pierced through my quiet rest. It was in easy reach. I answered it before the second ring. It was the dead of night, but I knew it could only be Howard, my husband calling.

"Hey."

"Don't come downstairs. You need to stay in the room," he spoke hurriedly. "I'll be coming in with some people from the office."

He hung up before I could respond.

What now?

I checked the clock. It was later than his usual check in time.

Despite the lateness of his call, I was alert. Over our nearly sixteen years together, I had developed an intuitive alarm which usually awakened me ten to fifteen minutes before Howard arrived, and no matter how late the hour, I seldom went into a deep sleep whenever I expected him to come home.

Usually, I'd use this grace period to prepare: for his wish to talk; to make love; or, to just enjoy some other small comfort I could give him.

I instinctively checked the condition of my hair, and which night gown I was wearing: sexy, sheer, or just plain cotton?

Cotton. Hair still in place. I'll wait until later to change.

I never told Howard "no" to sex, and I was usually always prepared. I gave as good as I got. He kept me seduced; the tender trap remained baited for a long time.

Up to this time, our marriage had worked. Happily? Debatable. Successfully? Yes, by most standards if material measurements were used. It had lasted long enough for me to become immune to his sharp and clipped directives. He didn't have to repeat himself for me to know what to do, or, as on this night, what not to do.

His barking took no skin off my back, but the barbs still stung. Each verbal jab rubbed at the tender wounds lingering just below the surface; raw from years of prolonged vulnerability.

"Who does he think he is?" I felt put out, being told to stay upstairs. It didn't much matter to me how Howard attempted to marginalize my existence. By now, I had not only learned how to resist him, I had cultivated a carefully devised and subversive way to fight back: I simply cared less.

Yet, I felt compromised. I sat upright in our bed.

Here I am, in my own home, after midnight, and told to 'stay in my place'.

But, that's what I did. I stayed.

I stayed: too long in love; too long in my marriage; and too long in that room.

Dammit! Sixteen years is a long time to remain tenuous about anything. When am I going to finally see the end? Ever?

Howard arrived home about fifteen minutes after his call. He was closely followed by several others, presumably from his office.

I knew his job of being the City Manager of Miami was 24/7. It was never done. On this night, he had been working in his position for nearly three years, but to me, it already felt like a lifetime. Our lives had been forever altered since the appointment, but I could not have imagined how this night would result in another shift of great proportions.

During the early years of his tenure, I enjoyed having a front row seat to many important decisions affecting the City of Miami. After-hour meetings to conduct city business at my house were nothing new. Oftentimes, I had prepared pot luck dinners of spaghetti, chili or other large bowl dishes for the occasional after hour budget planning meetings, or meetings on other key administrative matters.

At times, it felt more like an extended family gathering around my dining room table: I played hostess, Howard sat at the head, several assistant City managers, department directors, administrative assistants, and varying levels of other staff, sat all around.

This one was uniquely marked by its starting hour.

12:15 AM

I strained to hear his familiar footsteps come up the stairs, hoping that he'd put his head in our bedroom to at least say "hello." He did not. Instead I heard the front door being opened and closed. The big, old door made a solid thud at each closing. I stopped counting after a half-dozen times.

Fully awake and alert, I couldn't help thinking: *Howard may have been the City Manager, but I am the City Manager's Wife.*

I quickly confirmed my reality: the other half of Miami's 'first black couple', and also the mother to our two sons; Kito, seven years old, and Issa, nearly two. The boys were upstairs asleep. I could tell by their low snores that not much could disturb their rest. I smiled at the thought of my sons: *they were my anchor.* I had grown to depend on their dependence on me. I was grounded in, and I relished my role as mother.

It was very dark, and I couldn't see much detail. But from the second floor window of our bedroom, I could clearly hear cars pulling up to the front of the house. From my perch, it sounded orderly. They began to arrive in quick succession. I strained, but I saw a dozen or so cars parked along the street in tight formation, some spilling over onto the small lawn in front of my house. The sound of car doors slamming indicated how each vehicle carried multiple passengers.

Our house was built in 1936 and the original hardwood floors were uncovered, and every sound was magnified. It was difficult and expensive to keep the hardwood buffed, and I cringed at the sound of chairs from the living/family rooms hastily dragged around the dining room table.

I could hear folks scurry across the twenty foot expanse between the front door and the dining room, directly below my bedroom. Each set of staccato footsteps echoed with a unique signature. They were indistinguishable by status or gender, but they were heavy with urgency. There must have been, by my estimation several dozen gathered below. There were vague and teasing reverberations foretelling the weight of the matter at hand.

"God damn," someone uttered loudly.

"Oh, hell no!" An unknown voice snapped.

I remained as still as possible. Hard as I tried, I could not decipher any distinct thread of conversation. Hushed, anxious murmurings floated up the stairs on clouds of cigarette smoke. I had quit smoking two years before, but suddenly, the idea of a drag and a drink felt very appealing.

Low undertones droned on steadily. I felt and heard constant movement of people below. The refrigerator door was repeatedly opened and closed.

"Bring me one of those," I heard an unfamiliar voice shout out an order.

They are helping themselves to the canned soft drinks! Those people are foraging around for refreshments.

The parade of arriving cars kept up in a quiet, steady pace. Hurried footsteps echoed off the floors as more folk arrived and joined the business already underway. The heightened level of activity affirmed that the previous day's transactions could not wait for the next day's start of business.

My gut flipped at the notion of how our circumstances were about to change, again. I did not welcome another change. There had already been so many iterations in my life with Howard. I just wanted peace and stability. But here I was, an unbound hostage in my own house, restricted to passive listening. And adding insult, I had been uninvited.

Never mind that.

For almost three years, I had been taking a large measure of comfort from the many benefits I received from being Howard's wife; the city manager's wife. I enjoyed the deference given me across all sectors of society. I also expected the comforts and security inured to Howard's position would continue to flow to me and our sons, at least for a little while longer. I used his title and position as a salve to help soften the scar tissue wrapped around my heart, only to now have my wounds aggravated by the unknown threat wafting up the stairs in the middle of night.

As Howard's wife, I stood next to him in public, and I remained one of his most avid supporters. I went through the motions. I had a vested interest in his success. Of paramount importance, my children's welfare depended on him doing well. And, my face had to be saved at any additional costs. The total price I paid would add up quickly.

I glanced at the clock: *1:00 AM.* Time was passing slowly.

Muffled sounds of movement intermingled with an occasional outburst. My patience was being strained.

"Mother fuck!" It was Howard; his voice unmistakable. He was renowned for his cursing.

"Screech!"

I groaned at the thought of seeing the deep scratch from yet another chair being forcefully dragged across the wood floor.

I snatched at thin whispers.

I might be needed downstairs. What if there is another riot starting? Had something bad happened to Castro? Is the media gearing up for another assault on Miami? Perhaps, I could actually make a contribution.

Beginning in the early 1980s, Miami had suffered from a continuous threat of riots and civil disturbances. Additionally, there was the ongoing bombardment of immigrants from throughout the Caribbean, South and Central America, and deep, systemic corruption in its private businesses, and across the public sectors.

The November 23rd, 1981 edition of <u>Time Magazine</u> had declared on its cover: Miami, Paradise Lost. After two major urban riots, the Mariel Boatlift; street shoot-outs by the 'Cocaine Cowboys', the River Cops' corruption scandal, not to mention the popular Miami Vice television show, and a plethora of other cringe-worthy characterizations, Miami teetered on the verge of either greatness, or implosion.

I could only speculate what the caldron of the times in this special place must be cooking up downstairs: a recipe for more disaster?

Howard had inherited this mess. *But we went in with our eyes wide open.*

My bedroom was growing smaller. I felt imprisoned and I grew more conscious of my breathing: *was it too loud?* I couldn't pretend to be asleep, and I was reluctant to use my own bathroom, lest I later be accused of eaves-dropping.

That's insane!

"This is my house." I uttered to no one.

I was startled at the squeal of tires from more cars pulling up to the house. These new arrivals were in a really big hurry. Their racing footsteps registered an even greater sense of urgency than the earlier ones.

I hope our neighbors are not being disturbed.

By now it was after 2:00 in the morning.

I grew more anxious. Time slowed to a crawl in the closeness of my room. Finally, the activity peaked. It felt like forever, but after about another hour, the group began to leave.

The sets of footsteps grew faint. The cars began to peel off, one by one.

The meeting had ended.

Howard came upstairs.

One quick glance at his partial state of undress; rolled back sleeves, loosened tie, and opened top shirt buttons, and I knew. Howard had brought home more than either of us could have bargained for.

"What's going on?" I whispered. Even though everyone had left, I still felt under siege.

It was almost 3:00 a.m.

"I had to get rid of Harms." He sounded defeated.

Kenneth Harms had been appointed as the police chief shortly before Howard was selected as Manager. Howard had inherited him. Kenneth Harms belonged to a different administration, and was considered part of the 'old guard'. It was an uneasy fit from the beginning. Being a Police Chief is like sacred duty in large cities, and getting rid of one is tantamount to declaring war on the establishment.

Howard was Machiavellian in his relationship with Harms. Howard was like that. Clever. Deceitful.

To cultivate him, Howard became motorcycle riding buddies with Harms. They went out on long rides, sometimes overnight, nearly every weekend for almost a year.

Once I had asked him, "What's with all the Harley stuff? You have a Honda." I hated all the paraphernalia he bought to ride with Harms and their third mate, City Commissioner, J.L. Plummer. There was a leather vest, chains, a pocket book, etc.

"I need to at least look the part." He replied.

Howard, Harms, and J.L. Weekend bikers. I called them the unholy trio.

I wondered what had happened to their frequent weekend rides. They hadn't gone out much in the past few weeks.

"Why couldn't it wait until tomorrow? You've fired people before." I watched him slowly undress. "Because it would be too dangerous." He looked tired.

"We had to change the entire police department, change all the locks and computer codes, and, we had to reschedule the shifts for all of Harms' loyal officers before I could call him."

Then it clicked with me: *police + guns = danger*.

"You know the City has tons of weapons, ammunition, automatic guns, and tanks. And Harms had a personal army at his disposal."

I knew the City of Miami had amassed an arsenal to rival some small countries. The stockpiling began in response to the 1980 and 1982 police-sparked riots; and also in response to the flood of prisoners who had been released by Castro during the 1981 Mariel boatlift.

We were ready for a war.

Howard's shoulders slumped. "I had to appoint a new chief of police."

It was well within Howard's purview and authority as City Manager to hire and fire all department directors without having to get the approval of the City Commission. There were five elected officials, which included the Mayor.

For decades, the City had been governed by a strong manager/weak mayor structure. Only three votes were required for a majority to conduct the business of the City. But that governance model became more and more problematic as the elected officials became a majority Hispanic/Cuban; folks who had inherited a vastly different political legacy.

The police chief's position was sensitive. Harms was supported by the majority of the Commissioners.

"All hell is going to break loose, but at least no one will get shot," Howard collapsed.

There was no need for me to change gowns. *There'd be no sex tonight.*

I slept fitfully.

৩৯৩

THE TWO INCH HEADLINES IN THE LATE MORNING EDITION OF the Miami Herald read: **Gary Fires Harms.**

Harms' supporters in the police rank and file immediately declared war on Howard, and everyone else who supported his action. Sharp divisions were drawn along loyalty lines.

Political swords rattled. Threats flew. But no guns were fired.

My fears were confirmed. This was a life-changing event; so much more than I could have projected. For the next two years, a set of new nightmares were visited upon me and my family. I felt partly responsible; because I had stayed- in my room; in my house; in my marriage.

A foreshadowing of things had already taken place in early 1983. According to the news shapers, Miami had morphed into a 'banana republic', and we were in the middle of the growing list of incivilities.

People United to Save Humanity (P.U.S.H.), a new group primarily made up of black Cubans (who knew there were so many?), invited us to attend a dinner where they declared their support for Howard, and then Mayor Maurice Ferre.

Howard, well into his second year as Manager, was the guest of honor.

Ferre was preparing to run for a third term.

Notably, Ferre was not Cuban, but of Puerto Rican descent. He had been involved in Miami politics for decades, and was popular.

Just a few weeks prior to the dinner, the Commission convened at a special hearing to fire Howard. The Commission's action put the entire community on edge: the black community organized in protest; the 'downtown' leadership feared another civil disturbance; the Cubans were divided in their loyalty.

Masses of people stormed City Hall for the Commission meeting.

The blacks, many who arrived on chartered buses, took over almost all of the seating in the Commission chambers.

"Here comes Mrs. Gary", a voice rose above a small crowd. I was walking toward City Hall.

I was intercepted outside the building by a well-meaning black man who excitedly declared to me: "You're Howard's wife. You know he's ours, so you're ours too." I know he meant no harm, but his remark made my blood run cold. I did not want to belong to them. What they could not possibly know is that I didn't want to be Howard's either.

I kept my game face on. *Never let them see you sweat*, was my incessant internal mantra. I chanted the refrain over and over as I sought out a place to sit down inside the commission chambers.

There was standing room only. The restless crowd spilled over into the ante room and out into the parking lot as the hearing got underway.

People jockeyed seats to let a few recognized 'leaders' from the community get inside. I was escorted to the front row.

"You can't fire him. He's doing a good job for us", and similar shouts punctuated the Chambers, sometimes drowning out the remarks from the dais as the Commission debated the terms of Howard's employment contract, and the merits of taking an immediate vote on the manager's performance.

Not-so-under- current mutterings about another riot if they fired Howard ricocheted around the room.

I glanced nervously around the room.

This is so bad, it's good. You better get used to this. I hope they all know Howard is a fighter, and he's not going down easy.

My gut performed its familiar gymnastics. I held down the bile, but I felt like spewing out my anxiety on the floor. I took shallow breaths. *I wish I had a crystal ball- to know for sure what was in store for us over the next few months.*

The hearing ended in Howard's favor. He wasn't fired, but he had been put on notice.

Just a few weeks after the aborted firing, it was the Cuban community, nee, the black Cubans' turn. P.U.S.H. (People United to Save Humanity) wanted to demonstrate their capacity for having political clout. Their agenda? Ostensibly, to be considered a force during the upcoming election, and to show outward support for the City Manager.

The dinner was held at one of the most popular restaurants in Little Havana. More than 200 persons were crowded in space designed for 150.

The room was filled with the elected, the appointed, and folk with dubious political influence. It was a very diverse crowd, with a spattering of a few 'white' liberal Cuban leaders.

Howard's mother was there. She looked radiant. I had given birth to Issa less than a year before, but I was back to my fighting weight.

"You are so beautiful tonight, Mrs. Gary."

"Gracias".

"Y su pello es muy bonita. Como estan los ninos?" *Yes. I know my hair is just right.*

"Gracias. Mis hijos, Kito y Issa, estan muy bien." *Of course my boys were alright.*

Over half the City Commission was present; three members.

Howard's core staff was also there; his Department Directors.

The dignitaries were seated on the dais at the front of the room. Howard's mother and I were seated at a table near the front where we had a bird's eye view of the dais.

Many levels of conversation were taking place, mostly *en espanol,* and I was able to keep up with them during the cocktail hour.

Suddenly, halfway through the dinner, a very dark-skinned, middle aged woman, dressed completely in white, made her way behind the dais and kissed Howard on the lips. The room suddenly started buzzing loudly. The speed and volume of the conversations in Spanish increased, and I completely lost track of what was being said. The tone and tension in the room shifted, but as hard as I tried, I couldn't put my finger on any specific source. Next, I noticed a black man, also in a white suit, hovering behind Howard.

Who were these people? I wondered.

"What's happening?" Mom asked. She knew I understood conversational Spanish. "What does the kiss mean?"

"Mom, they're talking too fast and I can't understand them."

No one offered me any detailed explanation. After only a few moments, the dinner resumed with no further disruption.

The following week, photos from the event were delivered to our house. I hadn't noticed it at the time, but the photos showed that Mayor Maurice Ferre was the only dais guest wearing a red tie. Blue was the universally established power color for men.

"SO WHAT'S WITH THE RED TIE?" I ASKED HOWARD. HE WAS dressing to appear before another specially-called City Commission, once again scheduled to take a vote to fire him, or not. This was the second attempt in less than two years.

"You remember the P.U.S.H. dinner last month? Well the woman who kissed me was supposed to put a curse on me."

My mouth fell open.

As it turned out, the woman, Caridad, was one of the most revered Santeria priestesses in town. The man with her, Mr. Williams, was a well-respected Babalao, a Santeria priest.

"Someone hired Caridad and Mr. Williams to be at the dinner, and I have it on good authority that Ferre has his own personal Babalao, in New York."

Oh God, no. Ferre?

"So, I got myself a Babalao who told me to wear red, for protection, like Ferre had on the night at dinner."

I didn't know whether to laugh or cry.

"Oh Lord," I muttered. "Does this mean you are practicing Santeria now?"

"No, but I have to fight fire with fire," Howard shot back as he artfully tied the red shield around his neck. He then headed out to do combat with the multiple forces lined up at City hall: the known Commissioners and their minions, and the unknown dark spirits.

Howard already had a large, beautiful collection of self-tied bow ties, to which he then added every shade of red he could find. He could never be satisfied having just one of anything, and that included everything.

Miami politics was shot through and through with racial,

language, and economic divisions. And now, another front had been added: the battlefield of an unconventional religion.

In fact, the battle was fought all the way to the US Supreme Court which granted the right of the Santeria church to use live animal sacrifices in religious ceremonies.

Ironically, an often told joke was how all Cubans who practice Catholicism use Santeria as a backup. It was not unusual to enter a Cuban household to find both a hanging crucifix and one of the Orishas (African saints) displayed. Just in case.

As it turned out, the person who brought the case to the higher courts had been one of my former neighbors: Santero Pacheco. At first, I was unaware of his status as a Priest.

While still my neighbor, Pacheco, hosted what I initially thought were just great parties. His house was behind mine. The music coming from his yard was heavy on drumming; the beats were hypnotic, and his guests chanted into the night.

I couldn't help but move to the rhythm of the drums.

What struck me most about Pacheco's guests was how very diverse they were. Some of them parked in front of my house, and I watched as they pulled up in late-model, expensive cars, and showed off other outward signs of material wealth, i.e., clothes, jewelry, and elaborate hairstyles, worn by men as well as women.

The Miami style was real. The costumes on the popular show, Miami Vice, copied the residents, not vice versa.

So, there it was! Miami's third-world character was unmistakable, and undeniable. But this popular, unconventional religious practice was the last straw for many folks. A sharp turn up of negative rhetoric on some English radio talk shows reflected residents' frustrations.

So-called Anglo-Americans began an exodus out of Miami, prompting the display of one popular bumper sticker which read: **Will the last American leaving Miami please bring the flag.**

Miami's vice or virtue?

Everyone was under siege; competing ethnic/language/racial interests; declining economy; third-world characteristics; declining white-middle class; and under the leadership of what the Miami Herald labeled a brash and uppity black City Manager.

I could not guess where this would lead.

⚜

PARADISE LOST AND FOUND; AND LOST AGAIN: MAY 1983

"Reagan is a racist," Howard shouted at the end of an address given by the President during one of his many visits to Miami. Regan had come to talk about his trickle down economic theory.

Oh God! It's over now, for sure.

"What were you thinking?" I pounced when Howard got home later in the evening.

I needed a plausible explanation. Anything.

"Howard, its ok for you to be as brash and as uppity as you need to be on your job. I know how it keeps you on edge, but that was the President of the United States you called a racist."

I thought for sure our front door was going to get busted

down; and he would be hauled away and shot, or something equally horrible.

Paradise, indeed, was lost for me on that day.

"Baby, I was trying to speak out against his policies, which are racist."

"Well, I can't disagree, but did you have to be so ugly and shout it out at a public meeting?" I yelled.

"Shit, it just came out."

His remarks about the President set the conservative Cubans off in a fit of anger. They called for his removal from office. The English and Spanish language newspapers, radio talk shows-in both languages, and dozens of periodiquitos, the small Spanish-language newspapers (I called them the parakeets), were afire with rhetoric to get rid of him.

Fueled up and supported by the Cuban outcry, area Republicans and Reagan supporters joined in the call for his removal.

The media feasted at the trough Howard so freely provided.

It was awful. Our phone blew up from inquisitive reporters. Every day, for weeks, newspaper and television reporters, with cameras at the ready, showed up at our front door.

"Mr. Gary is not home, and Mrs. Gary is resting," Mrs. Ross, my housekeeper/babysitter/nanny, went into overdrive to keep the reporters at bay.

She and my dad served as the front line of defense for my children. They coordinated their schedules: Mrs. Ross kept them clean and fed, and daddy drove them to and from various sports practices and other after-school activities. It worked.

Howard tried to clean up his remark about Reagan. He

issued a statement, which I helped edit; explained the President's policies' negative impact on poor black folk, and what he meant was the policies were racist.

His feeble explanation didn't work.

One of the consequences of Howard's remark about Reagan was an increased number of threats on his life; over and above those he received after he fired Harms. A special unit of the Miami Police was assigned to him.

The unit, assigned 24/7, became an appended, inherited family. Like newly discovered relatives, having them around was bitter/sweet. It was not unusual for me to cook dinner for the group whenever Howard arrived home with them in tow. I served them along with our children. The regulars included Major Jimmy Burke, now a Reverend, Major Caroline Clark, who many thought would become the first black woman police chief, and Officer Christmas, who later completed his PhD.

They, and several others, became fixtures in our lives over the next year.

There were a few times when the police warranted extending their coverage to me and our children when Howard had to go out of town on City business.

On one such occasion, a friend of mine and I had tickets to attend the Marvin Gaye Sexual Healing concert, when my assigned officers arranged a tag team to cover me while they went home to change their clothes so they could look the part as our 'escorts' to the event.

"I'm not going with you if they ride with us." My friend was furious. I grew frustrated thinking I'd have to miss the concert.

"I will not ride in the car with you," I declared to my escorts.

"But, we have to be with you at all times, Mrs. Gary."

Ouch! There had to be another solution.

I agreed to take a two way radio if they let me drive myself. They followed closely. I played a silly game of hide and seek on the freeway, attempting to lose them on the busy expressway.

"Mrs. Gary, please slow down", the voice squawked. *This is going to be a long ride.*

"Remind me not to go anywhere with you again if you have those police with you all the time." My friend wanted to smoke her joint. I didn't approve. My preference came in liquid form. She did not drink. We were an odd pair.

"We lost them," I shouted as we pulled into a space in the crowded parking lot. We had momentarily shaken our escorts.

We dashed into the arena thinking we would remain incognito.

"Look again." My friend spotted the two officers several rows above us. They waved at us, smiling.

Of course! They were detectives!

I felt defeated. They had seen our tickets with our seat numbers. It didn't matter much, because their badges gave them access to any prime spot. They had a direct view of us during the entire concert.

Kill joys.

I became used to their presence.

But, it was not my first dance, up close, and personal with the police.

That took place in 1982. Howard was in his second year as

manager. On one Saturday, after being out all day shopping with my mom and the two boys, I drove up very fast in front of my house and parked on the curb, not in my driveway. We all needed to use the toilet; except for Issa. He was still in diapers.

Before I could get my car door opened, a large gun appeared in my face. It was holstered on the hip of a very tall man in civilian clothes. I froze.

"Who are you?" The gun with the man asked while showing me his badge at the same time.

"Look at that gun!' Kito, nearly seven, was impressed.

For a minute, I could not think straight. I began to mumble, much too fast.

"UmI'mMrs.GaryandIamcominghomeandthisismyhousethis ismymomthesearemychildrenandIlivehere," I gestured wildly, fumbling for my ID.

A large hand appeared inside my window and reached for my id. I still had not looked at his face.

The officer leaned inside my car window. We locked gazes as he examined my driver's license. His was a large, kind face. *But it was attached to the gun.* I could not reconcile the two opposing elements. Kito's excitement was growing. I could feel the very tight space in my VW growing smaller.

"Antonia what is going on?" mom nervously asked.

She leaned across me. "You're frightening my daughter and my grandsons," she talked up at the large policeman. She was a tigress, too.

"Not now, mom." I had gained a little control.

I pointed to myself and to my passengers, and in a more moderated speech, I said, "Officer, I came up to the house in a hurry because we all need to go to the bathroom," I gestured and spoke in slow motion. "This is my mother. These are my sons. Kito and Issa. As you can see from my ID, I am Mrs. Gary. And I live here."

He moved cautiously, stepping away from the car door.

A second man emerged from a vehicle which was parked on the other side of the driveway. He walked slowly toward my car.

He looks so young.

He had a round, cherubic face. He smiled sweetly and spoke with a slight accent. *Haitian? Yes, Haitian. He must be only one of a handful.*

I felt 'ok' with him. He was not so big, and I couldn't see his gun.

"Nice to meet you Mrs. Gary." He offered his hand to shake.

This was Officer Christmas.

After only a few moments, once properly identified, we were allowed into my own home. Officer Christmas helped us all get out of the car. He took Issa out of his car seat, and escorted me and my mom to the front door.

Hmmm. Old school, Chivalrous.

Christmas and the big officer stood outside waiting for us.

Bathroom break completed, I was better able to ask the officers a few questions.

"What are you all doing here? Is something wrong? Is Howard all right?"

"All we know is Mr. Gary has received a threat to his life and we have been assigned to the house."

"What about me and my boys?"

"Our job is to protect Mr. Gary and his house, Ma'am. You don't need to panic. When he is not here, Mr. Gary has his own personal detail."

"What am I supposed to do?"

"Just go about your business as usual."

Business as usual? They've got to be kidding!

❁

ONE DAY IN 1982, AND SHORTLY AFTER MY INITIAL encounter with what I began to refer to as our 'babysitters', I got a phone call. I was preparing dinner for me and the boys. Howard usually ate out before coming home. It was a quiet, late afternoon/early evening. It was still light outside. I had not noticed anything unusual.

"Hello."

"I don't want to alarm you Mrs. Gary, but the S.W.A.T. team is here at your house and we wanted to make you aware of our presence. You will not be able to see or hear anything, but please just know we are here," the male voice at the other end stated as a matter-of- fact.

Oh my! I can't get the boys alarmed. Where is Howard? The S.W.A.T. Team! What monsters were they fighting? Stay calm Antonia. At all costs, stay calm. He's never here when I need him. You can't let Kito and Issa know there's a threat.

"Thank you." I finished cooking dinner. We ate. I prepared the boys for bed. Howard finally arrived home, with his 'babysitters'.

"Howard, what is going on? Should me and the boys move?"

"Toni, I can't tell you what's going on, but you're safer now than ever. Just do what the police tell you."

Of course. Didn't everyone have the S.W.A.T. team show up on occasion?

Once, shortly after the S.W.A.T. team episode, the entire neighborhood got a taste of the police excitement surrounding our family.

The bomb squad arrived one Saturday, in the middle of the day. They brought a large, metal container which was used to detonate suspicious items, and parked it in the driveway.

Oh my God. Who's gonna believe this?

The neighbors crowded around our front yard and watched the experts go to work on a suspicious package they had retrieved near our house.

Where are the camera crews? Probably coming any minute now.

The problem? Someone had dropped a paper bag containing parts of a fresh killed chicken on the sidewalk which ran along the side of our house. Originally a bridle path from the early 1920s, the sidewalk ran several blocks- starting at the Miami River, adjacent to our property line. The proximity of the bag to our house was enough to trigger a call to the police from one of my neighbors who knew about such things.

Chicken parts could only spell one thing: a deadly curse.

Chicken parts. A bomb? Only in Miami.

Alas, there was no bomb- this time.

Living with a strong police presence became my business as usual. Sometimes I felt very annoyed, but at other times, really comforted.

❧

AFTER THAT FATEFUL NIGHT IN JANUARY 1984 WHEN Howard fired Harms, the police presence grew even larger, and even more intrusive.

"Baby, get dressed. We're going to see Nancy Wilson. I'll be there in thirty minutes." Howard often called me at the last minute for some of our dates. Not a problem; I always had the perfect outfit to wear.

When he arrived, he was accompanied by Major Carolyn Clark, one of the regular babysitters. Carolyn was one of Howard's high school classmates. I also knew her from when we both were High School debutants. She looked fantastic in her after-five dress, except her purse was oversized!

We had a front row table reserved at the beautiful Fontainebleau, Miami Beach.

Table for three? Check. Gun included? Check. It was concealed in her bag.

I must admit I grew to appreciate Carolyn, especially on the night she ran with me and Howard through the airport. The City had just concluded another grueling budget season; we were stressed beyond reason. Howard and I decided, at the last minute, to get away for the weekend. We ran late for the plane, but we got VIP treatment at the airport: our bags were expedited, and quickly checked.

"We have to hurry. The plane is leaving in ten minutes." Carolyn, who rode with us to the airport, took over.

The three of us ran through the terminal, when we stopped only for a very brief moment at the passenger's only checkpoint where Carolyn showed her badge and gun. After we were waved through, she continued running with us right up to the door of the plane. This was long before 9/11.

"Is that our bag?" Howard and I laughed as we watched our lone piece of luggage ride up the ramp. It was the last item to enter the plane.

Exciting? Yes. But exhausting.

Once I asked, "why does Howard need so much police protection?" The babysitters had just enjoyed my home cooking, again, and everyone was relaxed. Howard had gone upstairs to take a nap, his common practice. While he slept, everyone else tiptoed, lest we disturbed his rest. Once awakened, he'd go back to work regardless of the day or hour. There was no such thing as a normal, nine to five day while he was City Manager.

"Trust me. We would not be doing this if it was not necessary, and we didn't think the threats were not real." Officer Jimmy Burke bluntly shut me down. His explanation was enough for me, but I couldn't help think Howard was bringing this on himself, being himself: *calling the President of the United States a racist, firing the police chief, messing with Cuban politics, and walking around with a set of big ones.*

There would not be any more business as usual from late 1981 through 1984, when Howard left city hall, and not even then. It was always so bizarre.

Life in Miami was growing more insane. I needed some relief.

Having a third glass of wine during lunch sure helped.

❦

"Baby, can you believe my salary is more than double my age?" he was giddy. He was thirty four.

We were reminiscing about his climb to power.

"Well, you certainly worked hard, and your salary is on par with what other major cities pay their managers, right?"

"You damn right."

Initially, I had been proud of Howard when 'we' were appointed to the position of City Manager.

I say 'we' because I had been his help mate all along the way.

Early in his tenure as Manager, Howard began to get calls from around the country to make presentations to other municipalities and professional associations of public administrators. He accumulated a lot of recognition, and praise.

"Toni, can you believe they want me to come and speak at some conference? You know I'm not a good speaker. What do you think?"

"Go. Do you want me to help you write your speech?" I was still in the mode and mood to support his endeavors, and I wrote many of his public speaking presentations.

If he looks good, I'll look good.

Crazy? Still not as crazy as I got.

In 1982, at the end of his second year, The International City Manager's Association (ICMA), recognized Miami as the best managed city in the country.

It became widely publicized, when, after serving in his position for two years, Howard became the highest paid City

Manager in the Country. He was absolutely beside himself at times when we talked about his rise in fame, and accompanying fortune. But to me, he would remain, in word and deed, the little black boy from the projects.

His appointment came after our long trudge: starting with our leap-of- faith marriage in 1968; followed by 'our' graduate school experience at the University of Michigan; and after almost six years of laboring in the wasteland, aka the City of Newark, New Jersey.

I had strapped on for the ride, and I held on tightly, until I finally had to let go in order to remain alive.

I held secrets about him, about us. But those began seeping into the public eye, initially through the local, daily news-papers.

Speaking honestly, my gradual release on the marriage contract began in earnest shortly after Howard's appointment to City Manager, but I had emotionally disengaged from him long before.

I also realized shortly after his appointment how the socially stunted, once shy, and somewhat insecure man I married had changed his skin while occupying the offices of successively higher authority. He had transformed into a super bully.

My God, he really believes all the praise he's getting in the press.

Yes, he did have power and control over so much and so many. But, in just over a short three years, what I had already grown to loathe about him, and about our marriage contract, blew up into a nightmare from which I would not awaken for several more years to come.

Despite my inability to control his behaviors, and my eventual loss of myself, I remained convinced, if only I had better tools, I could have built a stronger defense against the tide ahead. I always thought I could fix everything. I nearly died trying.

ॐ

ON THE JANUARY NIGHT, 1984, WHEN HOWARD FIRED Harms, in addition to my full time job, I shouldered the day-to-day responsibility of making payroll for the staff at Fingertips; a chain of hair salons I had held ownership in along with nine other women: *The Dek Cartel*.

Fingertips opened in January, 1982, with great fanfare. The open house featured champagne, passed finger foods, and the popular Billy Rolle quintet performed in white tails. All of the Who's Who of black Miami celebrated with us. I was one tenth owner of a revolutionary change in the back hair care business in Miami.

Howard attended the opening.

"Howard, why don't you ever use the services of Fingertips? It looks bad for me." We had been operating for months; the other owners' husbands and boyfriends were regular customers.

"I don't have time for that bull shit. Ya'll just playing at being in business. I give it a year."

We'll see.

I thoroughly enjoyed my time as a business owner/operator. The Franchise included the opportunity to expand throughout Florida, and into the Bahamas.

I may earn enough to get my passport to personal financial security and independence.

I was prepared to give it my all, but I kept my day job with Miami Dade County.

Alas, under my leadership, Dek Cartel filed for bankruptcy protection less than three years after opening our first salon.

Through the bankruptcy, I proved to be stronger than ever. One particular exchange with our landlord was instructive and has forever stayed with me.

"How much will you take for us to just stay open for a few more months?" I asked the landlord. I wanted to be able to budget the right amount.

"Just bring us cash for the rent, Mrs. Gary," the landlord's agent said. "We don't want to be listed as a creditor."

"And bring it in person to our downtown office," he spoke softly into the phone. His voice sounded like he was a three pack-a -day smoker, and he quoted me a dollar figure only one tenth the 'normal' rent.

I was terrified on my first visit to the agent's office. The rental office, located on the fifth floor of a very old commercial building, had narrow hallways, low lighting, and a musky smell. There was no answer at the door, so I placed the envelope with cash in the slot and left.

"Thank you for the money," the same raspy voice called a few days later thanking me for paying the rent. I felt relief at first, but my anxiety grew throughout the bankruptcy proceedings. I was never asked to disclose this extra-legal arrangement to the Judge. He never once asked me how I was paying the rent for the salon.

Ask no questions, and get told no lies.

The bankruptcy tested me, except I remained in my marriage; weak and immobilized by my tender trap.

I had settled for being Mrs. Howard Gary.

One of the greatest benefits from carrying the title was I was released from the burden of needing to work. From all outward appearances, we had arrived into the upper middle class.

"Toni, you are just working for us to pay the IRS." Howard and Sujan, who had prepared our taxes a year after his appointment told me.

What did I do wrong?

Sujan Singh had worked with Howard in Newark and relocated to Miami with us. Under Howard's administration, Sujan became the Finance Director for the City of Miami and he had been preparing our taxes since we lived in New Jersey.

But I need to work to feel like I have some purpose other than just being your wife. That's what I got a degree for.

Solution? We acquired some tax sheltered rental property, and I continued to work.

Be somebody, and if you marry..............

I had always wanted a career, and it got jump-started in 1976 when I was pregnant with Kito. It got kicked into a higher gear after I had my second child in 1982.

So far, I was enjoying a good run: I had a professional positon; I was running a business, albeit a bankrupt one; I was a mother-twice; a daughter; a sister; and, a friend. I felt fulfilled in all my roles, and I remained tethered to Howard by a thread which was growing thinner; close to breaking.

Well, Howard did pay the bills, and there is always a little something left over.

However, no matter our appearances of success, in my family's eyes, I could never rest on my laurels. The second part of the family charge: if you marry, marry someone who will take care of you, continued to elude me; the directive had as much to do with my emotional well-being as it had to do with material well-being.

I worked and made very little money, comparatively. He worked and made a lot more money. The problem? I did not feel tenderly cared for by Howard.

How did I get to this place of pain and glory? It started a long time before midnight, January 1984.

❧ 2 ❧

THE BOY NEXT DOOR

"Who is that cute boy over there?" I asked Gwen, my best friend since I was 5 years old. She was standing next to me. He was standing alone in the corner of the high school gymnasium.

"Howard Gary. You want to meet him?"

"How do you know him?"

"My sister dated his brother. I met him once at my house."

I trusted her.

I liked his look. He was just over 6', and a little chubby, but athletic. He had a well-defined upper body. I could see the outline of his muscles against his crisply starched, short sleeved plaid shirt. I loved his arms. I saw a wisp of chest hair peek from the top of his shirt; like my dad's.

I soon learned about his uniform of choice- a perfectly ironed shirt, with a pair of equally starched jeans or khaki pants.

He had closely cut wavy hair. It was shiny and reminded me

of what my daddy always said about hair: "Keep it clean and well-groomed."

I later learned Howard was on the high school swim team. *Hmmmm. Explains his arms and his chest.*

There were nearly 150 high school senior girls and boys in the gym. We were the class of 1964, and we had gathered to practice for a cotillion; a well-established annual rite of passage for black girls to 'come out' into society. It was sponsored every year by one of the local Chapters of the National Sorority, Delta Sigma Theta, and it was considered a privilege to be invited to participate. The girls and their male escorts had all been selected for having good scholarship and high moral standards.

This was the first time the Sorority had invited girls from the Catholic schools, including me and three others. We were a curiosity.

"Does Howard have a girlfriend?" I asked three of Howard's classmates. One was my cousin Sandra Carey; another, Debra Perry, also my distant relative; and, Leslie Bridges, a girl who befriended me.

I got a clear "no" from each of them.

Peace, be still my heart. I was giddy!

Up to this point in time, I had had only one other 'boyfriend'. My parents would allow a boy from a good Bahamian family to come by my house to visit, but I still had not gone out on a date.

Howard stayed close to me during the weeks leading up to the cotillion. On the night of the ball, he performed the obligatory presentation 'waltz' with his assigned debutant, and then he joined our table. No one raised an eyebrow. His 'deb' was 'engaged' to a guy who had already gone off to college, who had come to town to attend her debut.

Several members of my immediate family, including my Aunt Lorraine, were in attendance at the Ball. They all seemed comfortable with me and Howard developing a romantic interest in one another.

The summer after High School graduation turned into a summer of romance. We talked about everything and we began to explore all the bases.

Young love.

❦

HOWARD CAME TO VISIT ME WHILE I WAS SPENDING A weekend at my Aunt Doris's.

He handed me a waded up bundle of cloth which I didn't recognize at first.

"What's this"?

"It's a shirt. Can you iron it for me?"

Was this some kind of rite of courtship? What's the point? To see what I was made of?

At the time I was at my Aunt Doris house. She was a champion ironer, but she was not at home for me to seek her advice.

I hesitated, but only for a minute. I proceeded to put up the ironing board and set the iron on a high temperature.

"I'm not very good at ironing", I confessed.

Daddy had done most of the family laundry- including the ironing, but I proceeded to go through the motions.

Actually, I was terrified. But I always thought I could do anything.

The joke was on both of us. One of the first things I had noticed about Howard was how particular he was about having just the right amount of starch in his clothing. His shirts and pants were always pressed with precision creases. I assumed he had his clothes professionally laundered.

Wrong. He did them himself!

Halfway through my ironing, I realized my grave error. I had set the temperature on the iron too high.

"I'm so sorry, but I burned your shirt," I mumbled and held out the ruined cloth.

He snatched it from my hands.

"Toni, I cannot afford to ruin a shirt. My family does not have as much money as yours," he sounded resentful

I had never felt more privileged than him. Where was the charge coming from?

Howard was upset about his shirt, but I was really torn apart. I was less upset about his tantrum, than I was disappointed in myself. I really wanted to show him I could iron; amongst other tasks.

Why? It's something females should know how to do, right? I wondered how many other tests I'd fail, as a woman.

It was a rare moment for me, but I began to doubt my own adequacy.

What else didn't I know?

"Don't worry, I won't ask you to do that again." I think he was trying to console me.

Thank God. I was relieved, but part of me looked forward to passing the next test.

I knew there would be another test. But what? When?

I know if I just put my mind to it, I'd be able to become an expert domestic or expert in anything. Just like always, before, in school.

⚜

"WHEN I FIRST MET YOU, I THOUGHT YOU WERE RICH."

He had come to pick me up in his mother's car. It was an older model Chevy.

"How did you get that impression?"

"Well, your mom was driving you around in a big Lincoln Continental! But I soon knew better after I visited your house and saw how dirty it was."

Ouch. That hurt.

"Oh no," I groaned.

My mom was never a housekeeper. In fact, my dad had done almost all of the domestic chores throughout my childhood, and beyond.

I had never been taught how to do anything domestic; there were few demands placed on me by my family except to make good grades. Of course, the aunts wanted me to also remain virtuous.

Our house was a mess.

When Howard first visited my home for our first date,

daddy had already moved to Cocoa Beach, and with him gone, the housekeeping fell to no one.

Our big car has brought nothing but tension. Howard's reaction was predictable.

"Bettye, why did you buy such a high maintenance car?" Daddy was perplexed when he came home on one of his regular weekend visits.

"The neighbors are going to think we came into some money." Daddy's comment reflected the sentiments of many middle class blacks at the time. Several of them kept their Cadillacs, or other luxury cars, garaged for use on Sundays only.

"I got a great deal on it, and we needed a bigger car," was all mommy could manage.

Daddy never thought mom made wise financial decisions except for her choice of private schools for all of her children.

❦

HOWARD WAS REALLY THE BOY NEXT DOOR I JUST HAD NOT met, yet.

He and I spent a lot of time together during our first summer of discovery, mostly in my Aunt Doris' pool, and under her supervision. What I did not realize, was he was also spending some in-between time with my cousin, Alice. We both attended Immaculata, and she and Howard met during the debutante practice.

It didn't take me long to learn how mine and Howard's families were tied together through social and community associations, starting before either of us were born. The educated middle class black community was insular. His mother's sister, Marian, and my mother's sister, Doris, had been best friends since the late 1930s when they both attended Florida A & M College (it was not a University when they attended). They were both elementary school teachers in Miami.

"We couldn't wait to get off from teaching on Fridays to go pick you up." Both aunts regaled in telling the stories about how, on weekends, the two friends would drive to Belle Glade, Florida, where my mother worked as a public health nurse with the migrant population. The round trip was over 200 miles.

"The conditions at the migrant work camps were too unsanitary for an infant," Doris and Marian concurred, so they brought me back to the city of Miami, where I remained for weeks at a time. My time was split between my mom's sisters: Doris, and Lorraine, whenever she visited from the Bahamas.

"You never cried." Aunt Lorraine was fond of telling me over her lifetime.

"You were the perfect baby. Your mother did not know what to do with you, so I kept you." Aunt Lorraine never gave birth to any children herself, but she had mother wit. Years later I would rely on her to keep my first born while I worked.

One of Howard's Uncles, Dr. Howard Hadley, and his family lived in *The Heights,* my neighborhood. He was a dentist.

I played with Dr. Hadley's children and was a regular visitor in their home. I used to hear rumors suggesting my dad and Dr. Hadley were gambling and drinking friends. Not too surprisingly, Dr. Hadley's first daughter, Carol, followed me into Immaculata High School, but it was a surprise when she also came to Marymount College. Carol and I were the same age, but I was two years ahead of her because of my early start in school.

"I always wanted to be like you," Carol once told me, "So I asked if I could go to the same schools you attended." Interestingly, in 1984, Carol's younger sister, Audrey, became my administrative assistant when I ran Greater Miami United. She completed my sentences and interpreted my awful handwriting.

After I was divorced from Howard, I once made the mistake of introducing Audrey as my ex-cousin-in-law.

"I am not your ex-anything. You did not divorce me. You divorced my cousin Howard. We are still family." Audrey was upset by my faux pas.

I felt terrible and vowed to not make that mistake again, with her, or any of Howard's family members. Audrey and I remain close, and I am still warmly welcomed by the Hadley clan as part of their family.

Growing up, Howard was part of a small group of boys who were pretty well known in our closed community. His cohort, including his brother, their cousins and friends, were reputed to be smart, handsome, and from good families: the Hadley's, the Dillard's, the Dobb's, and the Greene's, were professional, College- educated, and making something of themselves.

So, when Howard and I finally did meet at the rehearsal for the Debutant Ball, I felt I already knew him.

Early on in our relationship, Howard regaled me with stories of growing up in the ghetto.

"We were members of the Union gang. Harold was the leader."

I was incredulous. *A gang? He was from such a good family.*

"What kind of gang is that?"

"We wore Union brand overalls and mostly fought other gangs over having stuff and territory. Sometimes we got into real battles with weapons, but no one ever got shot."

"Did your mother know?" *I could not imagine she did not know.*

"No, my mom didn't know what I was doing," he told me. Didn't sound right.

Mom is too smart to not know what was going on with her sons.

"We kept our gang clothes hidden in our lockers to change into after school."

"I was in a gang too, at boarding school."

He laughed at my description of The Challengers- the good girls.

"Toni, you always try to make your bougie upbringing something it wasn't. You know you were spoiled and privileged."

Yeah, and you always paint a bleaker picture of your childhood than what it was!

In retrospect, I could more easily accept Howard's tales after having my own sons who told me about some of their on the edge of the law escapades when they were teenagers.

But from the beginning, I formed an image of Howard as being bad and bold. I liked it. In fact, I saw my dad in him. My dad was my first bad boy. Howard was my second smart, handsome, bad boy.

The fix was in. I was in love.

❧

DURING OUR SUMMER OF LOVE, HOWARD WORKED AS A certified Red Cross lifeguard. He earned a pretty decent fee. "Tips were usually good too," he bragged.

I had no inkling about work. I had a job once, for two weeks during the preceding summer. My cousin Alice had gotten a job waiting tables at a small café. My parents talked the owner into letting me tag along-I hated it. I was cured.

"Guess who I taught to swim this week?"

"Who?"

"Cassius Clay".

Clay, and his entire entourage, was staying at the Hampton House, a black-owned hotel where Howard life-guarded during the summer.

I was wide eyed as I listened to Howard tell me how the young boxer (he had not yet become Muhammed Ali) just sank to the bottom of the pool whenever he tried to swim.

"He didn't tip very well." Howard was saving for College. I had been awarded a full scholarship with a work study. Already, we valued money differently.

"You were both young." It was clear to me Clay didn't understand what was expected of him.

"No, he was cheap." Howard was unforgiving in his recount of his experience with the 'Champ'.

We used to trade stories about our experiences in Overtown, which remained the center of black social life during the many years of racial segregation. Adjacent to Miami's downtown, it housed many entertainment venues and outlets.

His were fond recollections of attending High School

football games between rivals Booker T. Washington and Northwestern HS, replete with competing marching bands. These notorious matchups were played out in the 'dust bowl', a rundown City-owned stadium.

"Aunt Marian would take me, Harold, our cousins, to see James Brown, Etta James, Aretha Franklin, and the other performers who came to town."

Those sounded so exciting to me.

As a retort, I told Howard about the time my family lived in Bermuda.

"I went to the matinees at the clubs to see the performers who came to the island."

"How'd you get so lucky?"

"Mom and dad knew most of the artists."

"Once, Daddy gave in when I asked him to take me to see Frankie Lyman and the Teenagers when they came to perform on the Island."

"What was so special about going?"

"Daddy thought I was too young to go to concerts. He teased me about their song, and asked me if I was a fool in love."

Howard and I both laughed.

"I had to rub daddy's head to get him to agree to take me."

"Once, only once, daddy took me to the 'dust bowl', but he told me he wouldn't take me back to one of those any time soon."

"Why? Were you too young for that too?" Howard sneered.

"No. He told me there was too much riff raff."

Riff raff was how daddy described what, today, I'd call youthful exuberance. Just after one experience, I was not allowed to return; not with any of my friends, nor was daddy going to escort me.

At the end of this exchange, I was nearly reduced to tears. I was shrinking from my own experiences. *Nothing I did seemed to measure up to Howard's.* My recollections of childhood and adolescence could never measure up.

After listening to Howard's childhood memories, I began to feel I had missed out on something essential. References to riff raff became code for what, much later, I labeled the authentic black experience. Howard had plenty of it.

The little hole in my soul continued to grow. Howard found it and picked at it, time and again.

My daddy's question continued to haunt me throughout my marriage. Too late. Alas, I was a fool in love.

❦

DESPITE HIS ATTEMPTS TO IMPRESS ME WITH STORIES OF HIS childhood lack, almost all of Howard's family were firmly in the black middle class. His mother was a college graduate, and was first a teacher, and later became a social worker. She retired as the assistant director of social work for the Department of Housing and Urban Development, Miami-Dade County!

Not bad for a woman who lived in the Scott Housing project when she first moved to Miami.

"I knew the Scott housing was just temporary," Mom told me how it took her years to save money to purchase their home. Howard was in middle school when they finally moved.

Then there was Howard's Uncle Charlie. His political weight was equally matched by his girth; he weighed close to 400 pounds at his peak, carried on just a 5'7" frame. His nickname, "pear shape", described him to a 'T'!

Uncle Charlie's 'weight' carried far beyond the halls of local political power and intrigue. His power extended to the bench as well. His connections would serve me and Howard many times over the years.

It was Uncle Charlie who helped get Howard's first appointment to the County Budget office after he graduated from Morehouse College in 1968.

Uncle Charlie and I developed a close and loving relationship as he continued to play an ever increasing role of political influence over the years as Howard and I became more involved in the City of Miami and the local community.

◈

WINTER 1967

Aunt Doris offered to send me to Europe for three months after I graduated from college.

"No," she said. "Stay as long as you want. Just don't marry Howard. What is the rush?" she wanted to know.

"What kind of fun will I have in Europe if Howard is not with me?" I couldn't believe she would ask me to give up my dreams.

"Everything you describe is exactly what I want to do with my husband," I told her. "After all, those wonderful things you describe for me to do in Europe, or anywhere else without him, would be an empty experience for me."

Didn't she get it? I had saved myself from dating and all that silliness. I thought serial dating, break ups, heart aches, and the associated drama was a waste of time, and energy. I had made my choice. I had negotiated my terms, and I knew what I wanted.

I was nineteen years old.

"Let's go to Nassau for the weekend," my mother offered. It was the Christmas holiday.

"Sure." I wasn't going to turn down a free trip.

My mother, Aunt Doris, and I went to the Bahamas, ostensibly for me to get Howard out of my system. While there, I clubbed, partied hard, and met lots of exciting new people in Nassau. I was given free rein- no holds barred- in hopes I'd meet another guy to help me forget about Howard.

"You know, Island men know how to treat women, and they love pretty American girls," my mom shamelessly pushed me out.

"Put on a little more lipstick", she urged me.

She's pitiful.

I could not wait to return home and to the ordered life I had already decided awaited me in marriage.

My family's intervention efforts persisted and extra recruits were drafted, including my Uncle Andrew.

Even my cousin Alice, Uncle Andrew's daughter, joined in the growing chorus of discouraging pleas.

"I never liked Howard. He's no good," was the best she could lobby. Odd, coming from her. Alice was always the rebellious one, and I thought she would join me in my efforts to go against the family elders. I turned a deaf ear to her, too. I had a made up mind. They finally all gave up.

I suspect Howard may have been getting similar kinds of advice from his family: to not marry me.

⚜

SPRING 1968

"She is our princess," Glendena shouted, "too good for your nephew."

"Well, he is our prince, and your cousin is not worthy of him," Uncle Charlie yelled back at her.

When the word got out to our respective families that Howard and I had decided to marry after college graduation, there was an unexpected hostile reaction from both. No one was in favor of the union taking place, then, if ever.

The daggers and hatchets remained raised and bandied about for months leading up to the wedding ceremony.

"Can you believe what they're saying to one another?" Howard and I chuckled over how proprietary our respective family members felt towards each of us. It was difficult to try to imagine the street fight: Uncle Charlie's 300 plus pounds shaking in indignation at one of my mom's cousins. Ironically, Charlie, Glendena and many of our respective family members were social friends; members of Miami's small and insular black middle class community.

A tragic comedy.

"Howard, didn't you tell your mother you asked me to marry you?"

"Yes, but I think she thought it would be later; much later. I think she's in shock since the wedding is only four days after I graduate."

A year or so after the wedding, I asked mom what she had thought about our plans.

"Well, I knew Howard had another girlfriend in college, so I couldn't help wonder when you and Howard had gotten so close."

She was always so honest with me.

"And", she continued, "I didn't have much time to adjust to the news, and plan for a wedding."

That's fair. She and I never discussed the matter again.

Howard never said he did not want to marry me.

The proposal was really a dare.

"Marry me by August, or never." His invitation came in a letter shortly after the Christmas break. We had enjoyed a few days together after I returned from the Bahamas, and I felt we had grown even closer.

At the time his proposal came, I was surrounded by applications to medical schools. It had always been my ambition to become a psychiatrist. Howard knew I was applying to graduate schools.

I did some math.

Let's see. Medical school, plus internship, plus specialty studies, etc., equals a lifetime of delayed gratification. Marriage equals immediate gratification.

I set the date for June 8th.

Once set, I went home for Spring break in April. Over the

course of one week, I bought my wedding gown and veil, placed the announcement in the local newspaper, ordered the invitations, worked on the guest list, and opened a bridal registry.

Satisfied the wedding would take place as I had planned, I returned to Marymount to march and receive my diploma.

I left the additional wedding details to my Aunt Lorraine.

"I will give you a beautiful wedding." Aunt Lorraine assured me. "I gave your mother a beautiful wedding," she reminded me. In 1947, my parents' ceremony was featured as the society wedding of the week in the Pittsburgh Courier, a nationally distributed Black weekly.

She had been waiting, all these years, for a repeat performance. She was the only member of my family who did not disapprove of my plans to marry Howard.

"The girl's in love," she flipped off my mom, and other members of the family who continued to protest; right up to the wedding day.

On hindsight, there really was no good reason for me and Howard to marry so quickly, if at all. In all truthfulness, I was in love, and I wanted to have all the benefits of marriage I had been taught to expect from my years of Catholic education: sanctified sex, mutual support, children (at some point), companionship, and, quite frankly, I feared being single (alone). Also, I had grown weary of studying.

I was a dreamer.

I dreamed how I would do it (marriage) better than everyone else I knew. Certainly better than my mom and dad. And, I'd show the aunts you can get married, only once; and stay married. There would be no divorce for me! "Till death do us part", was a sacred utterance.

I assumed Howard wanted the same. I recall we talked about those things, maybe, some. I also knew with the strongest conviction in my nineteen year old mind, my choice was a good one.

Howard should feel especially anointed. After all, hadn't I done the choosing?

❦

AUNT LORRAINE, HAD BEEN TELLING ME SINCE I WAS A child, "the man for you has not been born yet." After adding up the years, Howard was just right.

Remarkably, once we did marry, despite all the preceding storm and fury, our families immediately joined in total support of us-their Prince and Princess.

Neither of us had a job; we had no housing, and no income; just, our vows.

I had faith.

Miraculously, our folks pulled together and made sure we had what we needed to get off to a good, solid start: a bed; linens; cook ware; other essential household items; cash for a down payment on our first car; and, most importantly, the first job for Howard; compliments of Uncle Charlie.

Immediately after we got married, Howard's mother presented him with a paper-wrapped package along with a few wedding gifts which had been delivered to her house. It was a bedspread! She had it laundered and carefully folded. It was tattered and torn from many years of use.

"Toni, bring me my spread," Howard called out. It took me only a short time to realize his cry signaled he needed comfort during times of stress. Other times, it was a warning to me that he anticipated some impending doom.

It took a few months for me to figure out which one of his many wounds and/or dark moods Howard needed to soothe. His spread was his first source of comfort, and his cry out for it played out as a background sound track throughout our marriage.

I've never seen such a thing.

"Why do you do those things with your spread?"

"I like the way the fabric feels. The texture soothes me." He would strum his fingers over the threads like he was playing some invisible key board.

He'd had a spread since early childhood. He would discard one only after it deteriorated to a thread-bear condition. Howard held on to the things he loved for a long time.

The spread helped keep him sane and secure. Initially, it was all he needed.

Then again, I had my own sources for comfort and security.

"Toni, your toes are bleeding!" Howard was alarmed the first time he saw what I had done to myself. I hadn't noticed the blood.

At first, I tried to hide the mutilations.

I subconsciously ripped and tore at my nails and the surrounding flesh on my fingers and toes whenever I became anxious. I would use any sharply-pointed instrument I could find when my own teeth could not complete the task.

"Toni, doesn't it hurt?

"No." I had become so used to the numbness in my feet and hands.

My flesh was tortured and bloodied; much like some of the leftover feelings from my childhood when I constantly fretted about fitting in with my older classmates.

It began when I was three.

So there we were: newlyweds. Me, the young, smart, Catholic school girl. Him, the young, smart, inner city boy. Certainly, equally twisted

Ah, we are evenly yoked, after all.

3

NEWLYWEDS

1968-1972

As the fates would have it, our wedding took place at the same hour as Robert Kennedy's funeral: 10:00 AM, June 8, 1968. Kennedy had been assassinated on June 6.

Dammit. Why is this happening to me? I cried hard for two days. It was too late to reschedule our wedding ceremony.

The Gods are playing tricks on me. Is this punishment for something? No, I don't believe in that kind of God. Still......

Gwen and I spent all day before the wedding together. She tried her best to comfort me.

"Toni, if you don't stop crying, your eyes are going to be puffy." She was right.

But I did have puffy eyes, and, I suffered from very blurred vision from staying up all night, watching the news about the Kennedy services on my wedding day. It turned out to be my day of mourning, too.

Missing from the wedding, and presumably watching the

televised funeral was the photographer and more than half of those who had been invited.

Was this an omen?

Though sparsely attended, the wedding ceremony was a beautiful, traditional affair. I wore a simple, formal white gown: it was satin, with long sleeves and lace applique; and, it had twenty covered buttons down the back. I wore a full-length lace mantilla which cost more than the gown. The bridal party was large: six maids and six groomsmen, but there were no children participating. Howard's brother Harold, was the best man. Gwen was my maid-of- honor. The maids wore long, moss green gowns and small matching mantillas, and the groomsmen were in tuxedoes.

The day was also my grandmother's birthday, and hands down, she was the best dressed guest. She wore a periwinkle blue lace dress, with a matching hat, bag, shoes, and gloves. Outstanding!

"DADDY, JUST SAY WHATEVER IS ON YOUR MIND," I GENTLY coaxed him. Nothing.

The entire wedding party, my parents, Howard's mom, and a few select guests were being feted at a brunch immediately followed the wedding service. We had our glasses raised for a champagne toast.

"Ur ruh", "Ur ruh", "Ur ruh," he grunted. Daddy choked up in tears; unable to form two words.

This can't be my daddy! He was never at a loss for words. Was he hung over, too? Standing at the altar, I knew Howard was drunk from the night before. *Is he going to collapse? Thank God he had a chance to kneel throughout most of the ceremony.*

"Say something daddy. Anything."

This is disastrous. First Kennedy; no professional photos from the church; Howard's drunk; now daddy's melting down; and, I don't even have a legitimate marriage license.

Since I was under 21, according to Florida law, I needed parental permission to marry.

Two weeks before my wedding, I rendezvoused with Howard in Tallahassee, the State Capitol, to apply for our marriage license. Howard had come down from Atlanta where he was waiting to graduate from College the following week.

"Daddy's form didn't come." I had the form with just my mom's signature. We were standing in the Clerk's office.

"That's fucked up."

"I know. Daddy was expecting the form for me, but he got confused when the one for Gerald came."

"What do you mean he got confused?

My brother, Gerald, had graduated from high school in May, just a month before my wedding. He and his girlfriend had a baby on the way. Mommy told daddy on a long-distance call. He was on his way to college, and decided to get married.

"Daddy received two forms."

Poor daddy. He had so much to process. He must be traumatized: First he had moved to California; mommy and my little brothers weren't going to join him out there until after my wedding; and no one was expecting Gerald to get married. And having a baby, too?

"God damn, Toni. Everybody in your family is fucked up."

"Howard, please don't say that. He didn't know Gerald and Pearl were getting married. He thought he got a duplicate form for me, so he only signed one and sent back Gerald's."

"Shit. You better fix it or the wedding is off."

I panicked.

What am I going to do? The invitations are out. Plans are set. Commitments are made. Money has been spent. And, I am going to get married!

"Don't worry, I'll just forge daddy's signature."

Howard laughed out loud. "I sure hope you don't get caught and have to go to jail."

I held my breath and signed: **Adam G. Williams** in the space for applicant's father. No one knew.

And now, my poor daddy cannot find his voice for the toast.

"Say something, A.G.," mommy urged. "Take a drink. It'll relax you", she coaxed him to gulp his champagne. It was to no avail.

Uncle Ozzie, Aunt Doris's husband took over and made the toast while daddy collapsed into his seat and cried. It was a bittersweet moment.

The photographer finally found his way to the wedding party brunch where he took formal photos on the lawn. He returned in the evening for the reception: he took photos of the receiving line; the cake cutting; the party, etc.

Two weeks later, the photo album was delivered. Every single one of the photos was blurry!

Was this another sign?

Howard and I had exchanged vows at Holy Redeemer, a Catholic Church, where we attended a brief pre-marital counseling session the day before the wedding. We both made specific commitments and agreements according to the Church's teaching.

During our first year of marriage, it became more and more difficult for me to follow the church's teachings. Howard never did.

"It's a white man's religion," Howard spit out each time I went to mass. His attacks made it easier for me to fall away.

⁂

"TONI, I CAN'T FIGURE OUT WHY YOU MARRIED HOWARD IN the first place." For years, I'd hear something similar from Gwen. In her estimation, Howard and I barely knew one another, since we had only dated in between college breaks.

"Howard didn't have a job, and neither did you. I wondered what you were going to live on."

"We are ok." But, I was really scared.

I didn't want to show her any signs of just how unsure I was. I had started taking measures to save my face right from the beginning.

One day, after I'd already been married for about fifteen years, Gwen grilled me during one of her frequent visits to Miami to see her parents.

"O.K. Toni, how are you really doing?" Her volley barely masked she already knew. We were meeting for lunch; a ritual we continue, to this day.

I didn't think she actually expected me to tell her the whole truth, but I loved her for caring about me. Even though she had been living in Texas since 1964, when we both graduated from high school, she got a steady stream of news about me and Howard from one of her sisters who worked for the City of Miami.

"Everything is fine." I told her. I had told myself the lie so often, it began to feel true.

"If you say so." Gwen did not probe. We continued to enjoy our lunch, chatting about our families, and other less incendiary subjects.

From the very beginning, I revealed very little to her about my married life. I couldn't stand the truth. My truth? I did not have a clue about being married; and, once I realized I had made a mistake, I didn't know what to do. I had lied myself into isolation. I thought about one of the mantras I'd heard from early childhood: "You make your bed hard, you lay in it."

I was in for a long, uneasy sleep.

⚜

JUST HOW MUCH DID HOWARD AND I KNOW ABOUT EACH other before we married?

"I know you were a virgin," he praised me for letting him be my first.

He thought I was good looking. "Hey pretty girl," he'd address me from time-to time.

He knew I was an unhappy camper at home.

"I'm not close to my mother. She makes me nervous."

"So that's why you don't want to spend time with her?" My mother relocated to California soon after my wedding.

"It's so many things."

He listened patiently, at first.

"So what's wrong with your mother?"

It was hard to put my finger on it, but I told him a story about the time I lived in Bermuda. I was ten, my brother Gerald was eight, and Sidney was not yet two.

"One day, daddy, Gerald and I were frantically searching for our little brother's high tops. We were all trying to get ready for a family outing, but first we had to find Sidney's dress shoes. He had one good pair. Gerald looked in the refrigerator and found them. They were soaked with urine. Mommy put them in there to dry out. I pinched my nose and held the shoes out at arm's length. I announced, "At least she didn't put them in the stove this time." We all recalled how much that stunk up the whole house when she tried to dry them out with heat."

"Toni, what did your dad have to say?"

"The only thing he said was 'Bettye, that's disgusting'".

Well, it was disgusting.

"Yeah, I know. Almost every day, Gerald and I would get home from school to find Sidney in a very full diaper; he had not been changed for hours."

"That's pretty sick. Did you ever find out what she was doing all day?"

"Howard, I didn't have a name for it then, but on hindsight, I suspected mom had been self-medicating throughout the day."

"Did your dad ever say anything about her taking pills?"

"I never really grilled daddy about it when we still lived in

Bermuda. I was so young then. Only nine. He just seemed to accept her craziness."

Howard and I laughed when I told him the story, and at how crazy my mom was. Over the years, he'd see much more, first hand, himself. He would use this information against me during our divorce.

Once, when mom was a really old woman, nearly eighty years old, I lost my temper and yelled at her about her behavior. She was still abusing her medications. At the time, I, mom, and my dad were living together. Daddy, also in his eighties, stopped in the middle of his stroll and calmly and reassuringly, turned to me and said, "Toni, I don't know why you are so upset. You know your mother's a drug addict."

Of course. He knew all along.

❧

HOWARD HAD ISSUES OF HIS OWN WITH HIS MOM. INITIALLY we were both clams about our mother issues. More about mine would be revealed soon enough, but his remained closed over most of our entire relationship.

"Howard, why do you call your mother Arie? It's so disrespectful."

"Because it's her name." It was only after we had our first son, Kito, when everyone, including Howard, started calling Arie Gary "mom" and/or "moms."

At first, Howard seemed to like hearing my stories about being the first born. Unlike him, I had no competition at home. I had three younger brothers who worshipped me.

But, Howard always felt he was in competition with his brother; his mother favored his brother over him. More than once, "mom' denied she had played favorites.

On reflection, I did not know much about his day to day routine before we married, but I got highlights.

"I hated Morehouse," his fists clenched as he described those days. I was shocked. The college had a great reputation.

Howard's brother had preceded him there, by a year. Harold was a big man on campus. He was at the head of the Omega Psi Phi pledge line. The Fraternity is a very prestigious society for young black men.

"Harold beat me until I almost passed out." He was nearly in tears as I examined his butt. The scars were still visible from the hazing.

I cried with him.

"Why was he so hard on you?"

"He didn't want the other frat brothers to think he was showing favoritism toward me."

The skin on his back side remained darkened for years from the heavy-handed hazing.

"Is that why you and Harold have so many fights?"

"Partly. The fucker beat me in front of my line brothers, and I couldn't fight him back if I wanted to make it into the frat." Howard spoke through such tightly clenched teeth, his jaw twitched. He was still angry about it.

Howard's 'less than' feeling remained just below the surface whenever the two brothers got together.

Early in our marriage, Harold visited Miami at least once, or twice a year. The visit was peppered with a chorus of "fuck you." "No, fuck you," one or the other yelled out. I would retreat from their company to cry in private when I heard their name-calling, cursing, and shouting.

I've never heard anything like this between family members.

I felt like the brothers were always on the brink of some physical violence. On and on it would go, in every other conversation. It was war, whether they were playing a friendly whist card game or a $.25 stakes game of poker.

"Howard, it makes me sick to hear you and your brother fight."

Their conflict literally caused me physical pain in my abdomen.

"Well, Toni, you need to toughen up, and get used to it."

The tension did ease over time, especially after they both had children.

But, I was slow to realize just how angry Howard was, about so many things.

⚜

1968-1970

In the early days of our marriage, I used to like to recall how in addition to the Bahamian influences, there was a prevalence of Cuban culture infused in my immediate family.

"I'm tired of hearing about all your family of foreign people," Howard retorted.

But I held on to my warm memories and the stories I was told about how my grandmother was born and raised in Key West where the Bahamian and Cuban cultures blended.

It was in our food, our music, and even in the adult forms of gambling! We called the numbers game 'bolita' because the hit of the week came from the little roulette ball which was played in Havana, and not the results of the horse races in New York.

Grandma cooked chicken and yellow rice (arroz con pollo), or peas and rice using 'grandules verde' (green pigeon peas), and she even made a tres leches (three milk) cake by simply pouring a combination of homogenized milk and canned sweet condensed milk over a coarse yellow cake.

These dishes are typical Guarjia- or country-style Cuban food. They were what my family ate, including the popular snack: 'galletas' (soda crackers) with guava (paste or jelly), and cheese (cream or cheddar).

"That shit's not important," he'd say when I recalled some of my high school experiences I had with Cuban exile students.

He entirely missed the point. I intuitively knew my background could help him navigate the changes taking place in Miami.

If only he could see me as an asset. Immaculata was a great training ground for getting along with the new Miami and I had learned plenty. Didn't he know what I had to go through?

৩১৩

I HAD BEEN CRYING, AGAIN. ANY SMALL SLIGHT WOULD reduce me to tears.

"Toni, you couldn't fight your way out of a paper bag".

Fight? What did he know about me being a fighter? For years, fighting was all I'd done! What about my continuous fight to be on equal footing with my classmates from the time I was three? Or fighting to survive my mother's mental illness; or just fighting to be me. What did he really know?

Howard came home one afternoon from his job with Miami-Dade County as a budget analyst. We had been married for about three months. His salary covered all of our expenses. "You are nothing but a liability," he hissed.

Where was this coming from? I suffered in silence.

I was eager to prove my worth; I could accomplish whatever I wanted, once I made up my mind. After all, I'd been winning from a very young age, and I felt like I could do almost anything. I had usually arranged to get my own way, but with Howard, my weapons chest was empty; I had not yet stocked my tool box with the sharp retorts and other devises I would eventually accumulate.

What little armament I had, was dull, ineffective.

But there was a time, when I could work magic.

❧

"ANTONIA, I CANNOT AFFORD THOSE SHOES, SO STOP CRYING now." I can still hear my mother's voice as clearly as I can remember seeing the shoes in the window of *The Bootery,* a specialty children's shoe store on The Miracle Mile in upscale Coral Gables.

They were black patent leather high tops, with four buckles.

I don't remember what happened next, but I have a photo

of me in my Easter outfit in those shoes, clearly showing who won the fight. I was three years old.

It was also the beginning of my lifelong passion for fashion.

Where had that girl gone? What happened to my spunk and fight?

I had had no hidden agenda when we first married. It was no secret: I didn't have any work experience. I was an educated person; just bereft of any employable skills. But I was willing.

I applied for jobs.

"Mrs. Gary, you are certainly well educated, but you are too young for us to hire," was the typical response to my applications.

The minute I turned twenty, I applied for a teaching certificate and was immediately hired as a substitute teacher; qualified to teach science and biology, grades five through twelve.

After a few months of various school assignments around town, I got a permanent substitute teacher positon at Allappattah Junior High School, Dr. Kenneth J. Walker, Principal. The junior high schools included grades 6-9, and the eleven-fourteen year olds kept the hallways electrified from their constant current of energy.

The student population was all-black.

I loved it. I was eager, and I looked forward to the variety of daily challenges: a girl's first menstrual period; various acts of bullying; hunger, abuse, and parental abandonment issues; not to mention the actual teaching I got to do.

"I don't know why you're working so hard," a few of the veterans pulled me aside one day in the teachers' lounge.

"You're making us look bad. Don't you know these students aren't interest in learning what you teach?"

I looked much younger than my twenty years, and up till then, I had no worldly experience to call upon to help buttress me against the older teachers. Many of them had grown weary-some from living; others from being in the system, and from what I considered their utter disdain for the precious wards, the students, at this inner city school.

"You're not going to make any more money for your efforts," one of the most veteran teachers offered.

I started to protest, but I was cornered; outnumbered.

I lost what respect for those teachers who I'd known; peers of my relatives who were in the system.

I later learned several of them were either waiting for retirement, or to be transferred to so-called 'white' schools. A handful had applied for a promotion to work at the School Board administration.

I could not identify with their pain. I remained filled with zeal. I was employed! I was being useful! I enjoyed being in the classroom, and I took everything to heart. I was constantly frustrated with how the crazy system choked teachers with paperwork and planning meetings, effectively reducing the time remaining to actually teach.

I spent hours after work preparing lesson plans or grading assignments. Yet, I was careful not to cut into the time I budgeted to spend with Howard. He usually came home two-three hours after I arrived, when I would stop whatever I was doing to give him my undivided attention. It was my duty.

"Toni, you don't need this job. I make enough money to take care of us." Howard told me one night.

This from the same man who had called me a liability a few months before?

"Why don't you just tell those teachers to kiss your ass and go fuck themselves," he'd urge me.

I had given up cursing years before. It felt so wrong for me to have to resort to such base language.

I just wanted to give my best to my students.

I bought myself another pair of black patent leather shoes.

⚜

I MADE AN APPOINTMENT TO SPEAK WITH THE PRINCIPAL.

"There you go. Showing off and meeting with Dr. Walker." Mrs. Greene reminded me I didn't have a full time contract, yet.

I was not deterred. Dr. Walker didn't delay my request to see him.

"Dr. Walker, these kids (I was referring to my ninth graders), aren't paying any attention to what I'm teaching."

"What do you mean, Mrs. Gary?"

"They only have one thing on their mind and they need some education about their reproductive functions."

All the students, the boys in particular, were caught in a perpetual cycle of mis-education and ignorance. I was appalled by the conversations I overheard. The girls were especially misinformed about their menstrual cycle, and how they could get pregnant- a constant subject amongst them.

"Well Mrs. Gary, why don't you develop a curriculum to help them?" Dr. Walker encouraged me to work with the Vice Principal for Curriculum to get something together.

The Vice Principal for Curriculum gave me just two weeks to get the course ready. I threw myself into the task, and he approved the curriculum.

Victory! I felt great.

First, I conducted an anonymous survey of the students' knowledge of what they knew and understood about their bodies, reproduction, etc. I allowed them to use their own language.

Oh my God. They are so ignorant.

Once tallied, I substituted their street words with scientific labels. If anyone was shocked by what was shared, they kept silent; including me. We were learning from one another, and there were many moments of embarrassment, all around.

The class was wildly successful, and I felt redeemed after months of suffering at the hands of those veterans teachers.

Bingo.

Amazingly, my experimental mini-course was offered a full year before the system adopted a district-wide curricula on the same subject.

Double bingo!

Just before the end of the school year, I received a formal, full time contract.

"Dr. Walker, I want to thank you very much for

offering me a position on your faculty, but I will not be returning next year."

I couldn't tell him my husband had advised me to just cuss everybody out. Howard had also given me an ultimatum: to either toughen up, stop crying, or quit.

Quitting felt like the best option.

"I know Dr. Walker, but the system is not designed to just let people teach, and all I want to do is teach. I don't want to have to do all the other things required." I had grown bolder by this point in the conversation; I felt strong and confident.

Both he and his Vice Principal had been supportive. They took a risk when they permitted me to develop my sex-education curriculum. It was a big deal at the time. I was very appreciative.

"Besides, teaching was not what I studied in college," I leaned forward. "You know, I never took any classes in education or methods of teaching."

Dr. Walker smiled.

And that was that.

I had learned something valuable I carried into my successive careers: 1) I would not ever have to curse anyone in order to justify my worth, or my contribution to any organization; and 2) I could produce excellent quality work products which would become a hallmark of all my future endeavors.

I was also pleased Howard appeared to value my happiness and peace of mind more than my paycheck.

᠅

DURING OUR FIRST YEAR OF MARRIAGE, HOWARD BEGAN TO demonstrate his own proclivity for fashion. It was a harbinger of other monstrous, future obsessions.

He had to wear a certain cut of suit, with a coordinated tie, socks, pocket square, etc. At first, he depended on me to help him match up every morning.

"Baby, does this match?"

Thus, our morning routine began: he laid out several shirts (mostly solid blue, solid white, and an occasional blue and white stripe), a variety of ties, socks, belt, and a silk pocket square, to match up.

"Look at these," I'd point out several combinations for him to consider.

He seldom switched my selections.

Initially, Howard did not trust himself to put the right combinations together without always looking the same each time. It would take years before he began to dress himself with confidence.

I took my job seriously. I even extended to him the favor of placing all his blue and brown socks together in one drawer. I kept the black socks in a separate drawer. I always made sure he looked good. Polished. Professional.

In the beginning, we were budgeted to the penny.

We shopped together. Sometimes it took hours just to pick out one belt; it had to be perfect.

"What's wrong with the belt?" I got tired of looking at every inch of a belt with him.

"See that mark?"

"Howard, the marks are part of the natural leather."

It looked perfect to me. But to him, not even the natural markings from the cowhide escaped close scrutiny before it became acceptable to buy. He was not easily satisfied.

Howard had to have the absolute best our money could buy, and it had to have a certain cut, if a suit; a certain weave, if a tie; the feel of butter, if leather, etc.

I liked to look good too.

"Baby, you'd look good in a $2 dress," he told me often enough, I came to believe it. In fact, I have made it one of my life's mission to always buy low; looking as if I spent more. Over the years I have perfected the art of dressing up, and spending very little to pull off the look of wearing designer clothes.

But Howard never felt good in a $100 suit.

Twenty years later, toward the end of his career in municipal management and near the beginning of his years as an investment banker, Howard invited his personal tailors to his office to take his measurements for his $1000+ suits. He had all his specially designed shirts monogrammed. He ordered $200+ ties, and bought eyeglass frames in every shape and style to match his ensembles.

Years before, I had stopped caring much about this certain proclivity of his, but the matching glasses were too much for me to easily dismiss. By then, I was convinced his descent into madness had accelerated.

His obsession about his attire and appearance extended to his collection of cars. Eventually we owned more than twenty automobiles over the duration of our twenty three year marriage.

None of them got old. Even if we bought them 'previously owned', they had a short-lived stay with us.

Our first ride was a new, off the showroom floor, 1968 MGB/GT, British racing green; black leather interior; wire rims; and a cloth top we kept down whenever it wasn't raining. It was perfect for two young and newly married people.

"Baby, let your hair blow." It was a turn-on for Howard- to have my long hair blow around and then fall back into place after a wild ride with the top down.

I liked that he liked that about me.

There was no air conditioning in the first car. Just the natural flow of air from driving fast with the top down. I enjoyed riding in, and driving the car. It was my set of training wheels.

"Toni, Uncle Charlie can't keep getting your driving tickets fixed," Howard scolded me. "You need to learn to how to drive."

Our brand new MGB/GT, had 'four on the floor', and a fifth speed on the steering column. I tore up and down the roads of Miami, down shifting on three wheels. Speed(ing) was so addictive, and I got many moving violations and other 'minor' infractions resolved after a phone call to Uncle Charlie.

"Don't keep abusing your privileged access to Uncle Charlie."

I didn't.

Unfortunately, I completely destroyed my car, in one day. I had already been responsible for many minor scrapes and bang ups, but on this particular day I tried to fit it into a much too narrow space in a driveway. I was returning from running an errand while working at Operation Big Vote, on yet another political campaign.

Operation Big Vote was a powerful voter registration and political machine. It was started and run by Howard's Uncle Charlie, and was the mandatory go-to for anyone in Florida running for office who needed the black vote.

I was in a hurry (mistake number one). I misjudged the space between the car, the building wall and another parked car (mistake number two). I scraped along the wall going in to avoid hitting the parked car, backed out to try it again (mistake number three), and then I broke down and cried (mistake number four).

"How can you be so fucking stupid?" Howard cursed.

While I didn't agree, all I could do was continue to cry once I realized by how much I had miscalculated. Well I did feel stupid for taking this incident so seriously.

I was just trying to do the right thing, I rationalized. *First, I don't even like politics, and yet I was working on somebody's campaign. And, what was the big deal about some damn car? It could be repaired. The other car was not damaged. Hey, I'm not hurt. Isn't my personal safety more important?*

We had insurance, but we didn't get the car repaired. Instead, we purchased our next vehicle, a previously owned Mercedes. A police magnet. We kept the Mercedes for less than a year before we got our first Lincoln Continental. We nicknamed it 'Abraham'. It would be our third car in less than two years. The pattern was set.

"I'm going to buy you a Princess Rolls Royce, because that

would fit you best," Howard once promised. I groaned in protest about the grandiosity.

I would never.

But am I really his Princess, or just another item in his collections?

Howard's obsessions would continue to grow in proportion to his rise in authority and command. They eventually overflowed into every other part of his life, becoming so large they began to choke out, and eventually kill the life he had with me.

But then again, I developed my own set of monsters, and I started to act out with behaviors to fully complement his.

"You're just having an anxiety attack," the emergency room doctor proclaimed. It was my second trip in less than six months.

How do I cure it? Chocolate helped- some. Sex helped, too. Buying a new dress always felt good. Something's missing......

Where had I gone to? I wanted to get back to my fighter self; back to my long ago girl.

Just who was that girl, anyway? You know, Antonia.

BOOK TWO

WHO IS THAT GIRL?

❀ 4 ❀

ANTONIA, YOU WERE SUCH A BEAUTIFUL BROWN BABY; AND SO SMART

1949-1958 EARLY SIGNS AND INFLUENCES

"Mommy, I don't want to drink colored water."

I knew, even in my five year old mind, it was wrong to have a separate water fountain for 'coloreds'. We were standing in the basement of Richards, one of Miami's leading department stores. It was 1954. It would take another ten years before public accommodations opened up to people of color.

"Then Antonia, you can wait until we get home to drink any water." My mother didn't bother with any further explanation as we left the store. She always called me *Antonia* when the matter turned serious.

To this day, I talk to "Antonia" whenever I seek my own truth.

"Put on your gloves," Aunt Doris told us. I was with Alice and Sandra, my closest girl cousins. We were waiting to be seated at the Rooney Plaza. At age six, I was the youngest. They were both eight.

The Rooney was a Hotel on the ocean which looked like a big pink sand castle. It was one of my favorite places to spend a Saturday afternoon. I certainly felt like somebody special during those sojourns.

Before de-segregation, members of my family would go to Miami Beach to get treated fully as human beings. We could shop at the open-mall boutiques on Lincoln Road. All the high end stores were there, including Saks Fifth Avenue. Sometimes we went to the movie theater on Lincoln Road, and sat mixed in with the other patrons. On the mainland, we would have been relegated to the balcony, away from the whites. Our Saturday excursions were usually followed by having tea at "The Rooney."

Aunt Doris spoke enough Spanish to keep the hotel staff, restaurant workers, and store clerks on Miami Beach off-guard, so we got treated like any other tourists; not just some coloreds from the mainland on the other side of Biscayne Bay.

While on Miami Beach, we pretended to be visitors from Cuba.

Ours' was a pre-Castro Cuba, and it felt perfectly normal for us to pretend we were from the nearby Island. Since the later 1890s, there had been a continuous flow of people in and out of Cuba who went back and forth to Key West, Miami, and Tampa.

Many of them were blacks and browns, like us.

Aunt Doris's Spanish was good enough to get away with the subterfuge. She had learned from her own mother. My grandmother became fluent in Spanish as a girl growing up in Key West. Grandma, as well as her mother, also spoke a French patois they picked up from my great-great grandmother, an African woman taken to Haiti.

I would often use the same tactic while I lived in South Florida. Knowing conversational Spanish served me well, and it became a very useful tool I often used, especially as a young married woman in Miami. *En Miami, todan el mundo hablan en espanol. Es necesario, si?*

᭟᭟᭟

LEST ANYONE FORGET, THE MIAMI I GREW UP IN WAS THE near south.

In some places signs were posted prohibiting service to coloreds.

We were still on the cusp. We remained colored for a few more years, and then we became Negroes, with a capitol **N.**

While there were many softening agents at play during my most formative years (1949-1964); i.e., a steady flow of tourists from all over the world; the continuous influx of immigrants from the Caribbean; and, the great influence on our society by the developing civil rights movement which was broadcast nightly on television; 'Jim Crow' laws were still enforced, including segregated housing laws.

Choices were limited for anyone who wanted to move out of the inner city or other impoverished ghettos.

From a very early age, I became keenly aware of my parents' protective cloak around me and my brothers. I felt smugly protected.

I still admire my folks for their many acts of bravery.

My parents were fierce in their vigilance against the ugly world outside; racist barbs, being just one. There were many harsh realities of the times and place which threatened the tender psyche of little colored/Negro children. But my parents were brilliant in how they kept me and my brothers out of harms' way. I know it took cunning and finesse for them to navigate the vagaries of a fast changing society; and move them beyond the closed doors of their own pasts and into the promise of an opening society.

I was given more power than most kids I knew.

"Antonia," my mother would tell me, "don't back down from anyone. Speak up and ask questions."

Sometimes, her directive put me in precarious situations.

"Toni, I don't believe how you talk to grown- ups," Gwen would often remark. "I could never get away with talking back."

"I wanted to raise you all in a more conducive environment," daddy explained his decision to move us to the exurbs. At first, my mother wanted to live near her favorite sister, Theodora, Aunt Teddy, as well as her best friend, Jessie White, who both had moved to Ralph C. Bunche Park, another planned community for colored folk. Bunche Park was in the far north end of the county. We went south. Way south.

I was around two years of age when my parents bought their first home.

Richmond Heights was developed in 1949, primarily for colored/Negro veterans to take advantage of the VA/FHA loans which had become available. *The Heights* was a unique planned community located in one of the farthest places from the center of colored town. It became known as *The Heights*. Once, it was lauded in a 1950s edition of Ebony Magazine as one of the top ten places in the country to raise (colored) children.

The community was located twenty miles due south of the center of town, and accessible by US Highway1, a one lane road aka Dixie Highway where my mom and dad became well known for their contributions to the small, insular community.

"Daddy, can I help you roll papers?" I'd ask him every Friday and Saturday night before going to bed.

My dad held the franchise to deliver the Miami Herald daily newspaper to residents of *The Heights*. He would get up every weekday morning at 4:00 a.m. to retrieve his drop, 3 miles away on Dixie Highway, US 1.

To my delight, he would let me and my brother help him on the weekends. Spending time with my dad was really precious-he worked such long hours during the week.

"All right now, time to get up".

No matter how sleepy-headed I appeared, I did not mind getting up early if I could be in my daddy's company on those weekend mornings.

"A.G., you need to show Antonia more affection," mommy would constantly upbraid him. But, daddy was a man of few, but select words; with even fewer demonstrations of affection-except when we threw papers together.

Though scant, his gestures of affection worked for me.

Daddy would sit on our front porch to roll his papers before throwing them onto the individual porches. Daddy was athletic. A former College football player, he stayed in shape from laying bricks and concrete blocks on his day job. His was a legacy profession; a great many men from his family were builders. In between construction jobs, daddy also taught school-various subjects/grades, and he picked up a lot of odd jobs during the rainy season when construction halted.

Daddy had a good throwing arm, and he perfected his toss so each rolled up paper landed on the porches of the single family houses.

He threw the paper with his left hand over the top of the car.

"Touchdown!" Daddy shouted. He kept me and my brother entertained.

Gerald liked to ride in the back seat, handing the papers to daddy. They were stacked on the front passenger car seat. I did not like that part of the job. The smell from the printing ink overwhelmed the car interior, but Gerald did not seem to care about the fumes. Gerald remained in a happy mood about everything; lasting all his life. Sometimes I envied him for his sunny disposition.

The Sunday paper was challenging. Its larger content and the weekly advertisements required a thicker rubber band to put around the bulk.

"The trick is to wrap it tight enough to hold the paper together without popping the rubber band." Daddy only needed to show me once. Rubber bands were precious.

I can save him money from 'out of his pocket' if I get it just right.

My specialty job was to make sure the comics and magazine got inserted in each paper before they were 'rolled'.

"Is this ok daddy?"

He smiled in approval. It always made my day.

Throwing the paper on rainy days was an extra challenge. It took additional time to slip a plastic sleeve over the paper. That was Gerald's job. Daddy's near-perfect throw kept the paper dry almost all the time.

It was a treat to have breakfast with mommy, daddy, and my brother after we completed our paper run.

Daddy usually cooked. Except fish, which mom fried, Bahamian style- head and tail on.

I would often go with daddy to collect his 'paper money'. I was filled up with pride to hear his customers praise him for his spot-on delivery.

The Paper Man was oftentimes the only name daddy was called, but everyone knew him, and he in turn, knew just about everyone in the community. I was the Paper Man's daughter.

Daddy continued his Miami Herald franchise until we left in 1958 to live in Bermuda.

Alternately, I was the nurse's daughter.

Mom was one of only a handful of RN's in our community who had a college degree. An educated black nurse was still rather rare in the 1950s, and mommy took it to heart that she was supposed to help everyone who needed her.

"I'm going to report you for practicing medicine without a license," daddy half-heartedly threatened my mom. She ignored him, for decades.

Daddy was concerned about mommy losing her nurse's license if caught dispensing shots, but he also understood she was providing a vital service. Vials of penicillin, sterilized needles, and plungers, competed for space in our refrigerator along with other perishables.

"Antonia, bring me my bag," mommy commanded whenever one of our neighbors came over for some medicine, or a shot. I guessed not too many folk had medical insurance. We lived in a rural area where skin eruptions and other forms of infections from the soil were common. It kept mommy busy.

I remember hearing the grown folk talk about VD.

"You know VD is easily curable," I often heard my mom saying. "You just need three shots of penicillin treatment."

I grew up thinking penicillin cured everything.

"A little something won't hurt anyone," was my mother's abiding philosophy. For most of her life, she always had a stash of a wide ranging variety of drugs; the kind to make you feel good, or to take the edge off living. She especially liked her psychoactive medications.

My mother never stopped dispensing pharmaceuticals and/or advice, even well into her old age, and long after her hospital access dried up.

We were a popular household because of my parents' side hustles, and as far as I know, no harm ever came of my mother's medical practice on other people.

But some of her remedies for treating my childhood conditions and ailments were suspect.

"Antonia, you were so active. When you were a baby, I used to put a little whiskey in your milk so you would sleep all night. I did it with Gerald, too," she bragged about this peculiar parenting skill.

I was terrified of my mom's administrations, and when I could, I resisted her when she attempted to practice on me.

"I needed to give you an enema. You didn't have a bowel

movement for four days." Mom once tried to explain her actions to me.

She would trick me to stop playing and come inside the house.

Trapped inside the bathroom, I was no match for her grown up bigness, but I would kick and scream and flail with all my three year old might to get out of her clutches.

"A.G. I need help." She conspired to have my dad hold me down so she could insert the tubing carrying warm water to force my bowels to involuntarily move.

"Antonia, I had to spank you. You were being so rude; you wouldn't listen. I did it for your own good."

Each time, I died a little before finally letting go.

One of the only times I welcomed her shots was when I got stung by wasps. They hit me five times around my face, neck and upper arm. I had climbed a tree in my backyard and rattled their nest. The shot was to prevent an infection. It hurt. I cried.

I did not have much else to cry about in my early childhood, but I added those enemas to my list of things to drink over.

঺঺঺

IN THE FIRST TEN YEARS OF MY LIFE, MY FAMILY COULD HAVE been the colored model for a Norman Rockwell painting: we ate a cornucopia of red, yellow, and green vegetables; usually white rice; and, meat from the 'high' parts; i.e., steaks, chops, and plenty of chicken; we watched the nightly news on our black and white television; I practiced music every day on my own upright piano, the clarinet, and, the viola; and, I took ballet classes.

"What did you do in school today?" Daddy was the first to ask as the four of us sat around the table. We ate dinner together every day.

Gerald and I were required to talk only about our successes in school. Failure was not an option.

"Antonia, why did you get a spanking in school today, again?", either mommy or daddy would ask. It was a daily ritual; from the first through my third grade. If I was growing up in today's society, I would probably be prescribed Ritalin, or worse, Adderall.

I don't think my parents understood how hard it was for me. I was only three and a half when I started first grade, and only six and a half beginning the third grade. The half is important. I didn't develop the vocabulary to tell them how I felt for a long time.

Usually, if I received a spanking in school, I'd get another at home; by one, or sometimes both of my parents, depending on the offense.

I fought back. Sometimes, mommy would get tired of my resistance while she was spanking me and call daddy in to reinforce her punishments.

Let her fight her own battles. I resented daddy for stepping in as her relief hitter.

I never felt I had done anything to deserve any spanking, and I secretly gloated at my ability to get my parents so riled up they chose to spank me.

On hindsight, I now realize how frustrated they must have been trying to handle me.

"Antonia, you are too smart for your own good," my mother would say. I never figured that one out, but daddy would often say to me, "You have a lot of book learning but not a lot of common sense."

Strange, how after I got married, daddy's message was echoed in Howard's various derisions towards me.

"Those architects don't know what they're doing," Daddy's share at the dinner table was always about something he was building. He was happiest when he got to work at his trade.

"We can't build what they draw," he'd chuckle and complain about how the builders often had to 'fix it in the mix'.

Daddy became quite animated whenever he talked about his construction projects; that is, when he had work. Construction in Miami was seasonal, and the rainy season was long. But his work had standing and permanence. To this day, there are still several buildings around Miami which bear the mark of his signature brick masonry.

"You won't believe what happened in the OR today." Mom would regale us with stories about the surgeries she attended, sparing no details; blood, guts, and all. I have to admit I was turned on by mom's table talk and I developed an early love for biology and other 'medical'-related subjects. It's what spurred me on to become a premed student as an undergrad.

My mother was often the first or only black nurse with a degree wherever she worked, and she swelled with concomitant pride.

"I tried to expose you all to everything I could afford,"

Daddy boasted about his parenting choices. Society was slowly desegregating, and our family pursued all Miami had to offer, and which we could afford.

Daddy was usually always on time with the right amount of love, affection and discipline for me, and my younger brothers.

Mom was more volatile. Her love was often suffocating and, sometimes left me confused. She had a sleep walking disorder which worsened over her lifetime; her wanderings took her throughout the house and into whichever bed she came to first; usually mine. For years, I lost sleep fending off her near-death grip as she struggled through her recurring nightmares, fighting off her personal demons. I finally learned if I put a pillow at my back before I fell asleep, it would help cushion me against her grip, or grope.

"Gerald," I once asked my brother after we had grown into middle age, "Did mom ever get into your bed and wake you up at night when you were a little boy?"

I was desperate to put some closure to this vestige of my childhood anxiety. I had not had any success after working with a host of shrinks to resolve this remaining boogey man.

"Toni, you know I always passed out every night," Gerald was totally unaware of my experiences.

I envied my brother's ability to collapse at the end of his long days of hard playing. He always had a sunny disposition, and I'm sure if probed, he'd have his own stories of childhood trauma. His story.

Funny about what we remember and tell in our childhood stories. I easily and eagerly shared all of mine with Howard. In the beginning, he was a good listener.

While I had to probe, he finally opened up to me about some of his early memories.

"I remember my mom holding me in her arms when we fell down the stairs. I heard daddy screaming at her."

"What happened?"

"I think he pushed her. I don't remember too much more. And then we moved to Miami."

Years later, he admitted the early trauma left him feeling his mother would not be able to protect him.

I knew what he meant.

Howard and I continued to share stories about early childhood drama and trauma. In the beginning, it brought us close.

"We're soul mates," we agreed. When compared, there was an equal amount of mirth and misery between us; at least it seemed so in the beginning.

5

PASTELS, PREDILECTIONS AND PRECOCITY

1958-1968

Daddy went to work in Bermuda in early 1958.

"Bettye, jobs are tight in Miam, so I'm signing on for this job. You and the children can come over once I get settled."

We joined him a few months later. Our family had grown to three children: me, almost nine; Gerald, seven; and, Sidney, a second brother, then seven months old.

Daddy had joined the trowel trades union back in the mid-1950's; only one of a handful of non-white members in south Florida. His initial membership in the union created tension amongst the other non-white workers, but the upside of becoming a card-carrying member was he was selected to join the construction crew to build a new airport in Bermuda.

My parents always had a financial fallback position: mom's nursing license; the one daddy continuously warned her about not losing, because of what he called her "shady" medical practices.

"Bettye, you can always get a job, no matter where we live, but you know, my work is dependent on the weather and being called to a job."

Daddy was at the mercy of those two uncontrollable factors: Mother Nature, and the nature of men; usually white men, and/or the black men who did their bidding. In 1958, there were simply no general contractors in South Florida who looked like us.

"Why don't you get a teaching job?" Mom had repeatedly asked him. "It won't take you long to study and pass the teachers' test."

"You do have a college degree," she reminded him. It sounded more like a taunt.

"But I don't feel qualified to teach other people's children," daddy retorted.

Daddy was an exceptional brick mason. He would not have it any other way. For decades, he continued to bask in pride of his product, pointing out his workmanship as we drove around various areas throughout Miami.

"Toni, I just never felt I could be as good at teaching as I wanted to be; certainly not as good as I was at laying bricks." Daddy confessed why he hesitated to take up teaching in their early years of marriage. Classroom teaching was something he eventually did do for a few years, and it was made less painful for him because he taught industrial arts-his forte.

Whenever he did work at his chosen trade, daddy's rate of pay far surpassed mom's steady paycheck.

Before we got to Bermuda, my parent's waged a constant

tug of war about money: earning it, spending it, budgeting it, etc. We sometimes lived from feast to famine to feast.

"Bettye, I don't know why you would spend $35.00 on a pair of shoes for Gerald. It's foolish. He's only nine and you know how fast his feet are growing. He'll only get a few wears out of them."

I listened closely to my folks' dialogue/drama; hanging on to their every word and their nuances, just waiting for the storm to pass. It always did, but not before mom's recriminations.

"A.G., he needs to look nice when he dresses up, and besides, I'll spend my paycheck the way I want to."

Tension over money hung low; I could touch it.

I was growing fast too, but after hearing my parents argue about money spent on clothes, I grew reluctant to ask for anything new. I also feared another thing I heard them talking about: the union blackballing daddy and keeping him from being called to work.

I internalized my parents' conflicts, and I developed a life-long anxiety about money; mostly about not having enough. Even after Howard became a millionaire, my fears continued to plague me. I still feel my early childhood terror, even to this day.

But we got to live 'large' in Bermuda. Daddy's salary was scaled on the American rate of pay; much higher than the local standard. My mother got to 'stay at home' with Sidney. We dined out frequently, and we'd go to see all the 'first run' movies from the States. On Daddy's new salary, we never missed the matinees at either the Atlantic Beach Club or the St. Georges Club where we saw the top billed entertainers from the States.

It was a heady time.

༺༻

"Now Antonia," my mother said in her daily litany, "You are so smart; I know you won't disappoint me."

The last thing I wanted was to disappoint my mother.

When I started school at age three and a half, I kept up with all my lessons, albeit, I had to go to the Principal's office to take a nap every day during that year. Over my entire academic career, my classmates would always be older, sometimes by as many as three or four years. Even so, it was relatively easy for me to keep up with the lessons, and, I continued to excel, academically.

"I don't want to be put back," I stomped around in utter shock and disbelief I would be placed in the fourth form in Bermuda. I had just finished the fifth grade in my small, rural community school in *The Heights*.

I anticipated going into the sixth grade.

"Antonia, the schools here are different and the fourth form is the same as the sixth grade in the United States," my mother tried to reason with me.

"I can do the work. I know I can do it," I insisted. I loved an academic challenge.

This would be perfect.

"The students in the sixth form are already much older than you," mom tried a different tactic. "They are twelve and thirteen years old."

And what of it? I'm eight and a half. Old enough.

"I don't care about the older kids."

I thought my mother's concern was she didn't want me to 'fail' the lessons.

"I can do the work, and I don't want to be put back."

My mother invited the sixth form teacher to intervene. Mrs. Trout tried to explain how difficult the work material would be for me. No amount of her coaxing could get me to change my position.

"Please," Mrs. Trout, I pleaded, "Just give me a chance to 'try' the sixth form. If I fail, I'll go back to the fourth form."

Mrs. Trout allowed me to join her class on a trial basis.

The classroom was divided into two tracks: one for the trades, the other for academic preparation. I studied hard. I kept up, and the following school year I prepared to sit for the entrance exam to The Berkeley Institute, a prestigious prep school on the Island.

All the students in the academic prep track sat for the exam. Not everyone passed. I did. And, contrary to the initial concerns and fears, there was no apparent outward, or other adverse toll taken on me, or on my development.

⚜

BERMUDA WAS PRETTY PASTELS AND FRESH RAIN WATER. THE houses were painted in cool blues, warm greens, and pale shades of yellow, with lime washed, white roofs. The beach sand was pink.

Rain water was precious. It was collected in wells and used for drinking, cooking, and washing clothes, as well as bathing. It softened my hair when I washed it using Castile soap.

When I was just shy of my tenth birthday, I got my menstrual period. It was no big deal to me because I had long been prepared. Mom had been giving me 'the talk', along with various pamphlets on the subject since I was seven. Again, I was ahead of many of my peers.

I started to feel more grown up.

"He was a smooth operator," Sarah Vaughn's hypnotic voice came out of a scratched recording. We had gathered in the den of one of my class mate's homes. The lights were turned down low. There were at least a half dozen of us.

There was some beer being passed around, and I took a few swigs. I felt good. Too good. I was playing hooky with some of my older class mates, and sure enough, I got caught up in the giddy intoxication of everything wrong about the afternoon: out of school; young, naïve, vulnerable, drinking alcohol.

It frightened me.

I remember thinking, *this feels too good to be right* I worried about what my parents would do if they found out. They never did, but it scared me sober for the next five years.

But nothing could have foretold how I would eventually meet my own smooth operator, and have no defenses to call upon.

No matter how hard I try to think of anything unpleasant about the time in Bermuda, even my worse memory brings a smile to my face.

Fueled by my self-propelled academic accomplishments, the next leap into the unknown felt natural for me. I wanted to enter the annual fair's baking contest. I had gotten the announcement at school and, I thought it was a good idea. I felt invincible from my successes in the classroom.

"Antonia, you don't know how to bake a cake," my mom laughed out loud at my declaration.

"Don't worry, mommy, I'll be entering the contest as a youth and an amateur." I had it all figured out.

How difficult could it possibly be to bake a cake?

"But Antonia, we don't have any of the required items to bake a cake, and it will be expensive to get everything we need," my mother was still trying to talk me down.

I insisted on doing it anyway.

We borrowed baking equipment from Mrs. Godfrey, our neighbor from across the street. Since we had nothing of our own to support my ambition, we even had to borrow measuring spoons as well as the pans, mixer, etc. We went to the store to buy the dry and wet ingredients: flour, baking powder, eggs, milk, vanilla extract, sugar.

"We should buy a boxed cake mix."

I scoffed at my mother's suggestion.

"That will be cheating," I smugly pronounced.

"The contest rules said it had to be an original, home- made (from scratch) cake." I proceeded to follow the Betty Crocker cook book recipe for a yellow cake, and chocolate frosting.

I did not want any help, from anyone. After all, I could read, all I needed to be able to do to follow a recipe.

"That cake looks good," daddy offered even before the batter went into the oven. He never discouraged me from doing anything, but I knew he was just as skeptical as my mother. After all, this was a case of the blind leading the blind.

It took me almost half a day to bake and decorate my cake.

The end product left a lot to be desired. One of the two layers did not rise, and I had no clue about how to level it.

I'm an amateur, I continued telling myself. I was ready to take my contest entry to the fair grounds.

⚜

THE DAY WAS BEAUTIFUL; THE GRASS WAS MANICURED, AND the grounds took a gentle slope downward to where the cake table sat.

Several mature ladies in flowered hats were standing around, admiring one another's magnificent creations.

Those are the most beautiful cakes I have ever seen. I can't believe this. There're a mile high!

I wanted to run.

Please don't let me pee my pants. I held my breath and squeezed my legs together.

I slowly walked up to the table and placed my lopsided two-layered cake at the end. It stood out like an afterthought.

It's not fair. They should have had a children's table. Well, at least no one will ever accuse me of not trying.

I knew no one would recognize me, so I moved in and out as quickly as I could, never filling out the card to identify me as the perpetrator of this obvious joke. I went to join daddy and Gerald who were watching a cricket match on the other side of the fair grounds.

"Well, how did it go?" Daddy was surprised to see me so soon.

"OK." I answered and sat down on the grass to watch the remainder of the cricket game with them.

Daddy didn't probe. He never did. In fact, I grew up thinking all men would be like him. His style set me up for a great disappointment. Not one has measured up, yet; a few have come close, but still no A.G.

When the three of us got home, I couldn't tell my mother the pain I felt.

She will just say "I told you so". I couldn't admit I was out of my league; or that she was right.

And so it was hereafter set, the metaphor of my life: I just had to make up my mind I could do something; I would get it done- by hook or crook; by manipulation of the system; of people; and, certainly of the rules and regulations. And if I was wrong? Well, I'd never let them see me sweat. At least not outwardly.

My family spent a year and a half in Bermuda. I hated to leave. I was feeling good about attending The Berkley.

There had been some serious consideration given to me staying with Mrs. Trout to attend the prep school, but ultimately, my parents decided I was too young to leave behind.

⚜

"DINAH SURE LOOKED GOOD." MOM AND DAD WERE LOOKING at some of the photos from our stay in Bermuda. There was Dinah Washington, Queen of the Blues, doing a handstand on our front porch. We lived in the Spanish Point section of the Island, and our apartment had a view across Hamilton Bay into town.

Dinah, and her entire entourage had eaten dinner at my house. My parents had befriended her years before at one of the clubs back home in Miami. Dinah was diabetic and did not like to give herself injections; my mom was happy to oblige her.

"Yeah, but she was really sick, and almost went into a coma," mom recalled. "She could have died if I didn't give her that shot." I looked at the photo and saw a vibrant woman, mid-thirties, who was not one ounce overweight.

How could she be so sick and perform a handstand, and sing on stage? I wondered.

Also, I had observed how she had an appetite to match any man I'd ever seen eat.

"I don't know," daddy offered. "She must be on husband number four by now, and still can't take care of herself." Daddy was keen on grown folks acting responsible.

"Hush, A.G., Antonia doesn't need to know that."

I wondered what such a secret was. I also wondered how my mom could tell she was going to die.

"Could have died," or "going to die," I soon figured out, was mom's code for people who came to her for medical attention. She saved a lot of people's lives.

Mom was a good nurse. She simply was not good for much else. Thankfully, for her, she was able to get back to being a nurse as soon as we returned to the States

It was mid-school year when we got back to our house in *The Heights.*

There were few good local school choices for Negro students. Up for consideration were the very few Catholic schools which were beginning to integrate, or the away schools.

My parents had limited options.

In the meantime, I was enrolled in the seventh grade, second semester, at Mays High School. It offered grades seven to twelve.

"The teacher's stupid, and she doesn't know how to teach." My mother demanded to know why I was acting out in my seventh grade math class, and getting F's on my work.

"Besides, I already did the same work in Bermuda."

Everything looked dark to me: the hallways; the classrooms; the students, and the teachers' attitudes. There were accelerated classes, for sure, but, initially, I was not placed in one.

"You don't talk English like us," the other seventh graders charged.

You don't talk English like me.

For the first time since I was three years old, when I first started school, I began to fail. I felt like an outsider. I lost control. I became angry. I did not want to be at the school.

For starters, I had worn a uniform in Bermuda.

Stateside, my wardrobe had not caught up with the current trends. I had to fix it. Each morning I got up earlier than my parents to prepare for school.

I can't let them see me leave the house.

I had learned how to style my hair in an exaggerated bee hive (it took me fifteen minutes). I had tightened my skirts (I took them in by hand). I had adopted the trend of double bobby socks, and I applied makeup around my eyes.

Once I arrived at the school, I found my way to the corner store where I'd hang out with the boys, and a few other girls like me- other lost souls. A few times, I did not make it to my homeroom class before the second bell.

I was, simply, overwhelmed.

In Bermuda, I only had one classroom. At Mays, we changed classes. It took me a few weeks before I learned how to navigate through the hallways; locating the right rooms; and, getting to my seat on time.

How do the other students do this?

The biggest distraction? All those older students.

Those guys look and sound like men, and some of those girls are women!

"Antonia you had better stop acting so rude and spoiled. We will have to punish you." My parents defaulted to the one method they knew.

A sympathetic Principal, who knew both my parents, decided to test me and after some thoughtful consideration, he and my parents agreed I could do eighth grade work; their antidote to why I was failing seventh grade.

"Antonia can do the work. The only problem is she is so young." The Principal was reluctantly encouraging.

"Well, she did very well with older kids in Bermuda, so we'll give it a try," mom assured him. She tossed me a side-long glance, partly in rebuke, but also I felt, to let me know she fully supported me, and my promotion.

Yes, another academic challenge. I grew excited, once again.

So, despite my re-entry trauma, acting-out, and just plain unhappiness at the beginning of the semester, I was, once again, going to be with the thirteen-fourteen year olds.

That's more like it.

I had just had my eleventh birthday.

Alas, my semester of eighth grade remains a blur of insults and injuries: Alice, my favorite girl cousin, shunned me over the entire four months. She was two years older than me, and she hated that I had been placed in her homeroom.

"You need to stop trying to be with Alice," my mom saw how hurt I was. "She is too fast for you." I knew Alice had already been sent away, once, to live in Key West with our Great Aunt Mizpah. She was supposed to be getting taught how to be a 'lady'. It must not have worked for my mom to say such a thing.

Mommy didn't have to worry. Alice did not want to be in my company, ever. Her attitude toward me would not change for a long time; it would be years later before I came to understand more about her motives.

Back in Bermuda, everyone had a clear predestination under the British system. The tracking began at an early age. Good or not so good, it kept order in the classrooms. But back States-side, a more democratic environment awaited me.

I was not prepared.

⚜

"You will fail PE if you don't take a shower," the gym teacher yelled at me.

"I don't need to take a shower," I shouted back.

I didn't really 'play' hard at any team sports. My biggest 'sport' had always been marathon reading; I usually had three to four books open at one time.

I didn't exert myself enough outside to work up a real sweat. Besides, my small amount of perspiration didn't bother me. So why should I have to take a shower?

My problem? I was not physically developed, and some of my classmates looked like fully grown women. Their breasts fell into their brassieres! I was barely an A cup.

I was so uncomfortable. I'd grown used to saying 'breasts', 'buttocks', 'urination', 'bowel movement', and other clinical terms describing the body and its functions. They said 'titties', 'ass', 'pee' or 'piss', and 'crap' or 'shit'.

Their language assaulted me.

I couldn't stand to hear the girls' use such casual references to their body parts while undressing or taking showers.

I just wish I could be back in Bermuda.

"You can't make me take a shower, and I don't care if you fail me." I blubbered between my tears.

Antonia, stop crying.

The PE teacher favored the athletic girls. They were always sweaty.

Another problem to report home.

My parents were perplexed.

This was my first time feeling so apart from my classmates. Up to this point in time, all my competition had been in the academic arena. Mays High School threw me onto an uneven playing field; my parents had not prepared me for these adolescent rites of passage.

How can I get them to understand how much shock I was in? How the girls mocked me? How much it hurt to be so different?

And, to their growing dismay, they were unable to tolerate how I was attracting boys. Older boys.

"Who is that calling my house with a voice deeper than mine?" Daddy asked me one day after answering the phone. It was "T", a popular football player on the Mays High School team.

The real question should have been, what does a just-turned eleven year old girl have to say to a seventeen year old boy?

Above all else, my behaviors got my parents' attention, for sure.

"What are we going to do about Antonia?" Mom and dad openly talked about me in my presence; I felt I was invited into the conversation.

They should have left me in Bermuda.

I had heard about the glories of other schools in Miami where some of the kids from *The Heights* were attending: Northwestern (where mom once taught nursing), Carver (relatively close by), Booker T. Washington (the school from which all my mom's siblings had graduated).

"Why can't I go to (fill in the blank) with so and so?" I pleaded. "I can catch a ride with Dr. Hadley (who had an office in Overtown, near Booker T. Washington), or Mr. 'what's his name' (who taught at Northwestern), or ride with (I listed some students at Carver .....)."

"Antonia, those schools are too far, and the bus schedules are not reliable," Mom and dad agreed, dismissing my schemes.

"Yeah, but you were going to leave me in Bermuda, way away," I reminded them.

"Stop being impudent or I will switch your behind." My mother still thought she could control me with physical punishment. But we both knew she had lost the fight the minute she threatened a spanking.

My parents' logical response? They decided to send me away to a boarding school.

Other people don't just send their children off. Do they? Why can't I stay with one of my aunts?

At first I thought it might be their way of punishing me for my misbehavior at Mays High School. But after I got a chance to look at my neighbors' year books from their time at the chosen school-Holy Rosary, and I saw the boys were, with few exceptions, really good looking. I was sold on going.

"How long am I going to have to be there?"

"At least for this one year. Don't worry, you'll have your brother with you for company."

Gerald and I were still very close; the difference in our age- he was nine and I was eleven- didn't mean so much while we were living at home.

"Antonia, you're lucky. Not everybody gets to go to away school. Holy Rosary has a great reputation, and since you're a Catholic, you'll fit right in."

My mom's logic worked, for her.

The decision was complicated. My parents, in consultation

with my aunts, had already decided it would be best for me and my brother Gerald to go away.

Why? It was going to be a difficult time.

Mom was pregnant again.

Something else is wrong with mommy. She's too skinny to be having a baby, and she's just sick all the time.

As it turned out, she also had a tumor in her uterus which was growing along with the baby.

⚜

SEPTEMBER 1960-

Holy Rosary was a well-known institution serving black Catholics since the turn-of the century. It began as a school for girls in Galveston, Texas and moved, in 1913, to a hundred acres of land in Lafayette, Louisiana.

Several other children from *The Heights* had attended The Rosary. The school had seen better days by the time I arrived with my nine year old bother Gerald in tow (the boarding component closed in 1974, and the school permanently closed in 1993).

The place was literally suffocating! It was located near the great Atchafalaya Basin, a swamp, or Bayou, of the Mississippi River. The school was run by a group of black nuns who behaved as if they were in the nineteenth century, or an even earlier time. I was eleven and a half, and even at such a young age, I knew those nuns' attitudes were not very modern.

"Why don't they speak to us?" I asked my play big sister, Veda Joe.

One of the first things I noticed immediately after arriving, was tension between the boarders and the day students.

"Their parents told them not to mess with the boarders because we're not Creoles." Veda Joe, already fourteen years old, was from Georgia, and she knew a lot of things.

I had heard of Creoles, but I still had a lot to learn about the deep cultural, class, and color divides, even amongst Negroes.

I wasn't naïve about certain prejudices.

"You know you're not American," my aunts used to tell me. Somehow they felt if they held on to their ancestor's British identities, it would elevate them, and me, above being that much despised entity, a nigger in America.

My family had gone to great lengths to keep me from thinking like, or being a nigger. I was never less than, but I wasn't prepared for my encounter with those Louisiana Creoles. To this day, I have still not been able to plumb the depth of that group's peculiar place in American history.

The day students were mostly descendants of Blacks and French; were 100% Catholic; French-speaking, mostly fair-skinned people; and, did not 'mix' with anyone who was not from their same origins.

I know some colored people, even some of my family, who are whiter, and they don't act like them.

On the other hand, the boarders were a real mixed bag: many were non-Catholics, and their skin tones ranged from ebony to ivory.

The boarders and the day students only interacted in the classroom, or on sports teams. The two groups did not socialize with one another after school except at an occasional social/dance, and/or at the weekend movies. Even then, they stayed in separate groupings.

Several of the boarders were throw away kids.

"My mother is a call girl." One of my classmates proudly announced.

I enjoyed looking at photos of her mother in an array of ball gowns, in glamorous poses with various men and their fancy cars.

That's what I want to be, a kept woman.

I further confirmed my ambition when, on a visit to her daughter, the woman blew into town from a business trip to nearby New Orleans.

She looks like a movie star. She was accompanied by a good looking man who drove a new Cadillac convertible.

Yes, that's what I want to look like. I was an instant convert.

It took me years to absolutely reject the peculiar career choice. Or did I ever, completely? From a very young age, I used to often think about how women exchanged themselves for all manner of material comforts. I would hear the refrain from my earliest childhood: "....and if you marry, marry someone who can take care of you." It would take me years to disavow myself of this reasoning.

"You're going to be our valedictorian," the Priest/Principal told me shortly after my brother Gerald, and I arrived at the school.

I was stunned.

I shifted nervously on my seat.

"How do you know? I just got here." I remember looking

him straight in his eye, something my mother had always told me to do when speaking with anyone.

"Your grades and test scores tell me you can do the work, and excel." He was so sure of my future.

"The staff and the other administrators are delighted to have you join the class of 1964. We have great expectations for you."

"Aren't you excited?" He was giddy.

His declaration frightened me. It also threatened me. I did not seek nor did I want the responsibility. *No! I can't handle it.*

My heart beat quickened. I began to hyperventilate. I think it may have been the first time I ever felt mistrustful of my own capabilities in the classroom.

"I'm not so sure about that," I uttered, but I continued to look him straight in the eye, like I was taught.

I was alone. I felt trapped in his office.

I'm nearly a thousand miles from home, but it might as well be another planet.

I rocked in my chair and felt the room begin to swim.

I don't not want to be the Valedictorian, or anything else. I just want to be a normal student. I wish I could go back to Bermuda.

I did not realize it at the time, but looking back I was exhausted, and depressed. What eleven year old gets depressed? There was not much talk about that in 1960.

What no one could estimate was, for the first time ever, it was not the course of study or the rigors of academic achievement which was so daunting for me. I had always managed to rise to any academic challenge.

But, I was away from home for the first time.

Don't they know what I have to do? I don't know how to do my own hair. I've got to do my own laundry. Daddy had always done the sorting, washing, drying, folding, etc. I've got to budget my spending money and make it last between the times they send it. I've got to pick 'good' friends. Oh my God, I've got to make sure Gerald is all right. And, what about all these cute boys?

Almost from day one, I recognized that the place was secluded, sheltered, and overseen by a group of morally pure, but socially backward nuns who had dubious academic preparation and training to teach. I was overwhelmed.

Valedictorian? I don't think so.

In rebellion, I proceeded to do everything I could to negate the Principal's expectations.

I did the most natural thing. I joined a girl gang.

With the exception of my one semester at Mays, I always had had a group of older girls in school who defended me, and sometimes actually fought my fights.

At Holy Rosary, our group was called The Challengers. We were the good girls. We were academically advanced; we were not promiscuous; we were from intact families (more or less); and, we, not me, but my big sisters, were socially at ease. And, for the most part, we served as positive re-enforcers of one another.

My big sisters constantly came to my rescue. They immediately saw since I was so much younger than my classmates, I needed their protection.

There were only four of us Challengers; a small but mighty gang.

Our gang hung tight. We dressed alike, borrowing each

other's clothes, competed for top grades, exchanged our dreams and plans for the future, and we talked a lot about the boys we liked.

"Let me do Toni's hair." There was always competition over doing my hair. I liked the attention. I felt loved. I depended on 'my girls' to help me keep my hair presentable. They pressed it bone-straight, and I wore it in a pony-tail switch. They counseled me on how to dress out of uniform: like a big girl, but still modestly. And they kept me out of harms' way.

One of those harms were nocturnal sexual predators.

The biggest culprit, a fourteen year old girl, stalked the younger girls at night. She was also the most delinquent, in other ways.

"Now Antonia, there will be girls at school who like other girls." My mother had warned me to be aware of what she called stalking lesbians who were found in away schools.

Forewarned, I was not too alarmed when I was first approached.

"If you try to touch me, I will tell and get you expelled." I managed to turn her away and never had that problem again.

After my confrontation, I was never threatened again, but I was terrified how she was able to molest some of the younger girls who, unlike me, had no gang/group protection.

The nuns must know what was happening. I hated them for ignoring the obvious.

The predator was also an accomplished shop-lifter. Every week before we went into town to shop, she held boosting classes for anyone interested. I did participate once, but I was not good at stealing.

Once, I found an opportunity to use her to my advantage; to leverage her propensity for all types of delinquency with my budding curiosity about boys.

I needed a co-conspirator, but I didn't want to tell my girls.

"I need you to do me a favor."

She readily agreed, given her zeal for wrongdoing.

"Sure, what do you need?"

I got her to agree to stand in the hall in front of the broom closet in between classes so I could met up with Percy D. He and I had arranged to have my first tongue kiss!

Once was enough.

Oh no! He has bad breath.

I started trying on other behaviors to match my pre-adolescent sexual urges.

I grew bolder.

I began to stuff my bra with my red fox stockings to fill out my size A cups. To my horror, the first time I tried enhancing my breasts, the swamp heat caused the stockings to rise from my bra and push up through the front of my shirt! I hurriedly pushed them back down before anyone saw what was happening. Subsequently, I'd pin the stockings to my bra.

I pretended to be older in other ways: I regularly used makeup; I mimicked the older girls' mannerisms; and, I cultivated a flirtatious banter.

I was curious.

The age of innocence ends early, and I had a made-up mind. What was a girl to do?

GERALD AND I WENT HOME FOR THE CHRISTMAS BREAK.

"Everything is fine," we both reported.

Mom was recovering from a difficult pregnancy and delivery. Haywood was born in October by a cesarean procedure, and Mom's large tumor was removed from her uterus at the same time.

"The doctors said the tumor was benign." Mom didn't have to explain to me what the word meant. She knew if there was a word I didn't understand, I'd simply look it up in the dictionary. I had learned about that medical term from listening to her talk about her nursing experience, and from my own keen interest in medicine.

I also knew the declaration was a good thing.

Me and Gerald might get to come home.

Our little brother was born with blond hair and blue eyes.

"Mommy, is my brother white?" Sidney, then nearly four, was not so sure about the shocking appearance of his little brother. At first, I too, was uncomfortable going out in public with Haywood, but his appearance changed over time; he got browner.

Besides his fair complexion, at issue was Haywood's health. He was small. He was sickly.

"No, I don't want to hold him." He looked so frail. I was afraid I would hurt him.

"Mommy, when will I get to play with him?" Sidney constantly pulled on the baby which caused me some anxiety.

I intuitively knew that I and Gerald should not give mommy anything else to worry about.

"Gerald, let's not tell mommy and daddy about how bad it is at Holy Rosary."

It was easy to make a pact with Gerald to not complain about any of our experiences at the boarding school. I had many complaints, but Gerald was always happy about everything.

"The food is ok, and the school is great," I reported when my parents asked how we liked Holy Rosary.

Actually, much of the food was foreign to me, and I shunned the daily offerings: dirty rice; boudin sausage; peanut butter cut with molasses; duck; fried rabbit, and other local cuisine were usually left on my plate. I pined for the familiar foods of home, and instantly devoured the meager and humble contents of my care packages- usually tuna, crackers and olives. Sometimes there was a Cadbury chocolate bar- compliments of the British aunts.

To this day, Gerald still relishes boudin sausage. I worried about that boy.

The physical structure of the Institute itself also had intimidated me at first sight. The buildings loomed large in my child's eye.

There was one main girls building. It had three floors where the nuns also kept their quarters. The ceilings were high and the hallways long. There were open dormitories, segregated by age, but accessible to all; and, an actual co-ed refectory on the first floor with its attendant long tables. We ate in shifts, dining by age/grade groupings.

There were designated rooms to do laundry, study halls, and social spaces remained segregated by gender.

The campus contained many other buildings: the school; the boys' dormitory; a playground; and, an assortment of farm structures out back.

And of course, there was the church/chapel where I suffered through interminable masses, prayer services, rosaries, etc. I had only recently become a confirmed Catholic; but there was not yet any conviction in my heart.

There was also a long alee of trees leading to the street outside the school's gate; just like in the movie images of some southern plantations.

The campus had a community building where the religious order held socials and showed movies which were open to the public. Only religious titles were shown. They screened one film, in particular, which showed an early martyr's death from piercing arrows. I had nightmares about the bloodied body; dozens of arrows sticking out from every angle. It took years to get over the trauma, and I recalled it recently when I watched Mel Gibson's The Passion of the Christ.

"Yes, we want to go back," I lied once I realized what was going on with my family; it had changed. Mom was not up to par after her ordeal of having a major surgery; our brother Sidney, had been diagnosed as hyperactive; and daddy was not working full time.

"Money is tight," I heard my parents repeat.

"There are a lot of medical bills, and your tuition to pay," daddy explained why times were hard. I accepted my additional responsibility; it was simply not ok just to be great on my own. I had to help my parents get through this difficult time.

"Now Antonia, you have to take care of Gerald. He is

younger than you and he is your responsibility," mommy had told me before we first left in September to attend Holy Rosary.

My mom kept up her expectation of me years after we left boarding school: to take care of Gerald.

Shortly after we got back to the Rosary from Holiday break, word came to me that my little brother was the target of Dr. Goat, a fourteen year old boarder, who was a known homosexual predator.

Here we go. Not my little brother!

"Over my dead body," I told my informant.

I enlisted support from our cousin Ernest. Butch, as we called him, had come with us after the Christmas holiday, to enroll at Holy Rosary. Butch was in the tenth grade. He agreed to keep a lookout at night for Gerald, but I was skeptical about just how much he would/could do. After all, he was sent away to the school because he had become hard to handle.

He had started experimenting with drugs, and I didn't fully trust him to do right by my little brother.

"If you don't do something about it, I will," I announced to the Priest/Principal as I stood with my arms akimbo, wagging my finger in his face.

I felt safe behind his closed office door. He didn't speak during my tirade which only lasted for a few, electrified minutes.

I don't know where I got the strength and resolve to be so aggressive.

Mommy and daddy might as well be on the moon, so I've got to protect my little brother. Since we're away from home, I'm on the front line and I'm responsible for his safety.

"I'll call the police, and newspaper, and report that the school did not do anything about Dr. Goat," I declared with so much force I shook.

"And, I heard Gerald was not the only little boy who Dr. Goat has targeted," I shouted my parting salvo.

After making my case, I stomped out of the office, worried I might not have been effective.

"Gerald, you tell me if Dr. Goat says anything to you, at all."

He just nodded.

"He's not even supposed to speak to you, ok?"

I'm not sure if my brother understood the importance of what was going on. He still remained innocent. He had only turned ten in a few months before in October.

"How is Gerald?" I depended on my cousin Butch every day to give me a report.

"Don't worry." Butch tried to help me feel better. "I have him under my protection every night."

I never trusted Butch to look after Gerald the way I knew I could, but we were separated at bedtime; no exceptions could be made. I didn't sleep well over the following nights.

Dr. Goat was expelled a few weeks later. I was relieved when I didn't have to call our parents. *What can they do from so far away? They had put me in charge*

Since I had taken care of the matter, I was feeling full of myself, and despite my efforts of self- sabotage in the classroom, I was still on my way to becoming the Valedictorian.

"Damn!" I uttered to myself. "What do I have to do?"

During the remainder of the semester, I got loud, and I started to use profanity. Cursing gave me a physical release from the mounting tensions and pressures of just being there.

On one Saturday afternoon, while I was doing my laundry, one of the nuns approached me. She began scolding me in the middle of the wide hallway about something I'd done; or not done.

Unbeknownst to her, I had reached my limit.

Right there, in the middle of the common area of the girl's hall, I shouted in her face: "Why don't you take your religious shit and just go to hell?"

I proceeded to curse the school, the Principal and all the nuns for what I felt was their ineptitude, wrapped up in their false religious piety.

My head felt like it would explode; the cursing felt really good. A release.

I don't recall what triggered my tantrum. It may have been trying to get the laundry completed. There were so many phases to doing laundry, and I could never successfully complete it without some hiccup: running out of coins and ending up with damp-dry clothing; missing items from the dryers, etc.

I was not ready to calm down. I hated those nuns, all of them.

I cried a lot that day, but I got over it, soon enough.

Just let me get through the rest of the year, and wait for the summer to go home.

I had turned twelve in January.

⚜

WHAT'S THE MATTER WITH HER?

My mother had come to Holy Rosary during the Easter vacation to see how my brother and I were doing.

She was pacing the floor, wringing her hands.

I was wrestling with my image in the mirror: I had tried on a soft green, chiffon dress with a sash in the back!

"Don't you like it? I bought it from...."

She mentioned the name of some leading store. Mommy was so proud of the Easter dress she had brought all the way from Miami.

"I paid a lot for it." Her voice dropped to a whisper, pleading with me.

I was speechless.

How am I going to accessorize this dress so I could appear in public? The thought preoccupied me.

"My mother's intuition told me I needed to check up on you", she fussed over the crinoline slip.

"I was worried you weren't telling me everything." She could not find my eyes.

Right. She has no idea what I'm going through, and I'm not going to try and explain. She'd never understand. Besides, that was all settled during the Christmas break when I told her everything was fine.

No matter which direction I turned in the mirror, the dress was still hideous.

She is clueless. This little girl dress is insulting!

I remained silent, looking away from her.

What does she know about me being at an away school?

I silently proceeded to put on my garter belt to hold up my red fox stockings. I then applied my makeup. The look of the hour was an exaggerated Cleopatra cat eye I achieved by using a heavy application of black pencil.

My hair, straightened with a hot comb, nearly reached my buttocks, and I had it pulled back on top of my head to hang down into my customary pony tail.

I checked myself in the mirror: *Sophisticated.*

I felt good.

The finishing touch was a pair of Kelly green, suede high heel pumps I had purchased earlier in the year. *Almost finished*

I liked how I looked.

"Oh my God, Antonia." My mother gasped. She was beside herself.

"When did you learn to put on makeup?"

"And how can you walk in those high heels?" She had been watching me from her perch on the side of my bed.

"I sent you here a little girl, and now you're acting like a grown woman," my mom sat crying on the side of my bed.

"Well, you sent me here. And this is what ninth graders do." I put on my red lipstick. One last look: *Perfect.*

I pranced out of the room on my spikes.

She followed me out and we headed to the chapel to meet Gerald for Easter Mass.

He looked great in his suit.

I congratulated myself on what I felt was a masterful job; turning that pastel horror into something wearable.

Didn't she get it?

I did not return to Holy Rosary the next year. They would have to find another Valedictorian.

I'd won another battle. Hadn't I?

※

"HEADSTRONG, ANTONIA, THAT'S WHAT YOU ARE." MY mother was, once again, perplexed about what to do with me. Over the summer after attending boarding school, I told her how difficult it had been. She understood, and my parents decided not to send me back, but they were still faced with limited choices in Miami. It was 1961.

My mother got busy doing her 'research' into available, 'appropriate' schools for me to attend in Miami. I was still far younger than my grade group; and yet, so far ahead of my age peers. I would be twelve and a half going into the tenth grade.

During the year in boarding school, I had cultivated a 'bad' attitude toward adults and authority, yet I still needed guidance and structure.

"What's a mother to do?" My mother was out of her wits.

She had to petition the highest authorities in the Miami Archdiocese after the school administrators told her my class was 'full', but she was successful in getting me enrolled at Immaculata Academy a local, private Catholic school for girls. I was the only black girl on my first day.

"Antonia, this is a really very big deal- they let you into Immaculata," mom impressed upon me.

"There are only a handful of Negro girls in the Catholic high schools in Miami, and you have to be an example."

This time, the challenge didn't frighten me. I was operating from my home base, and I was welcomed at the school from day one.

"I'm just waiting to graduate so I can go to work, or get married," was a common pronouncement from the majority of my classmates.

Little did my mom know, according to the running joke amongst the students, Immaculata was considered just a holding cell for virgins; a far cry from the preparatory school she had expected.

It was called a *parochial* school, and was such in every sense of the word.

When I started at Immaculata, it was predominantly populated with white ethnic Catholic girls.

That quickly changed.

The year before I enrolled, the Cuban Air Lift project had begun. First there was a trickle, and then a flood of students; especially into the Catholic schools.

"You're not Cuban," I told Hilda. "And what kind of Spanish name is Hilda anyway?" I challenged a classmate.

She was blond with blue eyes. Not like the family friends and relatives I had known all my life; the brown and black Cubans from Key West and Miami.

"I was born in Cuba," Hilda retorted. She thought she had the last word.

Not satisfied, I asked, "Yeah, but where were your parents born?"

They were Europeans. *I won!*

It was like that with many of the Cubans who came over

during the airlift: Europeans, and first generation Cubans who were part of the upper classes who had left their holdings in the hands of Castro and his revolutionaries.

The culture of Immaculata began to change; as did the culture of Miami.

While at Immaculata, I got very involved. I joined the cheerleading team for LaSalle, the Boy's school which was opened by the LaSalle Brothers who also were exiled from Cuba. I joined the school orchestra where I played the viola. I was a senior class officer (Treasurer). And, I was a key member of the layout team for the Senior Yearbook.

But to my dad's great disappointment, I never made the honor roll because of my grades in conduct.

"You want me to be smart and good too?" I flippantly responded when daddy asked me why I couldn't get higher grades in conduct.

We didn't argue about it. My dad and I were so much alike. I knew he was called the 'black sheep' of his family; he was smart enough, but at the same time, daddy walked a fine line between good, and not so good. I was daddy's girl.

My zeal for fitting in, and behaving as if I was older than my actual age continued. I was tall for my age, but still not yet fully developed. I was barely fitting in a B cup, but I had hips, so I could pull off the look of an older girl with makeup and the hairstyles of the day.

Ours was a very beige uniform: a skirt and blouse, and black and white oxfords. It was beyond impossible to look good in it, but we managed. After school, to dress ourselves up, I would join my classmates and adjust my skirt length by rolling it up at the waist, put on a stylish belt, extra makeup, and hair adornments.

I held my own in conversation and debates, but I was totally devoid of one key experience typical of 1960's high school students: I was not dating. The closest I came to dating was my occasional attendance at house parties in my close knit community, *the Heights,* where, the kids would peel off in couples to slow dance once the lights were lowered.

The parties I attended were always chaperoned, and I had an earlier curfew than everyone else.

My dad would arrive somewhere around 10 PM, turn up the lights, and actually call for space between the bodies.

"Alright, I want to see some light between you all," he shouted out, killing everyone's fun; at the same time signaling my curfew was up.

"I'm here to collect my daughter," he announced, much to my embarrassment. On hindsight, I'm so grateful he did show up. There were too many little 'colored girls' who did not have dads who loved them enough and who watched over them.

Daddy's girl. The notion filled me with pride.

Daddy never left me.

Remarkably, in 2004, forty years after high school graduation, I had the distinguished honor of being the first alumnae inducted into the Inaugural Immaculata-LaSalle High School Hall of Fame for my lifetime of accomplishments which (have) brought great pride and honor to (our) Alma Mater. Funny, it was more than ten years after being divorced from him, but I secretly wished Howard would come through the doors; to acknowledge me. As it was, I had one and a half tables of relatives, and a full complement of friends who did come to honor me: Mommy, daddy, Aunt Doris, my son Issa, Robbie Bell, Donna Ginn, Rene Beal, Dr. Sandra Bontemps, Vivian Bryant, Dr. Evalina Bestman, and Lee Damus. In fact, Robbie Bell and Donna Ginn both made presentations to me at the event. I was honored.

◈

I TOLD HOWARD ABOUT ALL THOSE EARLY EXPERIENCES I HAD had: starting school early at a young age; living in Bermuda and competing with way older kids; the terrible semester I spent at Mays Highs School; the boarding school fiasco, and dealing with the Cuban exile girls, so I wondered what he meant about me needing to fight my way out of a paper bag.

Why do I need to know how to fight, at all, anymore? I thought he would offer me a cushion; he would protect me.

I'd learn what he meant soon enough.

In 1976, when we returned to Miami after being away for six years, I wondered how Howard could remain unaffected by the Bahamian and Cuban cultures prevailing in the City.

He's gonna need me now, for sure.

For too long, Howard's world view remained limited by his narrow black and white lens; colored over by the residuals of Jim Crow, and the cautionary lessons he had learned from being a black-male in the near south.

But his attitude would change, and quite dramatically after he came into power at the City.

Before then, and on at least one occasion during the first

year of our marriage, Howard offered me a backhanded compliment; his nod toward my ability to act free in his small world.

"You're not black enough," he'd shoot at me, only to return at some later time to ask me to use my not black voice and/or to draw on my larger world view to help us overcome some racial slight; perceived or real.

It was a lot like the times when my grandmother and/or Aunt Doris used their facility with Spanish to get over.

Confused? You bet!

But it was just the beginning.

6

EXPOSURE

1964-1968: The College Years

"Toni, I don't know how you could stay up there with all those white girls."

Was that a compliment? Howard sometimes praised me for what he considered my supreme act of bravery: going to Marymount College in Tarrytown, New York, where I was one of only four black girls in my class!

Besides us four, there was only one other African-American at Marymount: Fanny Chestnut, my big sister.

I never suffered from being at Marymount. I smiled at the memory. How I got there was another story.

"Howard, I didn't have a choice about going to Marymount, or not."

When did I ever have a choice about which school I'd attend? I just had to do the best I could with what I got.

There was no question about what I'd do after graduating from high school. Many members of my mom's and dad's families were college educated, and amongst them were doctors, dentists, lawyers, college professors, and teachers going back three generations. It was part of my everyday consciousness that I was to be somebody. Higher education was my ticket to reach a higher status.

Just before I graduated from Immaculata, daddy had taken a job in Cocoa Beach and the family was preparing to relocate.

"Why can't I just stay here and go to the new junior college?" I pleaded with my mother during another tug of war between us.

"I can stay with Aunt Doris and take the bus. The tuition is cheap, and I can work a part time job." I was so sure I'd win my argument.

"Antonia, the junior college just isn't good enough, and you still need to be with the sisters. You'll get the best education with them" My mother was firm.

Besides, my mom and Fr. Swift, my parish priest had already commiserated. They were convinced, because I was only fifteen and a half, I still needed to be in a sheltered environment. They had decided I would attend a Catholic college/university.

After years of being an exception, I just wanted to go somewhere to be one of many; to remain anonymous; and I did not want to leave home, again. My memory of Holy Rosary was growing dimmer, but the recall was still painful. I did not look forward to having to 'adjust' to another unfamiliar environment.

I was tired; I succumbed to their machinations.

Fr. Swift, my parish priest, had developed a network with college Presidents, Admissions Deans, and other high-ranking officials in many of the nation's Catholic colleges/universities, around the country. Who knew? He hardly fit my image of a power-broker. He was a jocular, ruddy-faced, hard-drinking, Irish priest who stood over 6'3" and easily weighed 300 pounds. But there he was, controlling much of my future from a little parish in Richmond Heights, the exurbs of Miami-Dade County.

By the end of the summer of 1964, there were at least five-six of us black high school graduate students, members of Christ the King Church who had been accepted into some of the Country's best Colleges and Universities.

Fr. Swift managed my applications; he told me which schools to apply. There were dozens, and I received several acceptances and offers. The largest award was from Marymount College, Tarrytown, New York, which provided full tuition for four years (contingent on my grade point average), and a work-study program.

Howard, was awarded a scholarship to join the swimming team at Morehouse College where he would join his brother who had gone a year before him. There were also three others from Miami already on the swim team.

So off we went: I, to Tarrytown, New York, and he, to Atlanta, Georgia, but the distance between us was already far greater than just miles.

⚜

WHEN I FIRST GOT TO MARYMOUNT, I HAD A STANDING weekly appointment with the college President.

"Antonia, I have Fr. Swift on the line," Mother Brendan handed me the phone.

"How are you doing, Antonia?"

"Fine, Fr. Swift. Everyone is so friendly. I've made some good friends and my classes are going ok, too." I always tried to sound upbeat and positive whenever I talked with Fr. Swift. Freshman year was quite an adjustment, but I was content.

My schoolmates were in awe of my intimacy with Mother Brendan, RSHM, President, Marymount College, who was akin to the 'Pope' on our campus.

Two and a half years later, mid-way through my Junior year, our close relationship would help grease the way for me and five of my classmates to successfully petition the College Board of Trustees, and Mother Brendan, who approved our request to become the first experimental group to live off-campus. Our experiment opened the way for a score of seniors to live off-campus the following year, heralding in a new day for Marymount. Another triumph was added to my growing lists of firsts.

Fr. Swift had been sending black students from all his previous parishes to the best Catholic Colleges and Universities in the country for more than 30 years. One of his students, Fanny Chestnut (Hairston) from his previous Parish in Wilmington, NC, was the only black student at Marymount when I arrived.

She told me how she had begged Fr. Swift to send another black student to Marymount- so she would not have to be alone anymore.

"Some of the girls were really mean to me," Fannie shared

how lonely she was for two years. "Most of the time, I stayed closed up in the library with Sister Joan d' Arc."

The library would become a great refuge for me too. It had a wonderful collection of classical and show music, which I listened to, alone, in a sound proof room.

Fanny and I started writing to one another during the summer before I entered Marymount. She had been assigned as my big sister, a system the College used to get new students oriented before arriving on Campus. She was a God-send.

I found mecca when I arrived at Marymount: there was one student from Africa; several other students (of color) from foreign countries; i.e., South and Central America, Mexico, Philippines, China, India, to name a few; but, there were only three other American-born black students in my freshman class.

Fr. Swift sent his third black student to Marymount during my sophomore year. Wanda came from his subsequent assignment to a parish in New Orleans, his last. Fr. Swift drowned there during a church outing that same year.

🪷

"Let me have a cigarette, please," I asked Fanny. We were between classes in the Tea House, a three-tiered, cafeteria-style underground space where students gathered to play cards, smoke, drink coffee, and sometimes, actually study. It was one of several underground rooms connecting the buildings which protected us from inclement weather, especially those New York winters. The room was always brightly lit. Sometimes, our professors would socialize with us at the Tea House.

"No, I will not give you a cigarette," Fanny, like many other students, smoked like a chimney. Her family in North Carolina kept her supply of Winston's well-stocked; sending cartons at a time. The Surgeon General's warning had not yet come out; smoking was socially acceptable, and it appeared to me as if the whole world smoked cigarettes.

"I will not contribute to you developing a bad habit," she demurred. "Besides, I don't want your mother getting mad at me." My mother fell in love with Fanny when they first met during my freshman orientation. Fanny took her big sister role seriously. She tried to look after me. I was not always cooperative over the two years we spent together at Marymount.

"Then, I'll buy my own," I huffed. The machine packs cost $.35. My allowance was thin, and I barely had enough to splurge on such a luxury as cigarettes.

I put my coins in the machine and proceeded to pull for a pack of Winston's. What did I know about the difference in brands? I wanted to smoke my big sister's brand.

I lit up with the free matches that were dispensed at the same time.

Puff. Inhale. Cough.

I choked so hard, everyone in the room broke out in laughter. They were in stitches, but I was never one to be outdone by anyone; my peers, or better. I got a glass of water and continued puffing, inhaling, sipping water, until I no longer coughed. It took about a quarter of the pack, and at the end, I was a bona fide member of the Tea House in-crowd.

First came the cigarettes, then learning how to play bridge. I became quite expert at both. It didn't take long before I had perfected smoking tricks: I could blow different types of smoke rings; inhale, take a drink, and swallow before exhaling; and, flip my lighter open with one hand to light up.

Next on my 'to do' list was to learn to drink! All I needed to buy alcohol was a fake ID from anyone whose name sounded American/English, and/or who had dark brown hair and eyes (no photos were used on driver's licenses at the time). I had plenty of classmates to select from, and as long as their surnames were not Italian or Slavic, I was good to go.

The first hard lesson I learned was to not mix beer (cheap at $2 for a pitcher, or $.25 a glass) with scotch. I liked drinking, and, if offered, I never turned one down. There were plenty of grown men at The Huddle, the local Tarrytown bar, who were quick to send a shot or two my way. I look back on hindsight and horror when I realized what cheap barroom entertainment I was to them.

Marymount, as it turned out, was a wonderful place for me go to grow up.

I was wrapped up in the folds of an academic and social environment which nurtured independent thought, encouraged exploration of self, and provided me with a strong foundation in the liberal arts. But it was also during the mid- to-late 1960s when everything was free, i.e., free love, free sex, free drugs, etc. Every type of drug was available, and offered.

"No, thank you." I took mine in a cup or glass.

Despite being a Catholic College, we were encouraged to push against all familiar boundaries. We were within the safety of a homogeneous population: catholic women. *In loco parentis* was the operating philosophy; we were protected.

Academic competition was fierce. Almost without exception, all the students had graduated in the top 5-10% of their high school classes. But outside the classroom, the playing fields were leveled by hormone-driven interests, and other competing endeavors. Clothing styles, hairstyles, makeup, etc., were critical, even if one had adopted the 'grunge' look. There was a standard for that too.

"Antonia, you sure know how to put together a fabulous look." I learned quickly what my quirks were: to never see myself coming, so I stood out with my unique ensembles and eccentric accessories. The same pattern continues to this day. I am reminded by friends and admirers that my sense of style is unique, attractive. I have always taken pride in my outer appearance, but too often, I used my clothes, hair and makeup to cloak and disguise my feelings.

At Marymount, we were growing from girls-into-women. Many of the girls had the single ambition to leave Marymount engaged to a fellow from Princeton, Harvard, Fordham, Fairfield, West Point, or some other prestigious east coast university. We regularly attended mixers with guys from these schools, guaranteeing we had many chances to meet up.

"Antonia, why don't you get dressed up and come to the mixers? You can meet a lot of black guys there". My classmates were encouraging, and there was always one or two guys who looked like me attending the socials. But I felt most of them were there to hook up with a white girl.

I was not interested in the white guys.

Like I said, it was the 60's, and I knew I would not bring anyone home to my dad who was not black, but I was entertained by the few white boys who flirted with me.

I didn't like those mixers. I only went to a few for the opportunity to get off campus. I was just a little curious, but, in truth, I found dating fearful.

"I already have a boyfriend." It was an easy out and besides, I did not like the idea of getting to know anyone else. I was in love with Howard.

My first year at Marymount was an adventure; so many new experiences opened up for me: I got my ears pierced; I learned about where to get an abortion if ever needed; I learned about social/class division amongst ethnic Catholics. I first heard about the lace curtain Irish and other such divisions amongst Italians, Poles, southern Catholics, etc. It was really strange, but instructive to me to use later on in my life.

One of the most disconcerting of those divisions was the clear divide between the order of nuns who administered Marymount: the 'little' nuns were not teachers (uneducated) and they performed the domestic and drudge work. They were mainly from foreign countries, primarily South and Central America. I know the small, but growing, liberation theology movement underway in the Catholic Church helped correct some of those practices.

And, I learned how to eat an artichoke; learning how to

scrape the 'meat' across the front of my teeth after dipping it in a tangy sauce. Wonderful.

Also while at Marymount, I learned more about the real Mafia than from any book or movie I'd seen or read; before or since.

"Where do you think they're going?" There was open speculation about a handful of our classmates, who, on any given Friday after classes, would disappear into stretch limousines with dark tinted windows. The students were similarly returned on Sunday evenings. It was an unspoken agreement; not to ask any details about how they spent their weekends.

Sadly, during our senior year, our class President's dad was hit, gangland style. They were an Italian family. It was messy; a headline story in the New York papers. Stuff happened.

I also learned a few other life-essential things: how to properly wear makeup; about philosophy/psychology/biology; about how to get around the entire island of Manhattan; about a few private men's clubs in New York; how to shop discount in the Village; and, how to kill God.

The Berrigan brothers, activist Jesuit priests, were fixtures on Marymount's campus. They represented the teachings of liberation theology which took a strong foothold on campus. Radical to its core, we were encouraged to question all authority and to act out in protest against any perceived injustice. It changed my perspective on what being Catholic meant- lasting over my lifetime. During my senior year, one of the Berrigan brothers left the priesthood and married Sister Elizabeth. The couple became renowned for their anti-war protests and activism in the underground movement over the succeeding decade.

The sixties.

Daddy would have been so pleased. I was being exposed to everything.

While I became more finished while attending the girl's school on the hill, I remained unprepared for my upcoming marriage to Howard.

I had miles to go ………

BOOK THREE

THE RE-EDUCATION OF ANTONIA

7

AN EXTENDED HONEYMOON

IT WAS NOT ALWAYS SO HARD BEING MRS. HOWARD GARY.

There were some good times woven into the threads of our twenty three year marriage.

Throughout the first year, we would both bring home little 'S's to one another. Those little 'surprises' were either bubble gum (Super bubble, long-lasting flavor from a lot of sugar was the favorite), or Wise brand potato chips.

"Baby, that was a really greasy bag," one or the other of us would utter; an indication the chips were especially wet from the saturated fat left over from the deep frying process. This was years before folks started reading labels to determine fat from calories. I usually washed the chips down with real Coke over heavy ice, chased by a Milky Way or Baby Ruth candy bar.

"How can you eat like all those calories and never gain a pound?" Howard's mother looked askance at me. She had a life-long struggle with her weight. The Hadley side of his family, his mothers', were all heavier than average. Uncle Charlie was not the only pear shape in their group.

It was hard for me, in the beginning, to feel comfortable eating in front of them.

Howard had been my first and only sexual partner, and despite my relative inexperience, we enjoyed each other.

"How's Roscoe?" I used to ask when I wanted to have sex.

"How's Susie? He'd alternately ask me.

I had no fears, then, of any type of STD. Also, there was no fear of an unplanned pregnancy. I was on the pill. We were totally unfettered in our sexual escapades and experimented, to my great pleasure, with great freedom and abandon.

"Let's make a baby," he'd often implore, usually as part of our foreplay. I knew better.

"Baby you know I'm not ready. Who will take care of it?" I demurred. We both knew I was not prepared to be a parent.

I knew he was not.

I held on to my decision to not have children for eight years.

During the first two years of marriage, our best and most frequent form of entertainment were our respective families. It was cheap, and his kept me laughing. They kept a joke going, usually about themselves and one another. No one was spared, and I had to quickly develop a thick skin to remain comfortable in their company. It didn't take me long before I was able to exchange barbs with the best of them. But I paled in comparison to those aunts and uncles of his. Mom, considered to be the most conservative of them all, was no shrinking violet. She held her own with the best of them.

No subject was out of bounds.

"Hey, stop fucking and open the door. I need to take a piss." Farmer yelled through our front bedroom window. Farmer was one of Howard's uncles. Farmer was their mothers' surname. He was one of the greatest characters I'd ever met.

On that particular morning, Howard and I had been married only a few months, and we were living with his mother.

Farmer was the shortest of the four Hadley brothers; standing well under five and a half feet. He was rough around the edges: there was always a cigarette, usually only a stub, hanging from his mouth, and he spoke in a rasping smoker's voice.

Farmer drove an eighteen wheel truck for a living, and his schedule often brought him to Miami; usually arriving early on weekend mornings. For years, Farmer's pattern was to stop by his sister's place whenever he rolled into town.

"You just jealous cause you're not getting as much as me," Howard yelled back and laughed out loud as he opened the door to let his Uncle Farmer inside. They both seemed to get the biggest kick from this rude, early morning wake up call. I could have just died from embarrassment.

While I was mortified, it would not be the last time I heard Farmer shout about one or another suggestive sexual activity Howard and I might be enjoying.

However, it didn't take me long before I understood, though often bawdy, the intentions of Uncle Farmer, and all of Howard's family was to express how much they loved and cared for us, no matter how off color their comments tended to be.

Once relieved, Farmer would unceremoniously join us at

the dining table to enjoy a breakfast with us. The raucous affair was enlivened when Howard's Uncle Charlie stopped by to join us around their sister's, Howard's mom, table.

⊗⊗⊗

ONE OF MY FONDEST MEMORIES OF MY EARLY BONDING WITH Howard's family was the day I finally got to go fishing with Uncle Charlie, his wife, Aunt Ella, and Howard.

Charlie and Howard had packed up a trunk-load of fishing poles, tackle, and assorted gear. They had frequently done that throughout Howard's boyhood, and I had heard many wonderful fishing tales. I was thrilled to be invited on this trip.

We left Miami early Saturday morning and drove leisurely for two hours down to the middle Keys. We stopped for lunch at a long-time favorite of theirs in Turtle Cay.

"Welcome back Mr. and Mrs. Hadley." The restaurant owner was genuinely happy to see them.

Uncle Charlie and Aunt Ella had been fishing in those parts for over thirty years, and I was impressed with how they were greeted like long lost friends. Being in their company made me feel important.

Howard was quite comfortable; he had been fishing with his Uncle Charlie and/or Ella, many times before.

"Let me get that," Howard reached for the check.

But Uncle Charlie grabbed the bill, and no argument could dissuade him from paying the tab. He peeled off a hundred dollar bill from his fat cash roll. He always carried a large wad in his deep pocket. Howard picked up the same habit a few years later.

After lunch, we stopped by another one of Uncle Charlie's spots to buy live shrimp for bait. We set up our camp on the bridge for an afternoon-into-early evening fishing adventure.

The day was scorching hot. It was a typical South Florida afternoon but it felt hotter in the Keys because there is little or no land buffer between the Gulf of Mexico and the Atlantic Ocean.

It was my first time fishing.

We had stopped at Whale Harbor, Uncle Charlie's favorite fishing hole. It was a little more than half way between Miami and Key West.

Howard and Uncle Charlie were very patient with me, at first. They baited my hooks, got my tangled lines off the rocks, and, they re-tied my anchors and weights.

After a while, Aunt Ella tossed me a side-way glance. "Toni, bait your own hook."

I was having beginners luck. I kept hooking fish, but I needed help pulling them in.

"I got one," I'd shout, holding on to my pole but struggling with the reel. It was distracting everyone from their own lines.

I hooked nearly a half dozen red snapper in quick succession; each seven to eight inches long. I was hot and sweaty, but I was having the time of my life.

This is nice.

"Charlie, it's time for Howard and Toni to buy the bait," Aunt Ella insisted. Even though I was hooking fish, I dropped many more shrimp than I got to stay on the hook, and I had also snagged too many near catches, losing bait in the process. Aunt Ella had tolerated me for long enough.

"And let her take her own fish off the hook." Aunt Ella had not caught anything, but neither had Uncle Charlie, or Howard. She was finished being patient.

I got the message. We got the message. Howard bought more bait. I was on my own.

I loved them. Ella and Charlie not only taught me how to fish, they showed me how to be part of another family. I got loved back.

On the other hand, my family loved Howard only because he loved me. It was clear from the beginning, and with few exceptions, if I ever felt differently about him, so would they. Their acceptance of him was always conditional, and I know he felt it. They were generous with their hospitality, and the welcome mats were always out. Aunt Doris and Uncle Ozzie kept their bar open and the pool was cleaned for us to use. And Aunt Lorraine always had something good to eat during our visits to her house.

Of my mom's three sisters, Aunt Lorraine said she felt the most responsible for our marriage. She had like him from their first meeting at the Debutant's Ball, and she loved to remind me of one early dating episode.

"I want to get married," I told her one night during our first summer of love. Howard and I had gone to a party where someone put alcohol in the punch. I drank too much. We were all underage.

Aunt Lorraine was a life-long believer in scotch as a cure for everything, so she was sympathetic to my youthful disturbance.

"Well I think you may be a little young to have such a made-up mind, but I know you are in love."

"I want to get married. I want to get married," I drunkenly repeated. I was nestled up in her bed, where she held me throughout the night.

Aunt Lorraine never stopped loving Howard, even long after I divorced him. She constantly wished we would reunite.

"You loved Howard so much. You need to forgive him and take him back." Aunt Lorraine reminded me of that night of my teenage drunkenness each time she tried to get me to reconcile with Howard. It was much too late.

"Love dies, Aunt Lorraine." But she remained a lifelong romantic. Before she died at age 93, she had buried five men.

"You're a femme fatale." I joked with her about her love spell.

"Don't say that," she laughed. There was not one bitter bone in her body, about anything. I wanted to be more like her.

"On the other hand, my mother's other sister, Aunt Teddy, castigated me once for cutting short one of my visits with her when I told her I wanted to go home to Howard. "Husband, husband?" She looked down her long nose at me. "Girl, you may have many more husbands after Howard before it's over."

Aunt Teddy was on her second marriage to the same guy, and had been married once before him.

Then there was Aunt Doris. The outlier.

"Your mother didn't raise your right," Aunt Doris would

taunt. She was right, at least regarding men. But Aunt Doris also scared me. She was on her third marriage.

"Always marry up," she advised.

"Aunt Doris, why do you always put on lipstick just to go to the grocery store?" I asked her once.

"I never know when I might meet my next husband," she flippantly tossed back.

I liked Ozzie, her current husband, I felt badly for him never knowing if he was Doris's final one. Uncle Ozzie had paid for all the liquor for our wedding, and he really liked Howard. They played billiards together.

I did not know Aunt Doris's first husband, and her second, a well-known figure in Miami, was a distant and fading memory.

Howard was fully aware of Aunt Doris's attitude towards men, and I knew he was never too comfortable around her. She liked to tell stories about her dust ups with men.

"You know, I left my first husband because he was cheap," she bragged.

"And I wanted to kill the second one when he cheated on me. I waited for him to fall asleep and then I hit him over his groin with the boom handle. I left him nearly crippled."

She loved to tell the story and how she had already packed her bags and called for her brother, my uncle Andrew, to pick her up. He was waiting outside for her when she whacked her husband.

Another story she liked to tell was how she once flushed an engagement ring down the toilet because the guy was unworthy.

I suspect Howard feared I might pick up some of her ideas, but, much to her chagrin, I never did.

"If I had raised you. Howard Gary would not have even gotten a second look, let alone a marriage." She told me more than once after she failed to get me to take up her offer to go to Europe, and not marry Howard at all.

Family. If only we could pick the ones we're born into.

⚜

DESPITE ALL THE ODDS, AT THE END OF OUR FIRST YEAR OF marriage, we celebrated with a series of surprises, large and small.

Howard and I had moved into our second apartment, where we were enjoying playing house.

"Baby," Howard said, "I need you to go to Aunt Marian's to pick up something, and when you get back we can go out to celebrate our anniversary."

I was expecting a celebration, and we had talked about toasting our one year anniversary with dinner. But I was in for a surprise. It was on a Saturday, late- morning, June, 1969. What a year it had been.

We still only had one car, the MGB, so I left Howard at home, doing his chores. We had divided up the tasks equally, alternating the laundry, floors, kitchen, etc. I still did all the cooking. Howard just didn't get the rhythm of preparing a meal. He did all the ironing. I had proven it was not my thing.

I arrived at Howard's Aunt Marian's, and found her whistling. That's what she did when she got excited. Entering

Aunt Marian's house was always a thing of wonder to me. There was never a sign anyone actually lived in it. There was not a spot of dust anywhere; no signs or smells of cooking, even though large pots were prepared every Sunday.

I was still smoking cigarettes at the time, and Marian would quickly remove the ash tray at the first flick of ash, and replace it with a cleaned out bowl before the time it took for the second flick of ash. Years later, whenever I left my infant-toddler aged sons with her for an overnight stay, they would return home cleaner than I could ever get them. Aunt Marian had scrubbed and groomed them like little thoroughbreds. She even laundered and ironed their clothes before sending them home.

I lingered for a short, obligatory visit before Aunt Marian hustled me along, whistling in between her words.

Giddy, she handed me two packages. One was gift wrapped, in a bag, with a note in Howard's handwriting which read: "Proceed to Aunt Gladys," another one of Howard's aunts.

"Have fun," she half spoke/whistled.

Aunt Gladys was clucking with merriment when I arrived. She kept me for a little while. We loved to visit. She was a great storyteller, and always made me laugh. She told really raunchy jokes. Her home was the opposite of Marian's, her sister. It was well lived in and was always filled with the sweet smell of something in the oven.

She handed me another wrapped package, and a bag, with another note.

I was beginning to enjoy this treasure hunt, and that more

than one person was invited to play along with me (us) added more joy to this adventure.

The note read: "Next stop, Uncle Charlie and Aunt Ella," where more beautifully wrapped packages awaited.

One can never just make a quick stop by Uncle Charlie's. Ella loved to show and tell, and she always had some interesting anecdote to share about her frequent shopping sprees. She regularly shopped for new clothing-especially shoes, furniture, and fixtures, which she loved to model or point out.

Charlie and Ella's aging dog, Ann, held a central place in their household. She, too, demanded her share of attention from visitors. Ann suffered from a very bad case of doggy flatulence, and she walked around the house freely emitting her gas.

"Stop that Ann," was shouted out at various Hadley gatherings whenever anyone parted with their own natural gases when they could not get out of the room, before releasing.

Leaving Uncle Charlie and Aunt Ella's house, when I got into the car, I picked up the aroma from a variety of seasonings. It was coming from the bags I had collected.

I was tempted to look, but I played along. My excitement was building up with each stop.

By now, I had gotten what was up with all the stops: gift packages and food. I was wild with curiosity, wondering what additional surprises awaited me at my next stops.

The next set of directions were for me to proceed to my Aunt Doris, where I had another gift-wrapped package waiting.

My Aunt Doris feared nothing and no one. I admired her for being bold and sassy.

By now, I had been gone for nearly two hours.

I visited with her for twenty minutes, the absolute minimum I could get away with before begging my leave.

"I never thought you and Howard would make it a whole year," she admitted she never thought it would have lasted this long. I accepted her back-handed compliment as she handed me my packages.

Finally, I made it to Howard's mother's house, my last stop, where she made no attempt at disguising a salad she had made. She also gave me the frozen top of our wedding cake. She had kept in her freezer for the past year!

I had forgotten about our cake. It was chocolate, my favorite, and it had been perfectly preserved.

"I hope you enjoy your dinner and this special desert." Mom had a broad smile on her face. She had been so supportive of me during our first year of marriage. She taught me things I never learned from my own mother.

I grew to love her, and to call her Mom.

"Mom, how did you keep this cake hidden all this time?"

I had never noticed it in the freezer, even though Howard and I had lived in her house during the first few months of our marriage.

"I had it wrapped up and pushed way back in the freezer," mom congratulated herself on keeping the cake hidden from me.

Oh yes, she also handed me a few additional gift-wrapped packages.

By the time I arrived home, three hours later, Howard was broiling some steaks. It was the one food item he knew how to cook.

And, he had set the table with candles. It was romantic.

Compliments of all the aunts and his mother, we had a feast with all our favorites: peas and rice from Aunt Doris, baked beans from Aunt Gladys, potato salad and macaroni and cheese from Aunt Marian, salad from mom, and of course that wonderfully preserved chocolate wedding cake topper.

I retrieved my gifts for Howard I had hidden in the apartment.

We spent hours eating and exchanging our mutual tokens of love.

We called to thank each of the co-conspirators and players in our celebration; to thank them for their role in support of our wonderful day, and more importantly, for their full year of support. Our families had demonstrated how much they loved us, as individuals and as a couple; some more openly than others. In their unique ways, they continuously showed how much they wanted us to succeed.

I was in love with the man, and his family. I felt content and I basked in the warmth of knowing our lives would continue to prosper together.

Over the short course of our first year, Howard and I had firmly established a ritualized gift-giving practice we sustained over most of our entire marriage. We both loved honoring one another with big and little surprises.

His gifts to me were always expertly wrapped with care and

attention, and lovingly presented. He usually got it right: my preferences; the right sizes; something elegant.

I'll treasure many of those gestures. I know at the times of their presentation, they were not empty; they kept me holding on to the dream.

The honeymoon period extended a little past year one.

He loves me; he loves me not........he loves me.

8

A NIGGER IN TRAINING

"BITCH," A LITTLE SOMETHING HAD GONE WRONG. THE other side of Howard would literally burst out of nowhere, and with little or no provocation, or from just some small slight.

It was still in our first year of marriage when he first called me that. It cut so deep into my soul, I literally lost my breath. I felt a sharp piercing in the center of my chest.

What have I done to him to deserve such a put down?

"I can't remake myself", I mumbled weakly after one of his attacks, but then, I'd set myself up trying to do just that.

I developed a slick exterior. I'd just let his sharp words roll down to the floor, to fall into a disappearing pool so I would not have to feel them, look at them, or let them stick. I began to alter my reality. I turned his strikes into what I relabeled as his affectionate, though twisted, call for attention. I turned myself inside out to make his put downs fit me.

He's frustrated because he lacks a strong vocabulary, or *he doesn't want to take too much time saying what was on his mind,* or, *I know, the word was just a shorthand he used to get me to pay attention to what he was saying; or about to say."*

Sometimes he would call me "bitch" in front of other people. I watched as folks waited for me to give them some clue about how to react. *They want some kind of signal from me.* I'd nervously laugh it off. They laughed with me.

"You know Howard, he calls me the sweetest bitch he knows."

I knew it sounded crazy, but I had accepted this reality of my life.

Words can't break me, I told myself.

As our first year ended in a grand celebration, I was also his 'bitch- at times. We were both working, and enjoying what I thought was a successful partnership. But my doubt counter was tallying up.

Sometime toward the end of our first honeymoon year, Howard and I made a date for lunch. We met in the Civic Center, where both the County jail and the Justice building were located. I still felt good about being married to Howard, and I enjoyed playing at being a couple: we continued to hold hands in public, and showed other outward signs of affection. I was still very much in love with my husband.

"Hey, Gary!" The voice came from 20 stories above.

"Hey nigger," he shouted up. "Who's that?"

"This is so-and-so mother fucker. Man you looking good."

"Good damn, mother fucker. What the fuck you doing in there?" Howard shouted up at the high rise jail.

"Shit man, you know how it is."

"Yeah, I know. It's hard for a 'nigger' out here. Take care of yourself."

After nearly a year of marriage, I would no longer cringe when I heard him curse in private, but this was out loud, and in public. The sidewalk could not open up wide or deep enough for me.

I had lost my appetite. *How is my husband so familiar with a criminal? And why does he kept referring to himself (and the other guy) as 'nigger'.*

When I asked, he nearly shouted, "Because I'm a nigger, 'nigger'!"

I folded in on myself. It remained a charge I never accepted, and one which remained a source of dispute between us over all our remaining years together.

"Toni, I have told you what it's like being a black man," he patiently reiterated the challenges he experienced as a young black man growing up in Miami; recounting the typical urban black male experience.

Much to his chagrin, I could not relate to his trauma, then, or ever.

It was becoming more and more apparent what different worlds we came from, or at least the perception of our worlds, were vastly different. He had already described serious material lack, competition with his brother for recognition and affection from their mom, and other forms of struggle unfamiliar to me.

As the first born and only girl, my position of privilege, I always maintained an outlook of optimism, joy and continuous reward. Howard and I agreed early on, I was incapable of understanding what he, a black man, had had to suffer or endure, and I would not try to. I would be accepting and agreeable, and whatever he had suffered from his experience, he would not envy me my feelings of well-being.

I had never heard my dad use the word nigger in reference to himself, or anyone else. Surely, and I knew, daddy had suffered from being discriminated against.

"My granddaddy had the only gin mill and smoke house in town, and the white folk burned them down, more than once," daddy used to tell me and my bothers. The stories he told about his childhood on the farm in South Carolina were often graphic, and instructional. With all their potential for blame and recrimination, daddy never used derogatory words like nigger, or cracker when referring to the jealous whites.

"We never went to the store for anything other than salt and shoes." Daddy used to brag about the independence he knew as a boy. Those lessons followed him throughout his life and he taught them to me and my brothers.

"You need to learn how to stand on your own two feet." Daddy taught us about racial injustice and how unfair the world was, but we didn't learn to hate. My dad was never a nigger.

Howard was an anomaly to me.

But my re-education was fully underway. I adopted an attitude of gratitude that I was not a black man.

I learned to walk a fine line: being the wife of an avowed militant black man, and just being my free-spirited self.

I hated it when Howard won our arguments about race and racism, showing me up whenever he and I actually did get treated like niggers. There were too many instances.

"Toni, keep your mouth shut," he warned.

It was around 6 pm; not yet dark outside, when we were stopped by a Miami-Dade police officer. It was a typical work day, and we were dressed in our suits.

Bags of clothing hung from a hook behind the driver's seat. The windows of our second car, a Mercedes, were tinted, and in a shade within the lawful limits allowed. Before we pulled over and stopped for the blue flashing lights, Howard dared me to say a word. He knew how I felt. I had nothing to fear, not being a black man, and up to then, I was certainly not a nigger.

The young, white officer was visibly nervous. His voice quivered.

"Let me see you driver's license," the officer spoke, nearly stuttering, in a very low tone. He stood erect and avoided eye contact with Howard. I was staring at his face, in an attempt to evoke some type of emotional register in the human being behind the hard set mask of his face.

Howard began to move and talk in slow motion as he retrieved his driver's license, registration, and proof of insurance.

"Officer, I am getting my registration and insurance from the glove box," he explained before being asked what he was doing.

"Look, there is nothing and no one in the back seat," Howard pushed the dry cleaned garments aside for the convenience of the policeman.

"What are you doing around here?"

That's a stupid question. We're taking a short cut through the side streets of Liberty City. These are familiar grounds to us. We are driving home.

We had made several errands: to the dry cleaners, and a quick visit with Howard's mother, whose house was only a few blocks from the traffic stop.

"Just heading home," Howard quietly offered.

I was itching to jump in the officer's face; to get his badge number; to call his supervisor on the spot. This was decades before cell phones with cameras.

The officer made a cursory review of Howard's documents, and then went back to his car where he called in the information.

I was jumping up and down on the seat, frustrated that I had to remain quiet.

"Just stay calm," Howard implored me.

He knew my first instinct was to ask why we had been stopped. He feared I would challenge the police officer about why he had stopped us when we had done nothing wrong (we had not). He knew my inclination was to challenge authority. I had a need to know why the rules were the rules, and I usually did not hesitate to ask.

The officer had not given any reason for the stop; he didn't have to. But we had to remain compliant.

"Sorry for the inconvenience, Mr. Gary," the officer kept his tone low and well- modulated when he handed Howard back his documents.

"Have a great evening, and drive carefully," he offered as an aside as he walked back to his patrol car. We waited for him to drive away before leaving ourselves.

"How could he just stop us for nothing and I couldn't ask him what for?" I was seething.

"Toni, didn't you see how he kept his hand on his gun? I didn't want the cracker to lose his cool and get scared." Howard explained what could have happened to us if I had provoked him.

"Toni, your attitude could have gotten us killed. The cop was clearly a rookie, and when he recognized his mistake, he just got more agitated."

"But we didn't do anything wrong, and he didn't have the right to stop us for nothing."

"Mother-fucker could have shot us, and you better get used to it." Howard shouted.

I had not noticed the officer's hand on his gun. It annoyed me how Howard knew what to do; how to behave with the police. I did not have a clue. It was 1969, and getting stopped for driving while black, I'd later learn, was a common occurrence.

I was immune to that kind of humiliation. Driving while being a black female, I had so few reasons to be treated as a suspect.

Initially, I thought Howard was just tilting at windmills; seeing bad cops around every corner. But I started to pay closer attention. I remembered the episode when I trained our sons on what to do when the police stopped them.

I would suffer another soul-shrinking episode just a few months later, and according to Howard, I put us in danger again.

Into our second year, we took an extended vacation. We drove to New York, Connecticut, and Massachusetts. We visited with one of my college classmates, Melissa Haddock, and her family who lived in a Boston suburb: Duxbury, Massachusetts, best known for its cranberry bogs. Missy, a Catholic from the Philadelphia area, had married Fred Hammel, a real WASP who had grown up in the Boston area.

Fred took great pride in showing us, Missy's black friends, around his home town. Missy had a PTA meeting and could not join us. We had dinner at a well-known restaurant in Chinatown. Fred was excited to take us to an Italian restaurant to get the best cannoli in town for coffee and dessert. We left Chinatown and drove to a place Fred referred to as the north end. The restaurant didn't look like anything special; it was a typical neighborhood spot in a residential area.

Fred was clueless.

Ten minutes after ordering our coffee and desserts, Howard quietly said to me and Fred, "Get your coats and let's go."

I hesitated. I was enjoying the fresh baked pastry; it brought back wonderful memories of when I visited the homes of my Marymount Italian classmates.

Howard demanded more forcefully that we get our coats and leave. I instantly recognized his tone as a call to action. Fred looked perplexed, but he moved quickly.

I started to protest when Howard barked, "Get your god-damn coats and let's get the fuck out of here, now!" Fred had already begun to put his coat on and to move out of the booth, while I tarried for another second. The cannoli was really good, and my coffee cup was still half unfinished.

What Fred and I had not noticed, Howard had not only seen, but felt in his gut, was a menacing gathering of a group of young white men (18-20 year olds) who had quietly filtered into the place. They had comingled around a billiards table in the corner of the room. But they were not playing a game.

The ominous gang of youth followed us out of the restaurant. The clomping sound of their boots bore an unseen, yet palpable threat. The crowd trailed behind us in close formation, for at least a block down the hill, all the way until we reached Fred's car. They stood in the street and watched us drive away, confirming their intent to get us out of their place, and out of their territory.

Once we were safely driving away, I was finally able to speak.

"I did not see those guys, did you Fred?" I needed some cushion against what I knew was coming. They looked like regular guys to me. I had seen their type many times before while I was at Marymount: working-class white ethnics. These guys had come in from the cold. They all wore jackets, scarves, wool caps, and gloves. Nothing extraordinary. What did Howard see?

"Well I saw them, but I didn't pay them any attention," admitted Fred. "I'm so sorry."

Howard and I did not know where we were going. We found out later about the riots over busing and school desegregation which had taken place the summer before in that part of town. It was now the following winter, 1970. Fred was embarrassed for not being more politically aware, or astute enough to see the danger. The busing issue did not exist where Fred and Missy lived. There was a zero black population in Duxbury.

He continued to apologize.

"Fred, you don't have to keep apologizing, but Toni, you should have known better."

"And when I tell you to move, you better move."

I felt overwhelmed; by the potential danger, yes, but even more so by my own naiveté. I knew I would suffer Howard's wrath. He berated me for days and the incident ruined the balance of the vacation.

How could I be so ignorant? Hadn't I learned anything yet about being a nigger? I was never going to be black enough, and, thanks to me, I almost got all of us killed, again.

Again, Howard won that one. I was growing more defeated in my attempt to uphold my humanitarian beliefs and attitude, so I internalized what I considered personal deficiencies. I just wasn't getting it fast enough, and I was beginning to feel more and more uncomfortable being around my husband in public. I grew anxious anticipating the next derogatory exchange, and preparing to be a nigger myself. What was I supposed to do?

I turned to my default remedy: I began to read a lot of books about the black experience- not mine- and I vowed to become more sensitive to the black man syndrome. I would go against my instinct to shout out against any slight of injustice, and remain quiet.

I was miserable, not being able to act out on my natural disposition of openness toward everybody, my inclination to love all, and make everyone ok with me until proven otherwise. My mom and dad had not raised me to be fearful. They encouraged me to question anyone, and they told me adults were not always right just because they were grown. I also felt authority did not automatically attach itself to the form of a white male, in or out of a uniform.

I had long ago accepted my orientation was not the usual one for a colored child growing up in the 50s and 60s in the near-south. I have always appreciated how my parents were special. I was never made to feel inferior to anyone. In fact, I was taught to think and be just the opposite. More importantly, I knew my folks were prepared to fight to the death if anyone hurt me, or, as my mother would say, "Tried to break my spirit."

My high spiritedness would take me many places throughout my formative years. It continued to serve me in many instances, but it did me no good when I was with Howard and was a nigger in his eyes. *Did that mean he loved me less?*

As quietly as I could keep it, I was fast becoming his nigger bitch.

Over the years, Howard's sting softened. Actually, I became numb to it. I remained vigilant, looking out for danger signs of attacks from him; and I became more sensitized about real attacks against him as he began his meteoric rise in the ranks of municipal management. There were a few times when I recognized instances of real racism even before he did; I became a helpmate in that respect. By the time I had my sons, my sensitivity and awareness was even more acute.

Years, later, according to my youngest son, Issa, who wrote this about me in his Kindergarten ABC Poem: <u>A</u> is for Antonia. My mom is "<u>b</u>raver than a <u>c</u>ave <u>b</u>ear."

If Issa only knew what it took for me to get so brave.

❧ 9 ❧

OFF INTO THE WORLD

1970-1976:

We were still enjoying the extended honeymoon when Howard was rewarded for his special genius in municipal finance. He had only been working for two years; first as a budget analyst for the Dade County Budget Department; and subsequently on loan to administer the Model City federal block grant, when he got recommended by the County Manager, Haley Sofge, to participate in a national movement to professionalize municipal administrators/managers. This initiative involved recruiting blacks, women, and other minorities into the profession.

"You know that Howard University does not have an existing program, and it may take them a long time to ramp up," I offered as we debated. There were three options up for consideration: Howard, Harvard, and the University of Michigan.

"Yeah. It was probably selected to be the token black

school," Howard rejoined. He literally saw the world in black and white, only.

"I'm not sure you'd like New England, anyway" I counter offered. Harvard seemed so remote, and I was sure Howard would not like it. I knew I would not, especially after our unpleasant experience in the Boston north end at the hands of the Italian escort group.

I was lobbying for the one place unfamiliar to me; the mid-west.

"That leaves Michigan." It was decided.

The Rackham School for Public Policy at Michigan was the most well-established, and the State of Michigan held intrigue for both of us. It was a large University. Attractive. And, everyone liked their football team.

The offer to attend the University of Michigan included a full graduate fellowship, with a generous stipend.

We thought we were going to the liberal mid-west.

"They won't have the same racist practices there," we both anticipated.

We were also excited about leaving the increasing volatility of Miami's political environment; to leave behind its crazy Cuban exile politics, its seething, angry blacks, and its nervous white rulers.

The hotbed of conflict could be measured by the diminishing power of the establishment whites, the emergence of Cuban dominance, and the growing marginalization of the American-born blacks.

The riot of 1968 was a harbinger of even greater conflict seeping into every transaction; seething over time.

Howard and I packed our meager furnishings and had them shipped to Ann Arbor. We had also entered into our third year of marriage. We had raised expectations.

"Toni, call triple A to get our trip tick," Howard instructed. I was still put in charge of so much of our daily routines.

"And, let's take the scenic route."

We drove up in our third car, Abraham, a four door Lincoln Continental.

Abraham took us comfortably across country to Michigan.

The drive along the mountain range skirted between North Carolina and Tennessee. It was beautiful in daylight. The trip was unexceptional, except, even though the speed traps were highlighted by our AAA route, we couldn't avoid one in a very small town. We were coming down the mountain........

"Shit."

The blue lights came up fast from behind a blind bend.

Howard found a spot which did not have us teetering off the edge of the hill to pull over.

I remained mum throughout the ordeal. Howard didn't have to worry about me this time. I knew we were in the old south; I had learned my lesson.

We calculated the total amount due would include the posted fine for speeding, plus the court fees. We had been stopped after the normal hours of a working day, so we were taken aback by the extra costs which amounted to a surtax for the judge's inconvenience.

"I bet they do this all the time," we managed to laugh it off once we were across the state line.

We knew we were never going that way again, and were

thankful we had enough money in American express checks to pay the ticket and get back on the road.

"This is pretty cool for August." I put on a sweater when we arrived in Ann Arbor. I kept putting on more clothes until spring came, the following April.

It got really cold. How cold was it?

Among other survival measures, we had to learn how to winterize our car. Not only did we keep Abraham finely tuned, and put chains on the tires, we had to place a blanket over its engine during the night.

"Toni, you can't gun the engine when you're going uphill." Driving sideways up a snow covered hill could be exciting when executed without a crash.

I had experienced four years of New York weather while at Marymount. I knew a little something about surviving the cold; dressing in layers. But I didn't know anything about driving on ice.

I wondered when Howard had become such an expert. This was his first soiree into a real winter land of ice and snow. *Surely, Atlanta's winters were nothing like this.*

"It's minus five degrees below zero!" It was the coldest temperature either of us had ever experienced, yet.

One night, while walking home after seeing a movie, the temperature had dropped so low icicles formed around Howard's mustache from the moisture dripping out of his nose.

It was too icy to run, and there were no vehicles on the streets.

"It wasn't this cold when the movie started."

We walked backwards, trudging up hill. When we got back

to our apartment, we peeled out of our frozen clothes, stiff from ice. It was a first.

Never again, I pledged.

Over the year and a half in Michigan, we picked up pieces of information about our home town and State, mostly from the national news: the Miami Dolphins' undefeated season in 1972; the manned-space launches; Nixon's Florida White House visits, etc. Regular telephone calls and, occasional visits with family kept us connected. Geographically and culturally far removed from the familiar, we underwent a culture shock.

The so-called liberal mid-west, an older and more established society than South Florida/Miami, was dominated by white ethnics and America born blacks.

Alas, we soon discovered how racism did exist in this area, albeit, it had gone underground. Jim Crow signs had probably never been posted, but the insidious American disease raised its head around every corner we looked.

And we probed.

"Where do the black folk live?" Howard was keen to tour the ghetto as soon as we arrived. We had been steered to the vast complex of off campus student housing; near the campus. It was an insular environment- mostly white, affluent, and filled with academicians.

We drove around town. It didn't take us long before we found the city's historic black community.

"Yep, here it is," Howard exhaled in relief.

The sharp differences in economic status were clear. The area was in marked contrast against the richness surrounding the University. Here was the other America: not the familiar south of mine and Howard's childhood, nor the northeast of my youth, but still the same story- just a different zip code.

৩৯৪

GRADUATE STUDENT WIFE WAS A PECULIAR TITLE. BEING IN that position gave me another perspective. And, to my great pleasure, I got to research, read, critique/correct, as well as write Howard's papers. I hung out with the other graduate students; and, of course, I went to work.

I developed my initial set of sales skills from my first job in Ann Arbor. I worked at the largest Ford auto dealership in the area where I sold new and used cars, and trucks.

"I sold a car today. But the commission check will be very small because I didn't close the deal by myself." I earned commission-only pay, virtually nothing for almost five months.

It was a rude lesson for me. Not getting paid for putting in time on the job.

"Well, you need to find a job that pays you for your time," Howard was supportive. I knew he was right.

I got lucky. Almost immediately after leaving auto sales, I found a job with a salary and benefits.

I became a City of Ann Arbor Limited Duty Police Officer; smart name for a meter maid.

"Get over it," my training officer shouted. "It's just like being on a bicycle, only faster," he tried to soothe me. I was with a half-dozen other new officers learning to drive our 'motors': three wheel Harley Davidsons.

I stopped in the middle of the training course. Crying, I was overwhelmed by the size of the motorcycle.

What's the matter with me?

I jumped at the sound of the large engine cranking up to full rpms every time I started my motorcycle.

I was trying to get comfortable straddling the chassis; I didn't have to open my legs that wide to have sex!

I was claustrophobic: the helmet entombed my head.

This was far more complex than just riding a bicycle, but I fought back my tears and fears and forged through the training until I was able to handle my motor.

In fact I was able to handle it so well, I eventually prided myself on being able to park it, uphill on a curb.

It wasn't long before I was tearing around the hills of the City, enjoying command over my hog.

I have to admit, I looked smart in my uniform: knee high, gestapo-style leather boots; a utility belt, with everything but a gun; and, a helmet.

Debra and John Pope, old friends from Miami, were also in Ann Arbor at the time. John was at the university studying for his Masters in Pharmacy.

"Strike a pose." John had a camera. I had been issuing tickets.

He and Debra had met up with Howard in the park in the center of town. The three of them had me pose on my motor in my full regalia.

"We will save this for the day when we might need some money," John teased. We all laughed at the prospect of that day coming. We were all enjoying relative prosperity.

Combined with Howard's fellowship, my salary allowed us to live larger than many other couples in the same situation. Our place became central headquarters for many hungry graduate students in Howard's program.

After only a few months as a meter maid, I was promoted to an inside job. I was put in charge of Juvenile records. What an eye-opening! I was utterly depressed to see first- hand, how so many, upper middle class youth coped with their lives by using drugs, committing suicide, and adopting other damaging forms of behaviors which had been foreign to me. I'll never forget how helpless I felt about so many lost, young lives.

"They're white. It's what they do," Howard remarked when I shared my grief. It saddened me to hear how he tied their fate to their race/class.

Howard and I both worked hard for him to excel in his graduate studies. I was equally invested in his success, and I studied along with him. But he had to constantly challenge his graduate professors to reward him with the 'A' we had earned for his work.

One of the Profs admitted to Howard that he was constitutionally incapable of giving a black student an 'A', regardless of the quality of the work. Howard was recognized as the leader of the group who had been selected for this special program; minority men and women who had come from around the country. Some of them did not complete the requirements for the Master's Degree.

"I have found black students are generally underprepared and have had inferior training before they get here," he explained, "so I assumed that of all of you," he confessed. We were shocked at his candor, but we knew what he said was probably true for most of the professors.

Of course, the professor's confession sparked another of mine and Howard's many discussions about racism and being niggers.

I still was not thoroughly convinced all white people thought the same. It just had not been my experience.

In fact, Howard felt differently too after he formed very close bonds with several of his fellow graduate students.

There was one couple in particular who helped him change his mind about white folks. He was in the same degree program; she was a stay at home mother. They already had six children, and she was pregnant with the seventh!

Howard and I were very comfortable in their company, and we spent a lot of time visiting their home.

They lived simply: in a sprawling house in a densely wooded area. They dressed plainly, and expressed very open ideas. We learned later they were independently wealthy; they both had inheritances from old family money, so they could afford to be liberal in their choices.

While at Marymount, I had seen rich folk adopt eccentric behavior, so I was not surprised by this couple's disdain for showing material wealth.

"I can't understand why they want to have so many children."

"Well, they're Christian and believe they should have all the children God gives them," Howard admired them for their choice. I filed his statement away for future reference.

The graduate student/graduate student wife lifestyle was nice. Howard had a pretty easy- going time. Plus, he had me!

Initially, the study group sessions were held in our apartment, and I felt very much a part of them. Over time, more and more of the sessions were hosted by others, and I began to lose touch with the group.

He started helping one particular graduate student more than the others. She was beautiful; blond.

Not too bright, I initially thought.

Left more to myself, I filled my time with projects. I started several crochet projects; it was a craft I had learned as a child. I made kaftans, belts, and purses for Christmas gifts. I perfected the popcorn stitch. I also did a lot of sewing. I took a course in tailoring. I wanted to make a sport jacket for Howard.

It was orange polyester, with wide lapels, flap pockets, and top-stitching. That style was the fashion rage. I took the unfinished garment with us when we left Michigan. I had every intention of completing it later.

❧

WE WENT OUT FOR A SIMPLE DINNER TO CELEBRATE THE Christmas Holiday.

We had agreed to not exchange gifts with one another since we were living on a very strict budget, and had reduced our spending. Our agreement felt right. Besides, I had made very little money selling cars.

Christmas came before I started working for the Ann Arbor Police Department.

Mid-way through dinner, Howard surprised me when he pulled a bag out from under the table.

"What's this?" Howard gave me an odd shaped package which he had wrapped in newsprint. He had drawn green holly and red berries on the corners.

"Open it," he blushed.

There was a total of four packages, stacked by size, and taped together. On top was the smallest package. It was a set of flash bulbs. Next was a package of Polaroid film, followed by the flash attachment, and finally the camera! He knew I wanted a camera, and there it was, the complete works! I gushed with excitement and gratitude. But I had honored our promise and did not have a gift for him. I felt badly, but he was giddy and quite pleased with himself to see how happy I was.

It was like that then.

I wasn't called bitch too many times either during those eighteen months.

Was this a turning point?

We continued to give to one another. I cooked his favorite foods. One was banana pudding which I learned how to make from scratch in a double boiler on top of the stove. It had to have Nabisco Nilla Vanilla wafers; no off brand would do. He also loved fried baloney sandwiches.

In turn, Howard honored me with gifts.

One of the requirements for completing his Master degree was an internship in a City.

Howard was selected to work in the City of Inkster where he was tutored by Sylvester Murray, a highly regarded and seasoned professional manager who was recognized as one of the first of his kind in the country: a black City Manager.

Inkster is a small city. It is only five miles square, and was notable because of its predominantly black population. Located midway between Ann Arbor and Detroit, everyone seemingly enjoyed full employment generated by the healthy automobile manufacturing industry in the nearby cities of Detroit and Dearborn.

It was the early 1970s and the Detroit Renaissance was fully underway. Benefits were plentiful and widespread.

I was enjoying a personal renaissance: working for a decent salary; crocheting; cooking; relieved from not being a 'nigger'; a size six; and falling back in love with a man with a plan.

❧

SPRING BREAK 1972

"You spoiled everything," Howard barked. "This was a trip for me and Sy, and you were not invited."

For spring break, Howard and Sy planned a trip to South Florida. Sy was born in Miami, and the trip was billed as an opportunity for them both to visit family. I decided, at the last minute to tag along. Granted a leave from my job, I prepared to travel home with the guys. They were going to drive down in 'Abraham'.

"I miss my family too and I want to go home," I pouted. I did not realize they had planned for a boy's only trip. Sy's wife was going for part of the trip. They planned to drop her off to visit her family who lived mid-way down the coast, so I insisted that I go, too.

We were speeding down the expressway when I realized my sweater sleeve was hanging outside.

"Howard, slow down. I got to get my sleeve out."

Before Howard could slow down to a safe speed, I opened the door. I lost control of my grasp on the handle, and the heavy door flew back. The Lincoln Continental's 'suicide' door opened 'backwards'. I could hear the metal on metal.

"Toni are you ok?" Sy surveyed the backseat.

We pulled off onto the shoulder.

"Oh my God, what have you done?" Howard stroked and petted the damage.

"God damn it, Toni, you done fucked up my car," he screamed in rage.

Oh my God! I'm so sorry. I didn't mean to hurt the car. I'm going to be in for it. Maybe I should just get on a bus and go back to Ann Arbor. Fuck it. Shit, it's just a car.

The door could still close, but it could not lock. The scar was very noticeable.

I flashed back two years prior and recalled the time I wrecked the MGB. Howard also felt a strong attachment to that car. It was obviously more than just a vehicle to him. I connected the dots: much of Howard's emotional well-being was deeply invested in his vehicles.

I never knew what to say to Howard when he was in his rages. He was inconsolable. I felt responsible for most of his mood changes.

If only I had been a little bit more careful; more beautiful; more loving; more.......; so next time I'll be sweeter.

Sy and his wife tried to make light banter, but the mood in the car had turned dark.

Inside the car, silence reigned for the next hundred miles.

Needless to say, the visit with family and the entire rest of the trip was miserable. I stayed knotted up inside for the entire duration of the spring break.

Howard and Sy remained friends over many years. We had a lot of laughs and shared many good times. Sy's wife liked to drink Jack Daniels and coke. I held the coke.

⚜

OUR STAY IN MICHIGAN COULD NOT END FAST ENOUGH for me.

When we first arrived in late August, I put on a sweater. By December we were in coats, hats, gloves, scarfs, boots, and thermal underwear. Besides the frosty weather, I was growing uncomfortable with the time Howard spent studying with one particular female graduate student.

We always knew our stay in Michigan would be short lived. Where we'd go next was an exciting speculation. We were still both on the same page. Or mostly. We were still reaching most decisions by consensus.

I prepared several applications for Howard to be considered for upper echelon administrative positions. We looked at opportunities all over the country, but only in places where the weather was less harsh, with shorter winters.

The graduate department at the University gave referrals. One of them was to the City of Saginaw, Michigan. I strongly objected.

"If you accept the position in Saginaw, I'll have to divorce you," I teased. Saginaw was even further north; the weather would be colder.

Offers from small towns were out of the question. After all, we were from the big City of Miami, and there was no going backwards.

Shortly before actually receiving his Master's degree in January 1973, Howard scheduled a handful of interviews, including the city of Newark. A job was offered to him to join its Budget office as an assistant manager.

Yes! We're going to New Jersey. Close to my old stomping grounds in New York. We'll enjoy four distinct seasons, not just the one and half seasons of Michigan.

I still had fond memories lingering from my years at Marymount, just a short four years before. But there would be miles to go before........

❦ 10 ❦

NEWARK

"MY GOODNESS, THIS PLACE HASN'T CHANGED SINCE THE riots." Howard and I were driving around Newark's inner city on a self-guided tour. He was scheduled to report to his new job the following week.

Alas, Newark should have come with a warning label: Caution. Life threatening situations ahead.

When we arrived, Newark was still recovering from the 1967 riots. But it was now January, 1972, and the place was abysmally grey. And those were not just the remaining burned out building shells. Many of the people appeared the same.

"I hope we won't have to live near here," I suddenly feared the inner city. This forgotten urban land was a far cry from Miami's palm-lined ghettos. I even began to long for the cultivated rolling hills and beauty of Ann Arbor.

Newark and New York were separated by only a short drive across the river, but the two cities were worlds apart.

Even folk from the same ethnic groups behaved differently across the river from one another.

Howard was excited about his promotional opportunities, and especially about working with Kenneth Gibson, lauded in the local and national press for his election as the new Mayor of such a big, northeastern city.

"Guess who I met today?" Howard asked me excitedly. We had been in Newark for less than a month.

"Who?" I could never have imagined.

"Uncle Jake." Howard had never met this relative. It was no secret Jake existed, he was his grandfather's 'outside child'. But, Howard did not expect to meet him at City Hall in Newark, New Jersey.

Jake had walked into the front office of City Hall speaking fluent Italian to several of the staff. He obviously looked the part, so when he told them he was Howard's uncle, jaws dropped. Hugh Addonizio, controversial, criminal, but popular, had been voted out of office two years before, and several members of his former staff were still working in the City's administration.

Howard instantly recognized Jake.

"He looked just like poppa," Howard said he so closely resembled his white-skinned grandfather, Heyward Hadley. They embraced.

Jake told Howard if he ever needed any help, or if anyone ever bothered him, to not hesitate to give him a call.

When Jake turned to leave, he declared to the onlookers, again in fluent Italian, Howard was his nephew and they were to treat him right. Howard was ecstatic. He had been given

instant street cred, and a promise of protection from his
newfound Uncle. We both took great comfort in knowing
Uncle Jake had our back when, a year later, we moved into the
North Ward, Addonizio's home base, and where the population
was still majority Italian.

We had been welcomed to Newark.

Shortly after we arrived in New Jersey, Howard came home
with a newer model Lincoln Continental: Abraham
number two.

"I thought we were saving money to buy a house." I broke
down in tears when I saw the car. "We had agreed we would
discuss any major purchases before going off to spend our
savings."

"Well half of the savings is mine and this is what I wanted."
Howard ignored my tears and dared me to just get over it. "We
can save some more money and buy a house later."

I assumed he shared my interest in nesting; after all, he
had demurred to my urgings and pleas to go house hunting on
the weekends. I felt we were on our way to fulfilling the
American Dream of homeownership; apparently, it was only
my dream.

"Howard, I am so disappointed in you and your choice. You
hurt my feelings." My voice never rose above a conversational
level. I had rehearsed what I would say. I really wanted to
violently strike him. I wanted blood. My response was so out of
my character.

I never did fight Howard the way he described some of the
girls he grew up watching; you know, street fighting with hands
and feet, pulling hair, etc. He admired that part of them, but I

didn't have it in me. But I imagined it; in vivid, colorful scenarios.

I wondered when I would be able to go toe- to- toe with Howard, if ever.

I wish I still had my younger self. She was a fighter.

Where had she gone? Retired.

What was the point? Fighting and arguing required so much energy. Besides, we're both intelligent people' we can reach reasonable decisions, can't we? That was my go-to position, to go with my head; to let reason win. I grew increasingly smug in my knowledge I was the more reasonable of us two; he was the most aggressive, and so we began to sink deeper into our default dispositions.

In truth, I was afraid I was losing him, and I didn't have a fail-safe plan in place in the event I did leave.

I thought a fight would push him further away. Left alone, I had nowhere to go. He had a career, and I had, what? I was vulnerable and isolated.

Besides, the second half of my guiding childhood mantra: "..... And if you marry, marry someone who will take care of you," was working. He made enough to keep me comfortable.

But that car purchase marked the beginning of my serious thoughts about leaving Howard. I resented a car. It was our fourth in just five years

And that's all I did: think about leaving. I conjured up different scenarios, but I remained paralyzed with questions and doubt about where I would go: *I can't go back home, to Miami.* I fretted. *How, am I going to support myself? All of my jobs had been below par.* I stalled with embarrassment about failing in the marriage I had so badly wanted four years before. I was just too handicapped to follow my first mind.

I stayed busy keeping house in our two bedroom apartment. I kept his things in order, making it easy for him to get ready for his daily grind. I played a little bridge on weekdays and on weekends with some of my old College classmates. I collected cookbooks, experimenting with a variety of recipes, paying attention to every detail of meal preparations. I cooked a lot; still no chocolate cake; and I pined for a single family house.

Then, there was the matter of the white rabbit fur. Not long after he bought the new car, I found remnants of a fur coat on the seat in Abraham II. *I don't own anything with rabbit fur.* But finding the fur did not bother me as much as his growing dismissal of me and my feelings.

Why doesn't he love me anymore?

Howard had changed. The changes were remarkable, and they stood in stark contrast to all the other slights I had suffered in the prior four years of our marriage.

A new car. Rabbit fur. Longer and longer work hours. Money.
Ok. I'm lost.

The mountain of straw had grown higher, but the layers of scar tissue had thickened enough to keep my feelings covered over. I went numb.

And then I got a car of my own.

I wanted, and got a Volkswagen Beetle. It was a used car, but I treasured the first of my bugs. It always ran. It was a little faded, leaned to the left, and had a hole in the floorboard which I covered with a metal plate in the winter. It started and stopped without fail, and it had a horn and a radio. I drove the car hard; up and down the Garden State Parkway from Newark to my job, as an insurance adjuster in Passaic, nearly 20 miles each way.

One day, about six months after getting my car, my precious 1966 bug 'seized' on the New Jersey Turnpike. I was travelling at a speed of 65 plus/minus, still the legal limit, when, suddenly, and without any warning, I lost my ability to steer, brake, or to change gears. It happened all at once. I coasted-it felt like for hours- across three lanes of highway, and finally came to a stop on the outer edges of the shoulder. All during rush hour. I like to say I was safely carried on the wings of Angels; a savings grace I would experience several times.

We collected many more cars in a short period of time. While in New Jersey, there was another VW Beatle for me, and a 12 cylinder, 1968 Jaguar XKE type which spent three weeks in repair shops for every week it was driven, mainly for him. Over a twenty year span, we collected Toyotas, Mercedes and BMWs. In between there was an Alfa Romero, a Cadillac, a Honda and several Mazdas.

The closest I got to the Rolls Royce he had promised when we were newlyweds, was a Mercedes S Class 500 series Howard presented to me one day after he had become Miami's City Manager. I refused to drive it. I felt uncomfortable just sitting in it. My ego did not need it and I did not want the attention the car would have brought. By then, I had begun my own career path as an executive in the not-for-profit arena, and I thought it immodest, at best, for me to drive around in such an ostentatious symbol of materialism. Not for me. I got myself a Honda, and it was good. It was very good.

"Why do you need so many cars?" I once asked Howard. It was around the purchase of our tenth car.

"Toni, Mom never could afford to buy a new car, so I promised myself I would buy myself any fucking car I could afford, any damn time I wanted one. Remember, I told you how I never got a chance to drive as long as Harold did, whenever Uncle Charlie gave us turns. I couldn't wait to get my own car."

There was his deprivation, again.

Once, while I was in high school, I daydreamed about having a convertible. I fantasized about a yellow mustang.

"Well, I was never old enough to drive a car, so my parents had to arrange rides for me with the older kids. It was fine with me, being driven around."

I didn't even get my first driving license until after I was married.

For me, cars were just a means of transportation; to get you from one place to another. Yet, I confess I did succumb to car fever, once. It was after the divorce. I purchased a new model Mazda 929, the top of the line. It looked like a Jaguar and made me feel like a big girl. It definitely boosted my ego, and I suddenly understood how Howard felt whenever he got a new car.

I wished Howard's acting-out would stop at car buying. I hoped and prayed his growing collection of cars, plus the comfort and well-being he derived from feeling on his spread, and subsequently his designer wardrobe, would help soothe him from his childhood slights. It did not. There was so much to fix in him, but in myself too.

During our stay in Newark, my soul started to get sicker.

Howard worked, and worked, and worked some more.

Me? I found a new friend, Casey Savoy. She became my lifeline.

❦

"YOU KNOW, EVERYBODY AT MOREHOUSE KNEW HOWARD was crazy, and I can't understand how you could be married to him." Casey wasted no time telling me.

Casey had gone to Spelman College, the sister school to the all-male Morehouse College, Howard's alma mater. They were both 1968 graduates. Casey taught school: English, French, and Spanish.

"Casey, we have been married for almost five years, and I think I should know him pretty well by now."

"I knew him for four years before you got married, and I don't think you could have known him at all to marry him." She insisted.

Despite being put off, Casey took me under her wings. We became bridge partners, traveling around northern New Jersey on weekends to play in duplicate bridge tournaments. We lunched and shopped together on weekends.

"If it was me, I would have left you long time ago," Casey tossed her sharp words over her shoulder as she turned to leave our place after one of our typical shopping and lunching days.

"Yeah, but your shit stinks, too," Howard shot back.

I didn't know whether to laugh or cry. But my tears started to flow, releasing my growing tension, and in celebration of my new line of defense. Casey was a warrior. My heroine.

Howard tolerated Casey. I continued to be amused by their mutual animosity.

An uneasy truce hung between Howard and Casey. I was growing increasingly more despondent about Howard's changing behavior. Casey was insistent I get myself together. She absolutely abused me of any temptation I may have to whine or complain.

"He may not be a good one, but at least you have a husband who takes care of the bills," she reminded me.

"Once you get yourself in a position to pay your own way, then you can think about leaving. In the meantime, just make Howard's life as miserable as you can, and spend all his money."

I could not, then, follow all of her prescribed methods, but she did teach me a few life-long lessons; namely, every woman needed to keep a black book with a roster of men: one to talk with, one to pay the bills, and one 'to fuck', and to not get them mixed up. I don't know if she actually practiced all she preached, but after my divorce, I would remember to use her advice, if not by her exact order.

Casey was my antidote to living in Newark, but she could not save me entirely.

Sometime around my second year in Newark, I started to cut myself on the bottom of my feet. I experienced, immediate, acute, though painful, sensations, which offset the perpetual numbness setting in my soul. Howard had put me aside and took up with something else (work), or someone else (whomever). I was constantly 'hobbling' around; bloodied, mutilated, hiding my wounds inside my shoes. But I was 'feeling' something, and pain was better than nothing.

No one knew.

I began to take baby steps toward independence.

For most of the four years prior to moving to Newark, I had been a 'marginal' worker: one year as a permanent substitute teacher in the Miami-Dade Public Schools; a car salesman; a graduate student's wife; and, a meter maid.

What now? Howard is on his chosen career trajectory. He seems very well-paced for rapid advancement. I need to do something!

❧

IN 1974, A MARRIED WOMAN STILL NEEDED HER HUSBAND'S permission, under the existing law, to get credit cards in her own name. I asked. He agreed. Once secured, I sometimes spent more money than I had, exceeding my credit limit. But I did not spend what I thought was Howard's money. I did not know anything about the adage: what is yours is mine. I felt I had to earn my keep. Funny, I wondered where this line of thinking came from.

I began seeing a therapist, primarily medical doctors who gave me a drug to treat my life. Valium was prescribed.

Oh my God, please don't let me get like my mom.

But it was so easy to just allow my emotions to go flat with the assistance of the latest mother's little helpers.

I just want the pain to go away. I want to walk without the bottom of my feet stinging.

Shortly after our relocation to Newark, I found a permanent position through a temp agency. The Hartford Insurance Company was recruiting women to participate in an experimental program designed to get women, the new affirmative action target, into the company's management track. I fit the profile. Many corporations were starting similar initiatives in the 1970s.

"Congratulations Mrs. Gary. You and two other women have been selected to participate in Hartford's corporate training program," the Franchise owner called us in to make the announcement.

There were five other women who had been hired along with me at the independent agency in Passaic, New Jersey. I was the only black. We all started as claims adjusters. Our claims were small-nothing over $7k, and all of the claims were settled in the office. The company policy prohibited women from going into the field to examine automobile damages.

Participation required we either commute daily, or stay in Hartford for a period of four months (going home on weekends). For me, commuting was out of the question. The travel times were prohibitive. My only choice was to stay in Hartford.

"This is a great opportunity and will only come around once." I was so excited to be selected. This was just the boost I needed for my career.

"You can't go." Howard absolutely refused to support my opportunity.

We argued, in my style.

"What do you mean, I can't go? I'll come home every

weekend. Or you can come to stay with me. It'll be fun for both of us."

"And," I argued, "We'll have more money after I've finished my training as a manager."

"Shit, no! I won't have you competing with me."

"How could I compete with you? I'll never be able to catch up with you." I was shocked at his concern.

"You are already far more advanced in your career, and I can never catch up or pass you," I attempted to reassure him.

This was untested ground. Up to now, my ambitions were to be a good wife; a 'help-mate'. Howard knew of my earlier interests in going to medical school while I was still at Marymount, but since we got married, I had not asserted any ambition for achieving much more than being supportive of his goals.

"I'm going anyway." I surprised myself.

"Yeah, and if you do, I'll divorce you for abandoning your marital duties. I have grounds for you even desiring to pursue any promotional training. You are denigrating my role as the primary provider for considering it."

Was he smirking? Was this a dare? What? Who knew? I didn't know he needed to always be the man on top. I can't compete with him, or surpass him. Where is this thinking coming from? Am I a threat to Howard?

I had gone from being a 'liability' as a newlywed, to a pariah for considering a corporate promotion.

Once again, I lost my back bone to fight back.

There was no place else to go as a claims adjuster, so I quit the company and retreated to my apartment to nurse my wounds.

I cut deeper into my feet.

As it turned out, this would not be the only time my effort for a career in corporate America would be thwarted as a result of my relationship with Howard, including my last attempt, in 1987.

TEXACO, South America, headquartered in Miami, was looking for a community relations director. By that time, I had accumulated a list of credentials which qualified me for the positon. I had gained access to many people of influence, and I leveraged what I thought was an asset: being Howard's wife. I lobbied hard for the appointment

"You are without question qualified, and you have a lot of community support; they like you, but your relationship to Howard is a problem," Ruth Shack, former County Commissioner and then President of the Dade Foundation told me. She was one of the strong supporters of my bid.

Crushed, I tucked my tail. It was not going to happen, ever.

҉

HOWARD'S STAR ROSE VERY FAST AT THE CITY OF NEWARK.

Sometime during our third year there, the City administration voted to take over the bankrupt Public School District, and Howard was assigned to the task, increasing his responsibility.

He had gone from being an Assistant Manager of Budget to Budget Director in a matter of a few years.

I was content to stay at home where I grew very creative in my homemaking skills. During one intense three month period, I made a macramé lamp shade, covered a table with fabric, and stained the wooden floor. I also shopped for those $2 dresses.

But, I threw away the unfinished sports coat I started in Michigan.

I continued to go to therapy. I took my valium, and I didn't give too much thought to my deteriorating marriage.

I hardly ever saw Howard. We did very little together socially. His paycheck made up for the indifference between us.

The kitchen became my principle domain, and I began to attend to all matters about food: preparing grocery lists, planning menus, cooking and presenting meals from cookbooks- picture perfect and tasty. I made everything from scratch. Home-made English muffins became a staple. Still, not a chocolate cake.

Thankfully, my funk didn't last long. After only a few months, cooking and meal preparations, bargain shopping, and playing bridge with Casey, were no longer enough to satisfy me.

"I want to go to graduate school," I announced one day over one of my designer meals.

"Do what you want, and don't worry about the tuition; I'll help you pay for it." Howard's generous gesture surprised me, but it also made me paranoid.

Does he really support me or is he just trying to help me leave him? Doesn't matter. I'm just going to do it!

"What do you plan to study?"

"Rutgers has a program in city and regional planning. The

whole country is focusing on urban issues and that should be interesting."

By then, I was a long way away from my earlier interest in medicine.

If we're involved in similar matters, maybe we would have more to talk about.

I still fantasized about our relationship: I love him; I love him not. He loves me; he loves me not. It was all topsy-turvy.

The Master's Degree in City and Regional Planning was being offered at the George Sternleib School for Urban Studies, Livingston College. It was the mid 70's, and the nation's attention had turned toward the plight of inner cities and other matters related to urban development: transportation; health; utopian designs; policy, et al.

I was hooked. As a full time student, I found a new freedom, and I was back into the books. I was elated.

"You know you're smarter than me, so I know you'll do great in class. You'll probably get a fellowship."

He was right. He paid my tuition for the first few semesters and then I received a fellowship for the second year.

Graduate school was a charm for me and I was determined to make high grades, including graduate level statistics. The course was designed to separate the men and women, i.e., the serious graduate students, from the crowded field. 'Stat' was feared by most of the black students; there was the persistent myth that blacks, as a whole, could not muster the intellectual stamina to perform at a passing level. I was irked. Sadly, several of them did not pass the course. I did.

Over all the years we were together, Howard often bragged how I was smarter than him.

"Brilliant," was usually his only comment after he read one or two of my graduate papers. Unlike when he was at the University of Michigan, I did not host any study groups at our place. Instead, Rutgers' suburban campus became my refuge from home, which had, by then, become a very empty place for me.

I distinguished myself in the Master's program. In addition to my fellowship, I was invited to teach a few undergraduate classes after I completed my degree courses.

I was pumped.

Life was beginning to look brighter for me, albeit, I was still in therapy, but I had put down the valium. I could not really focus on my studies under their influence. Besides, I was getting 'high' from my new-found sense of self-achievement. The last time I had felt so good was when I was at Marymount.

I'm on my way! Where? I don't know but I better start planning to leave Howard. Great! Once I get my degree and a job in my profession, I'll earn enough money to support myself, and be free to leave.

The thought sustained me for a few months.

※

IT WAS NOW 1975, SHORTLY AFTER I COMPLETED MY graduate degree, when my youngest brother, Haywood, came to live with me and Howard.

He was fifteen.

When he stepped off the plane, Haywood was wearing a

brown leather jacket, had a large afro-with a pick in his hair, and carried a basketball under his arm.

"Oh no," I looked at Howard with dismay.

My mom and dad had moved to California when Haywood was just seven years old.

"I'm afraid Haywood is starting to act like his brothers, and Butch and Andrew." Mom reported how he had begun to show outward signs of teen angst and rebelliousness.

My other brothers, Gerald and Sidney, as well as my cousins Butch and Andrew were all experimenting with drugs. The country was in the grips of a growing drug plague.

"Antonia, please take him. You and Howard can do so much more with him than me and daddy."

"But mommy, we don't have any children. What makes you think we know what to do?"

"You are young, and Howard is strong." She pleaded her case. "Daddy works up in the mountains and he only comes home on the weekends. I need help."

"I don't know how to handle a teenage boy!"

"Haywood loves you, and he admires Howard. He'll listen to you two."

Howard and I reluctantly agreed to help my parents. We thought we could offer Haywood a disciplined environment.

"Shit!" Howard looked at Haywood's sulking stroll toward us. It had taken a lot of persuasion to talk him into this arrangement. Now, we were both unsure.

We were living in a large, two bedroom apartment in Orange, New Jersey. Orange Park was directly across the street.

"Let's see what you can do with your ball." Haywood barely

had time to put his suitcase in his room when Howard immediately took him out.

"What took you so long?" It was after several hours when the two of them returned. I had dinner prepared and ready to serve an hour before they returned.

Howard lay across the bed gasping for breath. We both still smoked cigarettes – up to two packs a day- and his lung capacity was compromised. "I couldn't let him beat me so we continued to play until I got the highest score," Howard wheezed.

"So, you won?"

"Shit yeah. I had to pull out every trick I knew from the block," Howard panted. "He's good, and young, but I'm smarter."

I laughed as I heard Haywood moving around his new room with great ease, unpacking his clothes. He was breathing just fine.

"Well, you may have won the game by the scoreboard," I said, "but I think he beat you."

We both chuckled in agreement, but Howard had established the dominant pecking order. The fix was in. Howard was 'the man' and Haywood would conform to our house rules.

As it turned out, Haywood was secretly practicing the Jehovah's Witness religion. He became devout while living with us. He was a straight 'A' student and did not gave us one problem except the initial concern we had about his late night comings and goings. We soon learned he was going to meetings and on service calls.

"Haywood, please call us to let us know if you will be out late."

"Ok sis. No problem. I apologize for worrying you."

Haywood stayed with us for just under two years. Howard and I would occasionally reflect back on the time with warmth and fondness.

"This looks like an easy and delicious recipe." Haywood constantly combed the newspaper and magazines for meals he wanted, and I would take great pleasure planning the menus. We prepared them together, from 'scratch'.

"You can save money if you clipped these coupons," Haywood encouraged me. I had never tried to save money on food before. It was not something I had been raised to do, and it was never a source of concern to me and Howard. We always just bought whatever we wanted- price be damned.

Haywood and I bonded over this routine; sitting around the table discussing food- and life.

As it turned out, Haywood was wise beyond his years. Years later, he confessed to me he was keeping me company because of Howard's painful absence away from home.

"I knew you were lonely, sis."

Haywood is now a respected elder in the Kingdom.

⚜

IMMEDIATELY AFTER COMPLETING MY DEGREE, I GOT HIRED at the City of Passaic, New Jersey as a Planner I.

"Toni, congratulations. I'm proud of you." Howard handed me a large, wrapped box. In it was a top-of-the-line Hartman luggage brief case. It was a nice token, but I was looking for something in a little box. But the briefcase made a strong statement and I carried it with pride, until it was stolen from the backseat of my car after a few months.

"It serves you right that it was stolen. You shouldn't have left such an expensive briefcase out in the open. You can buy the next one on your own."

I don't care. I never liked it that much. It looked too masculine.

I immediately replaced the bulky piece of luggage with a soft leather, designer tote and bought myself a nice piece of jewelry, too. Congratulations to me!

I also consulted an attorney about a divorce.

I was tired. Tired of being less than Howard's number one. My clouded thinking darkened. It began to matter less to me if it was another woman, gambling, alcohol, drugs, cars, work, or any other vice. I had an active imagination. The fact is, it wasn't me he chose first, became the central argument inside my head.

Armed, with my graduate degree, I had a new sense of my self; my power.

Gainfully employed with the City of Passaic, I started searching for another job. I was interviewed, and got called back twice, to be a Health Planner for the American Lung Association (ALA) which was launching its anti-smoking campaign. The Surgeon General's message about the hazards of smoking was on all cigarettes packages, and a massive national education campaign was underway about the bad effects of smoking.

Ironically, I was still smoking cigarettes, but it was not a question during the interview.

This was a dream job. The ALA office was located in midtown New York. It paid over $40K, a fortune in 1974, and I would be able to leave Howard, and live in Manhattan. What a bonus. But on the third call, I was told the position was eliminated from the organization's budget, and would not be filled that year. I was so close.... And then I was back to square one.

I found another therapist.

Tom Ward, a Jungian, headed a Lutheran pastoral counseling service. I had tried Freudian-based psychiatrists, but they were too cold and distant, and I knew enough arm chair psychology, left over from my undergraduate degree in Psychology/Biology, to know our marriage was sick; not just me or him. But I needed immediate help.

"It could have been anyone." Tom responded. It was during one of our earliest sessions, when I bared my soul through a flood of tears.

In a fit of pique and anger, combined with a feeling of profound loss when the new job (my ticket to freedom) did not come to pass, I began a sexual relationship with one of my colleagues. He was someone I had known in graduate school. This was not a 'love affair'.

"Antonia, you're not fully to blame." Tom Ward was always so kind and supportive in his assessment.

"You are married, and married people should expect to have sex with one another." Howard had stopped having sex with me.

Of course I blamed myself, as if I had any control of Howard's behavior. I felt a little better after Tom's assessment, but only a little.

Antonia is in charge- of all things; people; and outcomes of every nature. Holding on to that kind of thinking and behavior almost killed me.

By this time, we had been married exactly seven years. *Could it be true what they say about the seven year itch?*

I still had Casey chirping in my ears about 'how to get over'. I did not tell her about my dalliance. She was in graduate school, working two jobs, and I was starting a new career. We were not spending as much time together. If she knew, she may actually have been proud of me, but I was too ashamed to share.

My default lines cracked wide open and exposed a side of me which was so out of character.

I can't keep this up. I had become a lair, and a cheat. What was it I heard as a child? If you lie, you'll steal. If you steal, you'll kill. I was on my way to hell!

I directed my regret and shame inward. I began to suffer from bouts of colitis, and I developed an extreme case of stress-related skin inflammation. There were days when I could not make it to the office. I had to bathe in a colloidal suspension and slather an oatmeal potion all over my body just to be able to wear clothes. The only unaffected parts of my body were my face, the palms of my hands, and the bottom of my feet which still smarted from the occasional cuttings, which I continued.

I was in bad shape; couldn't sleep or eat. The affair ended

after a few months, but the acute skin break outs lasted for almost a year. Minor breakouts would reappear at the slightest sign of stress. It began with a thought. It took me years to control that process.

Over the course of a short four months, my weight dropped from a norm of 120 to 106 pounds. I looked like a walking skeleton.

Just around this same time, my parents were travelling across country in their truck; pulling their trailer home. Daddy had retired from the Forest Service in California. It had been his dream to go back to live in his hometown, Elloree, South Carolina. They stopped in Newark to visit with me, Howard, and their youngest son, Haywood, where they found me in the throes of my madness.

By day two of their three day visit, my parents could no longer ignore the obvious.

"Want a drink AG?" Howard came home with a bottle of Jack Daniels each night. He had had very little to say to them other than to invite dad to share drinks with him. It was bizarre to watch Howard match drinks with my dad. Howard's stomach could never tolerate whiskey unless he mixed his drinks with milk, or egg nog.

"Of course," daddy accepted. He was always a heavy drinker and took his whiskey over ice, no mixer. Jack was always my favorite, but I could not drink with them. My colitis was in full flare-up.

Howard's 'show' of machismo, or whatever he was attempting to display, backfired and left him really sick each morning after.

"Antonia, what is really wrong with you?" My mother couldn't hold back any longer.

I had taken time off from work to play hostess. I took them to various places of interest in NYC, and to visit several of dad's relatives in the area. I was okay long as were busy moving around. Just sitting around talking made me too uncomfortable.

"Mommy, I'm really ok. I had the flu recently and I lost a lot of weight then from being sick. I'm busy with my work too, so it has taken me longer to get better."

Despite the obvious, everything was out of order, I begged my folks not to intervene.

"Howard is not always like this," I lamely excused his sullen, disrespectful behavior.

I lied to myself in order to make it sound right to them.

But, I had never seen him act so badly myself. Something had turned, again. I was seeing yet another side of Howard. This was a new behavior, using whiskey. I was too weakened by my own internal struggles to put up much of a fight with him. I didn't know how to fight him, anyway. Besides, I needed to heal myself.

After three days of listening to me explain away Howard's behavior as having a 'bad day' at the office, when they visited his job, they got a chance to see for themselves how crazy things actually were. It was in the middle of the budget planning season, and the entire staff was frantic.

He had banned me from coming into his office, said it was too big a distraction, so this was also one of the rare times I got to see him at work.

So I see. He's wearing some mighty big shoes: got a custom- designed office with custom Herman Miller furniture - nice; promoted to Budget Director-good; making pretty good strides towards becoming a City Manager. Check. But can't you see I'm suffering? And injured? Shitting my guts out and cutting my feet up?

The rabbit hole was getting deeper.

"Don't worry about Haywood, he'll be fine." My little brother still had another year to go before graduating, and Howard and I still planned to take care of him, until then.

"And I promise I will eat better and get well, soon."

Howard sent my folks an apology, by proxy.

"Howard says he is really sorry for his behavior. This is the budget season. You saw how much pressure he is under."

It would not be the last time I made up excuses for Howard to make others feel better.

I know my parents began to pity me. But they never abandoned me.

11

TRIPPING

SHORTLY AFTER MY PARENTS LEFT TO CONTINUE THEIR TRIP
south, I confessed my infidelity to Howard.

"I'm going to kick his mother-fucking ass. Do you
love him?"

"No, I did not love him. It's not his fault."

"God damn it Toni, how could you do this? What the fuck
were you thinking?"

I was ashamed. I was apologetic. I begged for forgiveness. I
was still thinking like a catholic even though I had not seen the
inside of a church in many years.

*Is he going to kick my ass? This is your out. It's the best time to
leave. You cheated on him. What are you waiting for?*

Howard and I revisited my transgression every day, for
weeks. It was the same litany: He accused. I apologized. We
made up. We entered into a couple's therapy with Tom Ward.

But I didn't want to leave like this. Compromised.

He remained ignorant of how I had been planning to leave

him; about the new job prospect which never came through. I'd never admit to my part: my cheating heart and mind.

"You better quit your job, now, and never see him again."

Of course, I complied; taking the easier, softer way.

We dove into couple's therapy. We also scheduled separate sessions with Tom Ward.

"We've got to move." I was too contrite about my affair to question him. Totally compliant, I didn't challenge the suddenness or urgency. Since I had quit my job, I felt like I was suspended in mid- air; untethered.

If I move too far out of his gravitational orbit, I'll just spin away, lose control. I'll be lost in a space bubble. I'd better keep still and do what he says.

Howard issued the directive to move a few months after my confession. Conveniently, our lease was about to expire. We made arrangements to temporarily move in with Howard's brother and his wife, Nancy. They lived in New Brunswick, a forty minute drive from Newark.

Our household goods went into storage, and we spent a week bunking in with Casey in the interim while Harold and Nancy got ready for us to move in with them.

I never questioned any of these moves or decisions; I was in a fugue state. I remained mum and let Howard direct every action. I was so afraid to utter a word, for fear he would walk out on me for sure.

I felt like I was living out of my body/out of my mind. There was so much going on and I just didn't want to participate in any decision-making. I seriously questioned my sanity.

How had our lives degenerated into this situation? What was happening?

What was happening to me?

A few years later, I got an aptly descriptive diagnosis from Tom which was reaffirmed years later by another therapist: Dissociative Identity Disorder. Wow! That explains it. The label helped me understand what was happening to me all those years, but only in hindsight.

⚜

"GIVE ME A DRINK."

I sought clarity at the bottom of a glass of Jack Daniels. Two double shots later, and it was not enough. It was on the second night at Casey's, and I was trying to figure out why Howard and I were camped out on her living room sofa.

"I want to get higher."

"You don't smoke dope." She knew I was against using any drugs, other than alcohol. "You don't know what's in this stuff," she warned me.

"Yeah, but I got me some."

I didn't care. I lit up the joint.

"What do I do?"

"Just like you smoke your cigarettes," Casey laughed. I was up to two packs a day, so I knew how to take a pretty deep drag.

I chased my next drink with a very deep inhalation of some unknown substance.

In a very short time, the room was no longer level. I tried to hold onto the side of the sofa, but I kept falling off. Or so it felt.

"Hold me down," I moaned.

Howard had come in and found me hallucinating.

I couldn't see, and I fell deeper and deeper into an abyss. I knew if I hit the bottom, I'd die.

"I'm holding you." I could feel Howard's body on top of me, but it didn't keep me from falling.

"Hold me," I screamed. "Hold me, tighter. Tighter!"

I lost track of time. *What had it been? Minutes? Hours?*

"What did you give her?" Howard lashed out at Casey after I came to.

"Don't put it on me. She's grown." Casey always had a laissez faire attitude toward adult personal choices, especially mine.

I didn't want to feel that paranoid again, ever. Thenceforth, I was careful to never mix my drinks with any outside substances. Never.

Just before moving in with his brother, Howard and I sent Haywood 'back home' to our parents who were now living in South Carolina. Howard and I agreed the trauma of our lives and our strained relationship would be too heavy a burden for Haywood, now ending his 11th grade year.

Everything was upside down.

The crazy thing about the timing of my confession is Howard's extra-marital affair (s), yet unconfessed, but were clearly evident.

"Do you have a boyfriend?" my Doctor asked. Somewhere during Howard's first year with the City of Newark, I started to develop gynecological problems; vaginal infections of mysterious origins. After the third bout, my doctor asked me about my sexual partners. I had not yet strayed outside of my marriage, but I had no delusions about what Howard may have been doing; his long hours, rabbit fur on the car seat, telephone calls hung up on when I answered, etc. I was prepared to tough it out- until I had a clear exit plan.

None of the infections were untreatable or incurable, and, I thought, *I'd just let Howard get caught in his own stew.* My line of thinking was another one of the ill-formed, egotistical self-talks I had adopted, e.g., *Howard=bad; Antonia=good, therefore, he'll never get to heaven if he breaks my heart,* a line from one of my theme songs. I had a growing collection. *I really don't care if he's having an affair (s), as long as I got to wear the title of Mrs., and he continues to pay the bills, and oh yes, does not make me irreversibly ill.* There was another toxic thought to add to my growing list of delusions. But it's what I knew to think.

"You know it's not always the man's fault," I recall my mom telling me about my dad's infidelities.

"Antonia, there are women who make a point of sleeping with other women's husbands. It's not ok, but as long as the husband brings his paycheck home, and is not disrespectful to his wife in public, then it's to be expected."

I was speechless. Why was she telling me this? I was only seven!

"You know, once your daddy even gave me a 'venereal disease', but I was able to cure it with penicillin shots."

Of course. The ubiquitous penicillin shots. They cured everything.

So, I had long been programmed to accept Howard's

infidelities, and some of their consequences, and to not leave the marriage because of them.

So there we were, cramped up in his brother and sister-in-law's townhouse.

Howard had to leave earlier than when we lived downtown to get to work on time. It was a forty minute commute. He usually left me in bed, so I didn't immediately notice when he took the local section of the Newark Star Ledger with him every morning. Initially, I didn't think his behavior was so odd. I had other, more pressing matters to address. Primarily, the shame of my infidelity, and making up for it was foremost on my mind.

"Let's make a baby." Howard pressed me from the time we first married. It was usually a teasing request, often a prelude to us having sex. I thought of it as part of his foreplay.

"Howard, you know I'm not ready to have a baby," was my usual reply. But not this time. Now, making a baby became part of our make-up strategy. We talked about me getting off 'the pill' so we could start a family. Insane? You bet.

Up till now, my fertility had been the one thing I maintained absolute control over. I had mastery over my ovaries!

"It's common," mom used to tell me about getting pregnant. She would have known for sure. Mom's earliest job was as a public health nurse in Belle Glade, Florida, where, she served as nurse/mid-wife. She delivered many of the women farm worker's babies, and she reported from her first-hand observation, how easy it was. Her long nursing career also included a stint as a hospital obstetrical nurse.

She told me how she had had no difficulty getting pregnant with me.

"Antonia, you are built to have children," something about a wide pelvic bone, "So, you'd better be careful."

Those were enough admonitions to carry me for a long time.

I did not want to be, nor do anything 'common'. Thank God there was 'the pill.' Ironically, oftentimes, Howard would remind me to take my pill, so I thought he was on the same page with me. I soon realized how not agreeing to 'make a baby' gave me what I needed; I could withhold, and perhaps even punish Howard for his many transgressions.

But for sure, all of my magical thinking kept me shackled and trapped for a long time. Funny, I didn't realize I also kept the keys to my own 'jail'. But even after I came to, I did not know how to use those keys. I believed at the time it was my fault, totally, that threatened the ending of my 'workable' marriage; we had to get out of dodge; to run away from my bad behavior, nee my affair.

I stopped taking my birth control pill.

Simultaneously, Howard and I embarked on a frantic effort to get out of New Jersey.

"I've outgrown this job, and I need to move on."

Once again, I helped him complete applications for openings around the country. His resume was now much more impressive.

The search only took a few months when, wondrously, the City of Miami hired Howard as the Director of Management and Budget.

I was relieved.

I'm going to be saved. Saved from Newark- the ghost town; saved from the dark shadows hovering over Howard every morning; saved from the lingering, and incomprehensible shame of my infidelity. Saved by the comforting notion of going 'home'.

We packed our bags.

We shipped our furniture.

We flew down with our dog, a beautiful large-boned German shepherd, named Smokey; my constant companion. Smokey offered me another life-line at the end of her leash, as we took our daily walks around our new/ old home town. She helped me to start over, again.

BOOK FOUR

MIAMI

🎋 12 🎋

THE *305

WINTER 1976 TO SPRING 1981

Howard and I carried our open scars and deep wounds to Miami.

I sought refuge in the love and affection from our families. They knew we were planning to start a family; it was joyously welcomed news. I looked forward to a fresh new beginning. Howard came home almost every evening.

His new appointment as Director, Office of Management and Budget brought him closer to his goal: City Manager.

Howard and I temporarily rented an apartment in Coconut Grove; nearby his office at City Hall. It was convenient. I spent my days searching around for my first house; mainly in the Grove, which had been one of my favorite neighborhoods, from childhood.

One early morning, while taking Smokey for her daily walk, she stopped and whined at the sky.

I looked up in awe.

"Smokey, this looks just like New Jersey." She started running around in a circle. We both looked up and watched as the sky turned darker from a heavy, low cloud.

"Smokey, it's snowing."

Dogs know. They often show us the way. They are usually right.

It snowed in Miami, January 19th, 1977, and the event made the national news.

This has got to be a sign; things will never be the same, ever again; for me, with us.

Shortly after the headline-making snow, my Uncle Andrew stopped by one afternoon for a surprise visit. He was on his way to City Hall, which was only a few blocks from our apartment.

As much as times had changed, much remained the same in Miami, and there were still too many black 'firsts'.

Uncle Andrew was the first black master electrician hired by the City of Miami. He had been on the job for at least two years before we returned to Miami. Howard was now his boss. Uncle Andrew had always prided himself on being a 'race man', so initially, he welcomed having a black man in charge.

I was happy to see him. He remained my favorite Uncle.

I offered to make him a cup of coffee. "It's never too late, or too hot for coffee," he used to say. It was close to three in the afternoon, at the peak of the heat.

"How do you like your coffee?"

"Black, I take my coffee black."

I had just started to boil water to cook rice for dinner.

"Uncle Andrew, this is a nice surprise. I don't get many visitors in the middle of the day."

I welcomed the break from my routine. I took down one cup and saucer. It was too hot for me to join him.

He sat down. I put a heaping teaspoon of instant coffee in his cup and poured in the water.

I turned to the sink and, in an instant, a flood of memories from childhood rushed through my mind. Uncle Andrew was always such great fun. He used to take loads of children; his five; me and my three brothers; and a myriad of neighborhood friends, to the drive-in movies. To avoid having to pay for each one, he encouraged us to hide under cover in the back of his truck until we cleared the entrance.

"But that's cheating," one of the kids would invariably remind him.

"Are you gonna tell? And, are you gonna pay?" He'd ask his accuser.

The whole group joined him in laughter when he dismissed this petty larceny. We loved being his co-conspirator.

"Toni, why does this coffee taste like salt?" He was frowning.

"Oh my God, Uncle Andrew, I'm so sorry. I forgot I already put in the salt for the rice," I giggled. My head was in a cloud.

What is he really doing here? If only he knew.

"Toni, I came to tell you something you might not like." He fidgeted with the coffee cup. I had gone back to the sink to prepare a fresh cup for him.

"You know what the paper is saying about Howard. And the people at the job are starting to talk really bad about him, too."

His great revelation began with was a rehash of a few stories and accounts about Howard: the new guy in town. He was labeled as brash and uppity by the Miami Herald. It was just the beginning.

But we just got to town. What do they know already?

The stories also covered some negative history during his tenure in Newark.

My Uncle had come to share a rumor he heard about one of Howard's transgressions. Another one.

But, I didn't want to hear anything negative, especially from this uncle.

"Uncle Andrew," I said in exasperation, "Those rumors are old news, and I can't do anything about them now."

Sorry, it's too late. It's been too many years since you joined with the other family members to stop me from marrying Howard. Don't you realize we are nearing our ninth anniversary? Besides, just a few days before you got here, I found out I was pregnant.

I had not told anyone else about the pregnancy, except Howard. I was excited, yet I was in turmoil.

"Do you still want me to make you another cup?" I had boiled a fresh, unsalted pot of water.

"No, I better get back to the office." He looked dejected.

"Please let me know if you need my help in any way," he offered.

No thanks, I don't want your help.

"O.K., Uncle Andrew. You come visit me again anytime you want. I'll be sure to make a good cup of coffee next time."

He left in resignation and defeat. Uncle Andrew retired

shortly after his visit. He told me years later he could not, in good conscience, continue to work under Howard's authority.

What he didn't know when he came to visit me was Howard had assaulted me earlier in the week with a demand that I abort the baby; a baby we had worked so hard to conceive. How could I tell my favorite Uncle, or, anyone?

After he left, I spent the rest of the day crying.

Smokey knew what was up. I was actually already pregnant on the day it snowed. Kito was born exactly nine months later, to the day, on October 19.

What is wrong with Howard? He makes me crazy. He keeps me crazy.

We had spent almost four months trying to get pregnant.

Howard's demand for an abortion was sudden, unexplained, and far outside the realm of our new reality back in Miami. I had just begun to enjoy being married again.

I'm finally being somebody, even if it's only as Howard's wife. It was good enough since we are getting so much praise and attention from our families and our new friends. This feels good- all the status and, extra attention. Maybe we're going to make it, after all.

I was aware of some of the rumors about Howard Gary; about the gang of loyal staff he brought from Newark: the Indian, a few other blacks, a woman. While he was labeled by the old timers in City Hall and in the press as 'brash', 'uppity', 'being too big for his britches', etc., he was also called 'brilliant', 'the best municipal financial analyst Miami ever had', and, 'Uncle Charlie's nephew', nee untouchable. These were just a few labels and characterizations that began appearing in the growing press coverage which would become a hallmark of his eight year tenure with the City.

I paid little attention to all the talk. I knew better. I had greater, more important matters to tend to. I was making a home, reinserting myself into Miami, working on starting a family.

I had learned from those hard experiences, gleaned from our years in Newark, to not interfere with his office, and to let the business of municipal management rest solely with him. So I left those matters alone and became immersed in my very private space. I was also trying to grow my love deeper, and to make up for my extramarital affair.

"This pregnancy is not a good time for me," Howard continued to implore me to abort.

After weeks of daily badgering, I pretended, one day, to be on my way to do just that.

"So you're going to the clinic?" He had called me early morning from his office.

"Yes, I'll see you later," I lied.

I was actually on my way to the airport.

On the taxi ride to the airport, I struggled to put my thoughts in order: *How could he even think about a termination of 'our' pregnancy, let alone utter those words? He had fully agreed to us getting pregnant. I was using all the modern techniques available at the time, even calling him to come home at times in the middle of the day when my temperature was 'right'. For months, he was an eager and willing participant. What is this darkness plaguing him?*

I had a strong feeling the answers to his new attitude must be in what he had left behind. I intuitively knew I had to return to Newark, to the source of the floating rumors, to find out for myself. I needed to understand what had triggered such a turn of heart.

After we moved to Miami, Howard had made a few trips back to Newark. He explained he was wrapping up some unfinished business with the City, and to help the new Budget Director with his transition. It was a reasonable explanation. But on the taxi drive to the airport, I began to experience clear flashbacks. I think the surge of early pregnancy hormones gave me a renewed strength, power, and, 20/20 hindsight.

I was coming to.

During the three hour flight, I began to recall our short, intense two month period of isolation at his brother's preceding our return to Miami, and how Howard stealthily secreted the local sections of the Newark Star Ledger every morning.

What was in those news stories? This time I'm going to dig around until I found out the why of it all.

It was in late afternoon when I called Howard.

"I expected to her from you a few hours ago. I was wondering why it was taking so long. Are you ok?" I felt a heavy pull on my heart. He sounded like he had gone through this before; like he knew how long an abortion should take.

"I'm calling from Newark." I did not stutter. "I'm having second thoughts about the abortion, and I need some time to think." I was speaking calmly.

"I'll return home in a few days after I talk with Tom."

He remained silent for a few moments.

"Yeah, and when you get back, we will have to see about

that," he promised, threatening me with some empty new form of punishment.

I stayed with Casey. She remained as stoical as ever. This time, I did not plumb her for any information. I wanted to find the truth on my own.

I spent two days in the library and read from the archives of the Newark Star Ledger. I made copies. What I found has remained a secret I'd never shared; with anyone. I didn't feel sharing the truth would serve any purpose, but it did provide me with was a little insurance.

For years, I kept adding up the dividends, until keeping the secret nearly bankrupted my soul.

While the facts of the matter were public knowledge; after all it was published in the newspaper, the secret is I never told Howard I knew he had been involved in a scandal. He was charged with taking a duplicate, unauthorized salary, aka double dipping, and the City was suing him for repayment, or, at worse, prosecution.

The amount was substantial: almost double his published salary as the City Budget Director. The whole matter was dismissed as a misunderstanding: There was no question he performed the work as both Newark City Budget Director and as the interim Budget Director for Newark Public Schools.

The trips he was making were to attend depositions, hearings, etc. The matter was resolved administratively.

The real scandal, for me, was I had no idea he had earned so much more money. How and where the money was spent was left a mystery for another year.

My God. Will there ever be an end to this madness?

This new knowledge marked the beginning of another era. I completely lost the little new faith and trust I had begun to build.

Did it even matter I had already experienced two failed attempts to leave him? All those tears spilled over the American Lung Association job, not to mention my loveless affair? I got a baby to think about. I'm keeping it.

So, I dug in my heels.

After I completed my research in the library, I went to spend two days with Tom and his wife at their home in a northern suburb of the City. Tom and I explored the myriad reasons how and why Howard and I had reached such an impasse. The lies. The cover ups. We did not come up with any definitive answers about what drove Howard, not then, but I did gain more insight into my own motivations.

I had to make a hard choice. I felt emboldened with the information I had found.

"No, I am not going to abort," I shouted and stood my ground with Howard once I got back home.

"I am going to be a good mother, and we are going to be a strong family, even if it kills me!" I cried. This time the tears were not for me, but for my unborn child.

I cried a lot throughout my pregnancy. I cried to think the baby might come to know he was not wanted by his daddy, and his mommy was such a fuck up.

I prayed the baby would be healthy.

I could not tell anyone in the family how much I was suffering. I didn't have a corps of girlfriends yet in Miami. I knew what Casey would have said: "Make him pay."

I didn't work during most of my pregnancy. I used the time to take a long pause- to look into the near future. I also took an even longer look back. I began to peel off the layers of rose-colored film I had used to filter my perceptions, imagined and real. I was quickly learning how to better use the guise of being "Mrs. Howard Gary" as a cloak of comfort and protection from the outside world, and at times, from Howard. It was enough to sustain me during most of my pregnancy.

And now that I had another person I was bringing into the mix, a separation and/or divorce was out of the question. "You've got to grin and bear it," Aunt Lorraine use to say, delivering her recurring lesson on how to cope with everything life throws at you. Aunt Lorraine had gone from rags to riches to rags. She knew a few things about life's ups and downs.

Stay. Stay married. Stay and grin and bear it.

By now, Howard and I were in sync: I well knew how to respond to the good, the bad, and the ugly of him/us.

Antonia, you can get used to anything, including hanging by a velvet rope, became my reset mantra.

Pregnant, bored, and restless, when I was seven months pregnant, I applied for and was hired to work for Miami-Dade County. My new career track was jump-started. It was a personal triumph. I was woman, and I could roar.

۞

I WAS BOLSTERED IN MY DECISION TO REMAIN IN MY marriage, partly because of my dad.

"You know, there are no divorces in my family," my dad used to brag. And mainly it was true.

He was proud of his track record with mommy; their marriage lasted until he died, after sixty two years.

"I never left your mother," daddy once declared, after recovering from another one of her frequent flights from him. Sometimes mom would just stay for an overnight, usually with one of her sisters. Once she left him in California, where they had moved, and came back to Miami and stayed for a full year. Her longest 'retreat' was for nearly five years when she ran away to Texas when she was in her mid-sixty's. He always took her back.

About five years after my divorce, the subject of infidelity came up during a great night of drinking and fun with my dad and my boyfriend at the time.

"Mr. Williams, how did you manage to stay married all those years and still have other girlfriends?" He dared to ask.

In disbelief, I choked on my drink.

The three of us were sitting on my balcony, overlooking Biscayne Bay. I had decorated the balcony with outdoor furnishings, plants, and a variety of decorative items befitting the Miami setting. There was a potted palm tree swaying in the light breeze blowing from the Bay.

In good humor, daddy began to search around and found an assortment of small items he had found around the balcony: pebbles, candles, coasters, high ball glasses.

"See, all these are the other women." He placed the grouping to the left.

"And this, this is my wife," he proudly pointed to an empty beer bottle, the largest item off to the far right of the others.

"I'll drink to that," Willie and daddy clinked their beer bottles in a toast. They both took long swigs of the brew.

I took a long swallow too. But mine was at least two fingers of Jack Daniels, on the rocks.

"I got to give it to you Mr. Williams; you're a good man. You're a good man." Willie laughed out loud as he continued to congratulate daddy.

I held my sides, joining them in laughter. Alcohol, the great social lubricant, helped lift my mood.

I always knew how daddy felt about mom, and I always hoped Howard would feel the same about me; and I might, in the end, be the central love of his life, despite, and in spite of the 'other' women.

So, I continued to stay.

❈

ANOTHER PHENOMENA OCCURRED SHORTLY AFTER WE arrived back in Miami. Howard was vetted by the private community for his business acumen. He was invited to join Sunshine State Bank as a compensated Director.

The principals of the Bank, the Corona family, were well known, and respected scions of banking in pre-Castro Cuba. The most colorful member of the large family was Ray, the oldest sibling.

"Ray is going to pick us up." Howard and I had been invited to attend our first Cuban wedding. The invitation read 3:00 PM, and we got ready to arrive at the church on time.

Ray was supposed to pick us up at 2:30.

The time came and went. We waited.

3:00. Still no Ray. Howard called him. "He says he is on his way."

3:30 and still no Ray.

By 4:00 I was ready to change my clothes thinking it was too late for the wedding and we would just not be going at all.

"No, let's just wait. He'll be here." Howard seemed not to be as bothered about this breech in wedding protocol, confident in his new friend showing up.

"But we can't show up at a wedding after it has started." I protested. "So I guess we're only going for the reception."

"Maybe. This is an important social commitment I made with Ray, and he knows these people better than us."

I prepared us a snack and we continued to wait.

Ray arrived in front of our house at 5:30! He was driving a Rolls Royce. Howard and I were seated in the back. *Chauffeured.*

"Howard did you know he had a Rolls?"

"Shhh, Toni. Yes. Don't act like you are surprised."

This was a first for me and I wondered what other surprises I was in store for with Ray Corona.

"Don't worry, we'll get to the reception on time!" Ray laughed it off, telling us that nothing started on time in Cuban culture, especially weddings.

Sure enough, when we arrived at the luxurious Fontainebleau Hotel a little before 6:00 PM, the bridal party was just pulling in behind us. Thus, we were introduced to Cuban peoples' time (CPT), and a new social order. Cuban culture redefined appointed time: you could add at least one half hour to any appointment to still be 'on time'. As it turned out, the time-formula applied to all situations. Business protocol was up to 30 minutes; lunches, dinners, and other informal gatherings, up to an hour; but with weddings, it was acceptable to add up to ninety minutes to the 'on time' window. Crazy, but we got used to it.

By the mid-1970s, Miami had undergone a spasm of identity crises. The area had become fully immersed in the Cuban culture. Miami/Dade County had the largest concentration of Cubans in the State; vast areas were punctuated with the ubiquitous aroma of mojo sauce in the air. The sharp and pungent garlic smell signaled Cuban-style meats were being cooked. There were entire zip codes, particularly in the City of Hialeah, where Spanish was the only language required to conduct all business and commerce, and other social enterprises (church, funeral homes, grocery stores, many schools, etc.). Great public debates were taking place about the efficacy of an English-only government/society.

Ray and Howard became fast friends from the moment they met. I enjoyed his company too. The Coronas were a large and loving family. The 'old man' had enjoyed a sterling business reputation as a banker in Cuba, and he had endured a long and hard struggle to gain another position of business leadership while exiled in Miami. Mr. Corona, Sr. was revered by his wife, children, and grandchildren.

I joined the Coronas' family gatherings on several

occasions, and I always felt warmly welcomed. Once, they hosted a baby shower for my second son, Issa.

"Howard, I can't accept this". Ray placed $1000 in one hundred dollar bills in my hand. It was a present for the baby.

"Take it. Take it," Howard urged me not to protest too much.

I was still overwhelmed by Ray's gesture, but I understood it was typical of how he treated people he liked.

Along with the bank directorship, another world was opened to Howard.

Seemingly, all at once, he held memberships in several private clubs: at The Mutiny Club, notorious for hosting the 'cocaine cowboys' and their entourages; Regine's, a rival eponymous club owned by the famous Parisian impresaria; and a membership at CATS, a men's entertainment venue.

CAT'S was owned by well- known restauranteur, Monty Trainor. Shortly after opening the club, Monty was convicted of a federal crime. He served his time, returned to Miami, where he is still immersed in community service projects.

"My cousin is a server at CAT's and she told me all the girls want to wait on Howard because he is a great tipper," one of my business partners told me shortly after the club opened. There are no secrets in public life. I knew Howard liked to reward good service.

CATS remained the 'in' spot for several years. It was located in a very upscale new shopping center built in the heart of Coconut Grove, Miami's oldest commercial village, on Biscayne Bay. No expense was spared in the club: a specially commissioned black onyx panther with jeweled eyes prowled out front, and the interior's marble, glass and brass was always polished to mirror perfection.

One night, Howard and I took his brother Harold and his wife, Patricia to CAT'S for dinner. They frequented Miami to visit family. The food was just ok. The evening's highlight took place in the ladies room.

"Oh my God, Pat, do you see that?" I whispered. Pat and I were standing at the wash basin.

"Those are a man's legs, and he's facing the toilet!" Patricia and I watched as a transvestite, in a dress, exit with a flourish. He/she smiled at us. Pat and I broke down in laughter.

"Welcome to Miami Vice, Pat." I played it down as we told the guys what we saw.

But Harold and Howard wanted to find the guy and punch him out.

"Wiillyam," Pat said in her sweet Alabama drawl (Harold's given name is William Harold Gary), "You don't have to do any such thing."

"It's no big thing. He didn't try to touch us or anything." Pat and I talked the brothers down. I always knew the brothers were cut from the same cloth: hit first, explain, if necessary, later.

I played by myself at CATS a few times. Always lunch. Once, I used my clout as Mrs. Howard Gary and used Howard's membership to host the members of my social club, JUST US, and their spouses, for a happy hour. Painfully, Howard did not join us.

Howard also had membership cards in several other 'clubs; around town. Some of these venues, and their clients, had earned questionable reputations, representing what Miami became renowned for in the 1980s: a fast drug-fueled cash economy, marked by glamorous, and loose living.

"You want to sample my hair?" Howard responded to one of the many charges from his nemesis, City Commissioner Joe Carollo, about alleged cocaine use.

I cannot attest to whether or not Howard engaged in any of the rumored behaviors. There were many allegations, but I certainly did not see any first hand. Howard did give his hair sample for drug testing and demanded the Miami Herald publish the negative findings. Yet, even after he tested clean, the news outlets continued to generate ongoing speculation about the 'company' the city manager was keeping.

One person specified was Ray Corona.

The Bank's deposits grew rapidly along with a high public profile.

Also on the Sunshine Bank Board was Roberta Klein, aka Bobby. She was married to Joe Klein, a very successful businessman who was invested in the bank.

I was pregnant with Kito when we first met. Bobby is thirteen years my senior, and I continue to admire her 'staying alive, living out loud, and loving whom I please' attitude. Her outlook on life, how she managed to survive turbulent ups and downs, of fortunes lost, regained and lost again, has remained positive. Thankfully, I have Bobby to model for me how to live a long life with grace, verve, and with a good dose of sensual sexuality. Bobby still has a well- proportioned figure, only going from a size 6 to her current size 8 over the nearly forty years since I met her. Viva the diva, Bobby Klein!

Bobby and I remain in the same orbit. We're planning to celebrate over forty years of friendship; coming soon.

Bobby became one of my best friends. We have similar stories. We loved our husbands and stood by them through the thick and thin of their lives. Bobby and Joe divorced, remarried, divorced, reconciled again, and now live harmoniously apart from one another. They remain great friends and share in their grandchildren's lives. It works for them.

Howard liked Joe and Bobby. We spent many wonderful, fun-filled times together. One night stands out.

We had made reservations for dinner, party of eight, at Le Ville Maison, well- known for its fine, French cuisine. We arrived late for our reservations. Everyone was feeling the effects of our earlier, protracted cocktail hour. We were in high spirits.

"Where are you from?" I think Howard started in on him first. Our waiter was putting on 'airs', speaking in a fake French accent. *Not a good idea for this group*. Joe quickly followed up before the waiter could answer. "Your accent reminds me of my cousin in Brooklyn, or was it the Bronx"? Everyone in our party broke out in laughter, at which point, our waiter chose to join us in poking fun at him. He laughed along with us. We ended the meal with amaretto cookies. The waiter set the cookie paper-wrapping on fire; and he joined us to watch as the ashes rose, and then floated high above the table. Much like our spirits that night.

SHORTLY AFTER HOWARD JOINED THE BOARD OF DIRECTORS, the bank, and its principals, came under a federal investigation for laundering drug money. He had become the City Manager after the investigation got underway.

The Miami Herald thought the city Manager's behavior might be of interest to its readers. Their coverage of Howard's relationship with Sunshine State Bank coincided with their coverage of the drug-laundering charges against the Bank.

His crime? Association. Howard became a repeat offender.

I read the newspaper along with everyone else.

Poor judgement. Bad choices.

But I also knew the Ray Corona fix was in when Howard began to, literally, change his spots. He always enjoyed dressing in the latest men's fashion trends, and his wardrobe began to grow beyond my wildest imaginings. His style changed; it got more colorful, more flamboyant.

"Howard why do you need so many blue ties? They all look alike."

"Yeah, but look at the weave of this one. Here, touch it. You can feel the difference."

That tie costs $200. I was sticker shocked!

"And, I got it at a discount. See it was marked down to $75.00." He was proud of his ability to bargain shop.

Once, the Herald reported, Ray allowed Howard to use his credit card to charge purchases from some very high end boutique shops at the Bal Harbor Shops, home to all the fashion designers.

While Howard palled around with Ray, the rhythm of his comings and goings shifted, and his habits changed.

"I didn't know you liked raw fish", I was stunned one day to hear him order sushi.

Howard had been a steak and potatoes guy, and he preferred his steak well-done. I was only mildly disturbed observing Howard's changes and new behaviors. I had grown comfortable with his chameleon-like responses to his surroundings; how he managed to fit himself into wherever he was placed. I attributed his ability to be a 'changeling' as one of his survival tools. It had not yet become unmanageable. Besides, I had long abandoned the idea of serving as his therapist. I was busy keeping myself sane and safe by making my nest more comfortable.

Howard got a lot of pressure from the City Commissioners to resign his directorship in order to protect the integrity of the job as City Manager.

Ray was convicted of the charges

Howard did eventually leave the Bank Board, and his association with the Coronas was curtailed, somewhat. Our socializing with the Coronas continued; I continued to enjoy the family gatherings.

Despite appearances, after he resigned from the bank board, Howard used his influence as City Manager to helped Ray's younger brother, Ricardo, open a grocery in the blighted Overtown area.

"Howard, are you going to get in trouble over this?" I was uncomfortable with all the press attention focused on Howard's private behavior. The investigation was intense, and I felt paranoid; they were scrutinizing me more closely, too.

"No, the Corona's won the bid in an 'open and competitive'

process. Nobody else wanted to do business in Overtown and they put up their own money."

I never liked the deal. The press scrutiny was just gearing up for a bigger onslaught.

Over the course of time, Ray worked out a deal to keep their father from being prosecuted during the protracted investigation. The bank remained open for business until 1986.

In the meantime, Howard began to attract all kinds of people to him. He was a living *tabula Rosa,* presenting himself to his new acquaintances to impress their peculiarities onto him; their sets of interests; their taste in clothes, food, entertainment, etc. There were times when it was difficult for me to recognize him.

⁂

IN ADDITION TO ME AND HOWARD, THERE WERE ONLY A FEW other 'native' born blacks who had returned to Miami after leaving to get degrees, gain work experience, or just to travel the world. Scores of African-Americans were coming to Miami at the invitation of a few industry headquarters; namely, Burger King, Ryder Truck, and a growing number of new banks were following the money into South Florida.

Howard and I did not socialize much with other couples from our natural social circles. i.e., the black middle class. It was growing harder and harder for me to continue living a lie; especially in front of folk who, from outer appearances, had what I considered trust-based relationships.

☙❧

"I KNOW THE FOOD WAS GOOD, AND I HOPE YOU LEFT enough room for dessert." I looked at Camille. She was loosening her tied belt. She had worn a shift-style dress.

"Camille and I are having another baby." Ignatius beamed at his blushing wife.

I had cooked a meal to end all meals: duck, lamb, and beef roast, with all the trimmings. I was proud of the production. I had been cooking for three days for this very special dinner party.

We had invited three other couples to come to our home. Also at the table were Ron and Regina Frazier and Ben and Sylvia Guilford. Everyone in the room was an accomplished professional; there was an easy camaraderie amongst us. As it turned out, all the women, including myself, were Roman Catholic. Teasingly, but lovingly, Sylvia's husband, Ben, called her the "Pope-ette'.

Circumstantially, we were all having our children at the same time; several of our pregnancies were in sync. I had had Kito, and we were working on another. We were only halfway through the dinner when Ignatius and Camille made their announcement. They already had two boys.

"This time is the girl, for sure."

We all hoped so, for them. It was a joyous announcement, but her news depressed me. I felt like crawling under the house. I had had an abortion shortly after I gave birth to Kito. I agreed with Howard to terminate that pregnancy.

I know everyone around the table could tell, just by looking at me. I know the shame must be written all over my face.

Actually, not then, but my shame actually did begin to show shortly thereafter when I broke out in a succession of skin outbreaks- all over my chest and back. The eruptions persisted, off and on, over several years.

Déjà vu.

It seems I always wore my sins and shame on the outside; open for interpretation. The experts would surely have recognized a woman under siege, but this time I did not seek outside help for another few years. I was grinning and bearing it.

Here I go again, I punished myself for being so compromising: keeping one baby; aborting another. *When was this going to end?*

But it would be the first and only dinner party-for couples I'd host. Every other entertainment at my house would be big, anonymous events for the masses, and my parties soon became legend. Also, I felt better being out in the public arena with Howard where we both could wear our respective masks of respectability and general deportment. Over time it became harder for me to keep my mask on straight in intimate settings. I felt I would crack, and the whole charade would be over.

I also feared being called out in small settings for putting up with how Howard talked to me. His general and spontaneous outbursts of disrespect grew more frequent; unpredictable, and they kept me in a hyper vigilant state. I never knew when he might call me "bitch", or 'nigger' or some other soul-stealing word.

On one rare occasion, a girlfriend asked, "Why do you let him talk to you that way?"

"I know he loves me." I gave my pat, weak response. It was a lame excuse. "He doesn't really say it to be mean", I'd explain.

My heart knew differently.

By now, the grip on our long marriage had loosened from lies, cheating, feigning, and feckless excuses. Both stubborn; neither of us made the first move to physically leave. I had voted with my feet and remained committed to the long haul, to remain as an intact family unit in an environment of lunacy. It was messy trying to hold on; to hang in there.

And, by this point, I had grown accustomed to my velvet-rope 'hanging'. The unknown was too fearsome. I retreated into an unhealthy, but sustaining combination for survival: being "Mrs. Gary"; shopping; three servings of wine lunches with the ladies; running a business: Fingertips; Executive Director of GMU, etc.

Part of what kept me content was the lifestyle I had managed to cobble together where a major component included my house.

⚛

HOWARD'S POSITION AS A CITY EXECUTIVE REQUIRED HIM TO live within the City boundary, and we found the perfect setting.

The Oak Grove community dated from the 1920's. It was one of Miami's earliest suburbs. The neighborhood was marked by stately and palatial homes tucked between the Miami River and a set of sacred Indian burial caves; near downtown. Some of the houses were built directly on the Miami River. A few were as small as two bedroom cottages, serving at one time as vacation homes for the leisure class.

I loved the house the moment I saw it.

This would be a great place to raise children.

There was a small, beautiful park directly across from the house. Families from all over South and Central Americas; a few American born whites, a black family from the Bahamas, an Asian family, 'straights', 'gays', and, interestingly, only a handful of families from Cuba, called it home. It was a unique neighborhood in the City of Miami where most of the population still lived in areas segregated by race, language, or ethnic groupings.

We were not the only blacks, but we were the only African-American family.

My side yard had the sweetest mango tree on the block. Several royal palms towered over the house; and at least three other variety of palms were planted on the property. There was also an old Florida oak, and a variety of other native shrubs.

The house, and the 'live and let live' attitudes of our neighbors, provided me with refuge from the everyday madness surrounding Howard. I could unwind there and breathe easily before jumping, whenever I chose, into the fray with him.

I had grown 'content' with my home and all the challenges which came with repairing, maintaining, and decorating the 1936 classic. My tastes changed every five to seven years, and besides redecorating, there was always so much to do to keep the house from deteriorating. The house, along with every other home in Oak Grove, was custom built and hand-crafted in most instances: every window was double hung, sash style; all the doorways were arched; the closets were few, and tiny; and the wood floors were cut from non-standard size planks. The prize feature: an old world Cuban tile floor in the Florida room! Every change had to be carefully considered in order to preserve the character of the architecture and its special features: the exterior and interior walls were hand- applied stucco, now a lost art. Those were just for starters: the original plumbing and electrical wiring continued to plague us; and, while we never fired up the fireplace, it made a great 'planter'.

Howard called it my house.

He was right.

I had looked in vain for my own place in New Jersey, and while there, I decorated my long-deferred dreams with disposable furniture and temporary fixtures.

It took almost a year after moving to Miami to find and secure this house.

So, yes, it was my house, and there was something sacred in the naming as well as in the claiming of it as mine; it is where I found my authentic self.

Our first child, Kito, was born a few weeks after we moved in and I was forced to make a painful choice: my baby versus my precious pet, Smokey.

"Why are you crying?"

My brain was foggy from Demerol.

"Howard you know I cannot bring the baby home with Smokey in the house."

"Why not?"

Didn't he remember how Smokey lost control of her bowels and left piles of shit throughout the house when I went into labor, then hid, whimpering under our bed?

"Well, because I raised her since she was just six weeks old and she is too close to me. You know shepherds don't like to share their affection, and I can't risk having her around the baby."

"Why can't you just put the dog outside?"

"No, that would be cruel. She has always been an inside dog."

I don't know where he took her. I didn't ask. The tie was cut; once and finally. It was hard, but now I had a greater purpose: to be a mom in my new home.

A new leaf turned over.

The house in Oak Grove was also symbolic of my steadfast, dogged determination to stick it out with Howard, raise healthy and happy children, and to be somebody, at last.

It didn't take long before the neighbors came to benefit from Howard's increasing responsibility with the city. Four years after moving, when he became the City Manager, the surrounding streets had an increased level of police patrol; there was a major improvement to the small, pocket park across the street from my house which included landscaping and a great set of play equipment for children of all ages; and I helped organize, and was active in our neighborhood crime watch. We were good neighbors, and our presence was benign, at first.

❧

"LET'S GET AWAY FOR A WEEKEND". HOWARD HAD BEEN promising we'd take a break once the gruesome budget season ended. It was his tenth year in municipal finance; each succeeding one came with more responsibility, and he had worked himself up to be one of several assistant City Managers.

I was moved by his gesture. I was not blind to our share of ongoing trials, but he was my husband, I had had his baby, and I was still dreaming of building a stronger union. I relaxed into the promise of the weekend.

We drove 80 miles north to Singer Island, Palm Beach County, where he had made reservations at The Hilton, an upscale resort on the Atlantic Ocean.

After checking in, we went to have dinner at the Hotel's ocean-side restaurant. It was a romantic setting. I felt light-hearted; hopeful for a relaxing time.

I remember ordering lobster with drawn butter, steamed vegetables, and I had placed my dessert order in advance; something chocolate, I'm sure. Less than halfway through dinner, Howard left the table.

"Keep eating. I'll return shortly."

He must have eaten something bad. Going to the bathroom.

I wasn't too put off. He had a long-established allergic reaction to certain foods which caused him to either throw up or have to use the toilet. It remained a lifelong affliction for him. A life-ending affliction.

I continued eating. He didn't return.

Alone, (*what's new?*) I completed my meal. When I got to our room, I opened the door and saw Howard pacing the floor. I stood in the threshold and watched him nervously walk from the bed, to the desk, to the window, and back to the bed; repeating the pattern.

Is he crying?

I quickly closed the door behind me.

"What's wrong?"

He immediately broke down in a fit of sobbing.

I've never seen him like this before. Not even when I confessed my affair a few years back when we both cried a lot, out loud.

He continued to blubber.

I was really perplexed about this behavior. I had seen him demonstrate tenderness and kindness, and he was known to display a generous heart and open hand. But just as often, those gestures were often offset by his hard, calculating meanness.

What could the matter be? I thought we were here for a relaxing weekend 'break' on the ocean.

"I'm sorry." "I'm sorry," he kept muttering, over and over.

"Toni, I've got to tell you something."

"Tell me."

"I'm so sorry."

What? Did he find out I knew about the scandal he had left behind in Newark? Is he ready to confess? What could be worse?

I let my imagination run wild. *I was prepared to forgive him anything; drug use; homosexuality; even stealing more money than I already knew about.*

Wait. Is he involved in someone's murder? What could be so awful?

Howard repeatedly worked up his nerve to speak, only to break down, again.

"I'm sorry," "I'm sorry." Then he'd become paralyzed by body-wracking sobs and loud, haunting howls.

I sure hope the hotel security doesn't come knocking on the door.

I checked to make sure I had put on the door lock. I was at a loss about what else to do.

Oh dear God, I can't take much more with this man. How can I comfort him? This is going to be a long night.

"Hush. It's going to be alright. I'm here. Whatever it is, you can tell me. It's ok."

I attempted to hold him, but each time I tried to comfort him, it brought more sobs. By now, I was feeling conflicted. One side of me was in complete sympathy with his pain; I could certainly empathize. On the other hand, I thought he was simply getting what he deserved, from whatever source of pain he was feeling.

"Why don't you call Tom? Maybe he can help you calm down long enough to talk."

Tom Ward had been a great source of comfort to both of us when we lived in New Jersey. We highly regarded his counsel, and I knew Howard trusted him.

"Yeah, you're right. I'll call Tom."

Howard left me alone in the room and took his cell phone. I waited for nearly a half hour before he returned with Tom on hold.

Howard sat down on the bed. He looked up but he could not make eye contact with me.

Here it comes. I held my breath

"BabyIbroughttwootherpeoplewithmefromNewark." His words ran together in one inhalation.

I was standing, looking down at him. He looked smaller than his 6'1", 225 pounds.

"I moved my daughter and her mother to Miami with us."
He exhaled.

His confession was tortured. He curled up on the bed and broke out in another spasm of sobs.

I quickly did the math: *Kito was only eight months old. This had been going on for at least three years!*

Howard confessed his affair began shortly after we arrived in Newark.

More than five years?

The daughter was now two years old.

"Are they still in Miami?"

"No, they left."

"Baby", he assured me, "She can't hold a candle to you".

He calls himself flattering me. For what? My intelligence? My book smarts certainly can't help me with this.

His words had an empty echo.

Finally, he turned the phone speaker back on.

Poor Tom. He has been waiting all this time.

"Tom, I told her," Howard was still sniffling. "I'm ok. Want to talk to Toni?"

I assured Tom I was ok, and then I let him off the hook.

I was exhausted. I was somewhat relieved Howard had not confessed to any murder, or similar transgression. Actually, I felt vindicated.

I silently congratulated myself. *At least you didn't get hysterical. Good.*

But I wanted him to feel really awful; I also needed to be redeemed; to justify my continued devotion to our marriage. A big piece of me had died to the ideal of 'us', but was still alive. I had placed it on a low simmer, moving closer to a back burner. I knew not to let myself get swept up in an imaginary "never again" pledge from either of us.

We were laying across the bed. It was awkward; I was uncomfortable. I had turned my back to him.

"I hope you're paying child support."

"Of course. I send payments every month."

Ordered by the courts, I bet. I didn't ask about the amount. *He can afford to send whatever amount of money is due.*

"Well Howard, children are innocent and should not be punished for what their parents do."

Just knowing of the child's existence is a big enough pill for me to swallow. I don't want to think she was being neglected.

Howard took a deep breath. His confession seemed to lighten him. He undressed and slept soundly. I tossed and turned.

His albatross, tossed off, became anchored in my soul.

The weekend 'retreat' over, we returned to Miami the next morning. On the long drive back, we made a verbal commitment to continue in our marriage, to be better spouses, and to be great parents to Kito. It felt right.

But during the drive, I felt something shift in me, again.

Who else knew?

A tight circle of conspiracy had formed around Howard. I learned, after-the-fact how several of his loyal followers had closed ranks and had drawn a curtain of secrecy; partly in support of him, but equally in protection of me.

"Toni, we really didn't want you to have to worry about that mess," one of his closest staff told me a few weeks later, and at the risk of inviting Howard's wrath.

"We all debated about how and when to tell you. Howard had us make sure the two of you never came into contact with one another. And after they both left Miami, we thought we didn't have to tell you anything."

Oh, that explains why I was always shut out of his office in Newark.

Oh my God. Did Mom know? I could only speculate.

I did some additional calculations: the timing of my first pregnancy; his insistence I abort; the birth of his illegitimate child; and, the malfeasance charges from the City of Newark, had all came into play for him at around the same time.

Bastard! What did he think? Out of my sight, out of his mind?

For the next twenty years, I never spoke to him about his daughter, or her mother. Never.

Four years after the night of his tortured confession, Howard was handed the keys to Miami.

He was 34 years young. I was 32 years old.

*The 305 refers to the telephone area code. It was also the subject of a popular rap.

❧ 13 ❧

THE CITY MANAGER

Miami. The place and its politics had remained an enigma for so long. Mostly identified as a place for sun and surf; a tourist mecca, it was always a cauldron of political intrigue, corruption and questionable characters.

Miami's history and development was held hostage by its geography: it was the 'near south'. But, there was just too much sunshine, too many palm trees and beaches, too many New Yorkers and other northerners in residence, as well as a continuous stream of international tourists, for Miami to be a 'real southern city'. But make no mistake, the Klan rode through the streets in the 1920s.

Howard's appointment came shortly after a four day, nationally televised urban outrage, known as the McDuffie Riot. The 1980 riot was sparked when four white police officers, who had provoked a motorcycle chase causing the death of the rider, Arthur McDuffie, a black man who was innocent of any crime, were acquitted.

The conflagration left many dead: blacks and whites; tens of millions of dollars in property damage was lost.

Miami was still recovering.

Every person in the City was touched in some way. I had many friends, whites and Hispanics, assure me they were not in agreement with the acquittal. They were also eager to let me know they were not racists. My response? I wrote the following:

"Right thinking white folks, don't bend my ear,
with your wasted breath and sympathies.
Talk to you mothers, fathers, daughters and sons;
Your neighbors' the ones you should exhort."

The pressure was keen. The City was rocketed into another dimension after the McDuffie riot. We were all thrust into a cauldron of raised and, often unrealistic expectations, and demands from unelected power brokers and 'thought' leaders.

Everyone was all on high alert to avert another outburst from the black ghetto.

The police riot ripped a rotting seam along the tender racial alliances which were tentatively held in place by a delicate coalition. Everyone knew the business of the City was never confined within the walls of City Hall; the thumbs of the private sector leadership remained firmly placed on the Commission dais.

Before the smoke cleared, the town's power-brokers starting making commitments to 'fix' what was happening over there, in the black community.

This group, collectively known as the 'non-group', was all-male, all white. Their membership list was unpublished; they met in secret.

After the riot, they actually built a 'war room' to plan the head-on attack against whatever was ailing the City and its inhabitants. They made efforts to more evenly distribute the weight of the solutions amongst blacks, whites, and a few 'liberal' Cubans to begin to work on healing the community.

New leaders from the black and Hispanic community emerged.

Shortly after the 1981 riots, South Florida suffered another debacle when Fidel Castro opened his jails and mental institutions to allow the inmates, and anyone who could find a boat, to leave from Mariel, Cuba.

The regatta brought more than one hundred thousand new refugees from the communist stronghold. The US Army Corps erected tent cities throughout the Miami downtown neighborhood: the inner city was littered with folks; mostly young men, living under highway overpasses, on every vacant lot available, and on the infield of the Orange Bowl.

"Mommy don't go this way. That's where the bad people live." Kito was upset. I was taking a short cut home and passed by the tent city. Even at his tender age, he knew something was wrong with so many men walking the streets near our home.

"Don't worry baby. Mommy won't let anyone bother us."

It was an ominous time.

"The commission is going to take another vote tomorrow." It would be the twentieth round to find a new City Manager, and Howard was anxious.

"Howard, you have as good a chance as any other candidate."

Howard was obviously not the most favored candidate. There was a national search underway and several other local applicants were vying for the job: Assistant City Managers, Department Heads, et al. The field was crowded.

There were two other black men up for consideration.

"Well you know you're more qualified than anyone else." I continued to bolster his confidence. His appointment meant more money and prestige for me.

"Yeah, but you never know what those damn Commissioners will do. I think I have support from Ferre, and I know I have J.L.'s support, but I'm not sure about the other three."

Howard rapidly felt on his spread.

Only three votes were needed to pass any item of business from the five member elected officials, which included the Mayor. This Commission form of government was a weak Mayor/strong manager type. It was an arrangement augured for extreme conflict and compromise government.

"Why is it taking them so long to select someone?"

"They're just playing fucking politics." But Howard was thrilled with the intrigue.

It had been weeks since the selection process began. I was feeling anxious too.

"Fr. Gibson wants me to come to his house tonight."

"That's unusual. What does he want?"

"I'm not sure, but I think it's about the voting. He wants you to come over too, to talk with his wife."

Howard had distinguished himself as Management and Budget Director for two years, and then as one of several assistant City Managers, for one year. He was responsible for several vital departments: budget, finance, and communications.

Was it enough?

"How was the meeting with Fr. Gibson?" Uncle Charlie had stopped by for his regular, routine check-in; and, to see what I had to eat.

Howard's Uncle Charlie was the unelected "Sepia Mayor" of Miami. He had held the title and position of favor since the 1950s, when he first helped Claude Pepper get elected to a Florida State office. With Charlie's help, Pepper went on to become a popular and powerful US Senator.

Charlie was the founder, chief organizer, and guru of Operation Big Vote, a voter registration, get-out-the- black vote machine every person running for elected office supported- from US Congressional candidates, to local officials. He was very powerful.

"He told me to be patient. He is supporting me, but he was concerned I might not be ready to take the job. He's worried I may be too young; and, I have such a young family."

Kito was just four.

"Yeah, and I was interviewed by his wife, Thelma. She has known me since I was a little girl, and I told her she doesn't have to worry about our young family. I got that covered."

I was confident in my ability to manage our household and take care of our son.

Round 42.

Commissioner Joe Carollo, never a 'friend' of his, nominated Howard. It was an extraordinary move. No one saw it coming. Howard had gotten the first nomination from Ferre or Plummer on several prior rounds, but he could never muster the additional two needed for a majority.

Until now.

Comm. J.L. Plummer cast the second vote.

The third vote was cast by the Rev. Theodore R. Gibson, a black episcopal priest/politician. Fr. Gibson made sure his prior votes were always cast in an order so as to not tip his hand: he never was the first to nominate Howard. Sometimes during the balloting, Fr. Gibson would vote for another candidate to keep the other four Commissioners thrown off guard about his ultimate plan. He needed the count of two prior votes cast 'for' Howard before his 'third vote' was cast.

This high political drama serial accompanying the selection of a new city Manager, played out daily in all the local newspapers. There was national news coverage too, driven by widespread general interest in Miami since the 1980 riot; the ongoing conflicts in immigration policies; Cocaine Cowboy drug wars in the streets; Miami Vice on television; etc.

Intrigue had filled the air in English and Spanish on local radio talk shows for weeks leading up to the 42nd vote. By this time, Miami was a majority population of Cuban/Hispanics, but whites, commonly referred to as "Anglos" were still in charge of all the major financial, business, and government institutions, with one exception: the school district had a black superintendent.

The declining number of white males held tightly on to

their power which was shrinking by the hour. Anyone chosen to lead the City would have to be able to walk along tumultuous fault lines: the shrinking but still powerful white power base; the Cubans, who were increasing their power base; and the black community, which remained marginalized, but continued to hold the swing vote during elections. (It must be noted the black community was primarily non-Caribbean black, i.e., historically African-American. Haitian immigration was still only a trickle in 1981, and it was not yet popular to self-identify as a Jamaican, or being from any other English speaking island nation. That would come later- much later).

Was Howard's appointment part of the answer to this growing strife?

Nearly ten years after getting his Masters in Public policy, Howard was determined to show the world what he had.

I took a deep breath and prayed.

At last.

Blacks across the entire community erupted in elation at Howard's appointment. But tension over his appointment was palpable with anticipation: would he be able to lead a City with a majority Hispanic electorate; the majority foreign-born?

The elected Commission aside, Howard also inherited an infrastructure of predominantly white, male department directors and managers, and a nearly all white police department.

I gave a congratulations party for him. His brother and sister-in-law came from Virginia. Mom beamed with pride. Kito clung to his daddy throughout the evening. Spirits ran high.

What did anyone really know about this man?

"Are you sure you're ready for this?" I asked him before we went to bed.

"I've never been more ready."

I was ready too, to welcome anything different. Something new. It excited me. But I privately doubted Howard was 'man' enough for the big job. A chasm existed between the man at home, and the man at City Hall. But, by now, I had come to know, and keep my place: I stood beside him in public.

During the early months following Howard's appointment, I remained anxious, and fearful of so many unknowns. My breath came in short, shallow bursts. There was one thing I knew for sure: there was so much more demanded of him than what was printed in the job description.

"Baby, I'll show them." Howard privately swore before me he was prepared for war.

Over the course of the next three and a half years, there were two elections which resulted in a radical change in the profile of the Commission: Gibson, Ferre, and Plummer were cast out for a majority Hispanic electorate.

The result? A battle royal, Miami –style.

The City had always been managed under an American-style of governance. Historically, Cubans were used to a more informal system, something they called 'botela', the way business was done in Cuba, 'before Castro': on a handshake, amongst relatives, school-mates, and/or using some other form of 'favoritism'.

This was a new normal for all the players to adjust. There

was Howard, professionally trained and educated, versus raw political animals.

Howard had to be politically deft. Actually, he had to be more politically adept, at times, than the elected officials. Howard became masterful in this regard. In fact, toward the end of his career with the City, he was charged with being too much of a politician, and in some cases, stronger than the elected officials.

"Did you get your three?'

Sometimes at night, from my private reviewing station lying next to his pillow, I could watch him alternately grow (in stature) or shrink (from defeat).

"I got my three"= victory parade. "I did not get my three"=let the fight begin.

I watched and cheered. As his fortunes rose, so did mine. I enjoyed the political drama, but my role was clearly defined: helpmate. I did not have to get my hands dirty. It was a matter of academic interest to me to know and understand how the political machinations worked.

There was never any predictability.

۞

TWO YEARS BEFORE BECOMING MANAGER, HOWARD HAD begun to practice Tae Kwon Do, a form of Korean martial arts. His training took on a nearly religious zeal after the appointment.

"One, two, three, kick. Four five six, punch."

I coached him at night in our bedroom, counting out the

movements for each form until he mastered them all. I also made sure he always had a clean supply of gees (uniforms).

During the early months following his appointment, our days were filled with equal amounts of promises and pitfalls, teased out from the precariousness of pecuniary City politics.

It didn't take long for us to settle into a daily routine: showing up for our respective jobs; attending the obligatory social engagements; getting Kito to and from school and after school activities; etc. I privately struggled to make our lives appear normal. Most of my time and energy was devoted to designing and executing a balanced life for our son. I assembled my 'village'; the extended family was on call, especially my dad.

One year later, after Issa was born, having a full-time housekeeper, Mrs. Ross, was an essential ingredient to any success I had.

But despite all my efforts, I never felt in balance. I teetered on the high wire in Howard's three ring circus. I never fell off, at least not in public, but whenever I dared to look over, I would lose my breath again and again when I couldn't see the bottom. My breathlessness turned into blindness as I settled into the title of Howard's wife. I pulled a mantel over my fears, doubt, and plain frustration at seeking a normal, normal. Having our Miami-based family around helped, a lot.

Right from the beginning, it was clear to both of us - Howard's appointment was another one of the measures to be used to assess how the community's healing was taking place. At first, I was fearful of how his growing role as the appointed leader of the City would affect me, us. Yet, it didn't take long before I, too, became enmeshed with the strange balance of power, and the power brokers myself.

Power serves up three fingers of intoxicating elixir.

Did Howard have a clue of what was expected of him?

"Toni, those crackers expect me to fix their fucked up mess."

"Well you have all the resources of the City behind you. And now we have the federal government camped out here, too."

"Yeah, but I don't know if they're really ready to let go some of their fucking power." In the beginning, he shared his daily experiences with me.

"I have a meeting with the Miami Herald editorial board and Alvah Chapman," Howard told me, excited to go to the mountaintop. Alvah Chapman, publisher of The Herald, was also the recognized leader of the non-group. He was the man.

"This is a great opportunity for you to get him and the non-group to know what the real problems are, and how the black community feels."

"But I wouldn't trust them as far as I can throw them."

A lot was riding on Howard's shoulders. His appointment would become heavily symbolic of what was either the matter with Miami (bad performance reviews,) or what was the hope for Miami's future (good performance reviews.).

Shortly before he became City Manager, and by some small savings grace, I had started to come out from behind Howard's shadow. Initially, I took baby steps; I was still picking at left over scabs I had accumulated while in Newark, and I still felt raw, sore, and vulnerable. So many of my wounds were self-inflicted; others derived from the times when I did not get out of Howard's way. No, he never had to physically strike for me to suffer grave injury. I supposed I could have gotten away. It was complicated.

What's next, dear God? What about me?

As the City's highest ranking appointed public figure, many sets of eyes were cast on Howard. He was scrutinized: his public, and soon, his private gestures. And a certain set of eyes were also turned on me. I entered into the limelight, and I started to love saying, "This is Mrs. Gary calling."

As the city Manager's wife, my status automatically elevated, and I was granted a level of authority I had, up to then, only partially earned.

In late 1983, I took a leave of absence from my job as community planner with Miami Dade County and assumed the leadership role at Greater Miami United (GMU). GMU had been organized after the McDuffie Riot, by the same members of the 'non-group' which controlled City Hall.

GMU was still forming when I took over. I immediately had to address the organization's mission, board development, fund-raising strategy, and program development. The GMU mandate was to design a set of responses to the pressing issues of racial/ethnic, economic disparity, and language differences throughout the County. These had been identified as some of the underlying causes of the two preceding riots; not excluding the police actions.

So, on that fateful pre-dawn January 27, 1984, while Howard was firing the police chief from my dining room, I was resting from one of my typical days as the executive director of GMU.

I had been on the job for almost a year. I had gained access, with a certain amount of ease and finesse, to those in a position to say 'yes' to my requests for funds and other resources in support of GMU's mission. Doors opened when "Mrs. Gary" called. I leveraged my advantage, and I enjoyed the mounting benefits from sleeping with the boss.

❧ 14 ❧

FULL MOON OVER THE
MAGIC CITY

1982-1984

"How are things going?" Howard was calling me from out of town.

I was sitting on our back porch where I could see a thin plume of smoke rising over a section of the inner city, already in flames.

"Things are good at home. Kito is fine. But you better come home because you have a riot in Overtown." The reporter quoted me when he asked me about Howard's reaction to the news of the Nevell Johnson shooting.

It was early into his tenure as City Manager when Howard gained national notoriety. He was given credit for quelling the outrage during the 1982 urban riot, when people rampaged in the streets of Overtown. It was in the historic black community where Nevell Johnson, a young black man, was killed during, yet, another police misconduct. The incident took place on the eve of the annual Orange Bowl Festival.

Miami was still reeling from the effects of the 1980 four day urban cataclysm. Suddenly, there was so much riding on the young City Manager to keep Miami's volcanic fires from erupting, again.

Howard's 'heroism' thrust him into a long, painful, but successful initiative to overhaul the Miami Police Department.

"Can you believe all the press attention we're getting?" Howard was exhausted, but stimulated at the end of every evening during a tense two week period.

"I let Kito watch you on the early news tonight. He couldn't believe his daddy was on T.V."

"How did I do?"

"You did great." And he did.

He was a hero: he saved the City's face before a national television audience; the Orange Bowl public relations machine, which included all of the community's leadership, was grateful; potential loss of life was averted; and hundreds of millions in projected property damages was prevented.

On the night of the shooting, Howard went to the hospital to comfort Nevell's family.

"I've never seen anything like that before," he sobbed to me. He was shaken to his core. Nevell's brain had exploded.

"It made me sick to look at him." The magnitude of Nevell's head wound haunted him for months.

"He didn't look human. The gunshot took off his face." Howard was further outraged when he learned the 'boy' had done nothing wrong.

"He was just a 'nigger' minding his own business."

The incident pushed many of Howard's old buttons which

had remained in check for years beyond his own youthful experiences with white police officers. I knew they were still seething below the surface. He had successfully covered them up with the thin veneer of his suit and tie, and his title and position of authority.

"It's so damn easy for one trigger-happy racist cop to fuck things up, Howard ranted.

"Was the cop white or Cuban?"

"What the fuck does it matter? Probably some cracker. They're all the same."

The officer was Cuban.

"Shit, they better watch out. I got something for them."

"I hope you don't do anything stupid." I was worried he had gone dark. I knew his natural instinct was to pick up his own gun(s) and join in the street fight.

"Don't worry, I got something they never saw coming. I got something for them."

Yes, what you have are many more bullets and guns at your disposal than are stored in your small personal cache. You have control over and demand of all the ammunition at the Miami City Police Department. You have the power and authority to reshape the police force to reflect your own philosophy of community policing to respond more judiciously to the people.

I hoped he could see it clearly as I could.

Time will tell.

"MOTHER FUCKERS. THE POLICE ARE A FUCKING PROBLEM."

Nevell Johnson's murder ushered in a new era for the City of Miami Police. Hallmarked by the peculiar relationship between City Manager Howard Gary, young black man, City Commissioner J.L. Plummer, an avowed 'Florida Cracker', and Chief Kenneth J. Harms, a highly respected and nationally recognized veteran Police Chief; it was also the harbinger for the demise of all three.

"Howard, what do you guys talk about when you're on those road trips?'

"Toni, that's the only time we can get away from City Hall and all the prying eyes and ears to strategize about how to change the culture of the police. Especially the motors."

I resented the time Howard was spending with J.L. and Kenneth Harms, but I could appreciate how much strategy was needed.

But why always on a weekend trip?

The entrenched police culture they were so concerned about was dominated by the 'motors': a tight, small bunch of good old boys who were hell bent on keeping their power contained within their small 'club' of a whites-only motorcycle police squad. They were renowned for altering their short sleeve shirts to fit tightly around their bi-ceps. Their bulging arms made them look more intimidating riding on their polished motors; in their shiny boots; wearing dark aviators, and gunning large Harley engines.

They always rode in groups of two or more. Intimidation as policing policy.

There was a consent decree already in place which required more affirmative action hiring practices and allowed for tougher negotiations with the Police Union. J.L. was committed to securing political support for Howard's proposed new measures.

J.L. was a popular politician.

He was effective; there was no doubt.

"Howard, you ready?" J.L. yelled from the front yard. I could hear his motor coming from blocks away.

Though his family was originally from Key West, The Conch Republic, J.L. Plummer considered himself to be a 'Southerner'. He had cultivated and practiced sounding like someone who were born in a rural area of the country. He had perfected a just right 'twang' belying his roots. He called Miami, 'Miamuh'. It was always funny to me, and his unique accent brought a smile to everyone.

"Yeah. Where's Harms?" Howard was eager to get going.

It was a beautiful south Florida Saturday morning; usually our family time. Howard bounded down the stairs to join J.L.

The boys and I looked on; Kito wanted to ride with his daddy. I wanted him home.

"We're meeting him on the road. He got an early start."

Howard was dripping in Harley-Davidson regalia.

"Toni, I'll be back on Sunday evening."

"Don't they make clothes for Honda riders?" I resisted laughing out loud.

He brushed it off and spun off with J.L.

J.L. had a boyish quality to him. He appeared to have fun playing politics. He was good at the game, until the majority Hispanic voters issued him off the Commission. He was instrumental in getting Howard hired; he wasn't around to save him from being fired.

But he was in office long enough to help Howard change police policies and practices.

※

HIS PHOTO APPEARED ON THE FRONT PAGE OF THE MIAMI Herald. He had gone straight from his office, and, still in his shirt and tie (he had removed his shoes and coat), he proceeded to break several stacks of boards with his elbow, hands, and feet.

His mouth was twisted opened in a shout deep from his gut to gain maximum strength. Repeatedly yelling so loud it would raise the hair on my arm, Howard showed he was a ferocious, big, black man, who could kick your butt and anyone else's.

Bow.

"Thank you."

Bow.

Any questions?

I got a little tingle, in amusement, when I saw the photo. I still admired his chutzpah.

※

I KNEW, FIRST-HAND, THE AMOUNT OF DISCIPLINE, AND THE number of hours he dedicated to practice, and what it took for Howard to accomplish this high degree of skill. He had earned multiple degrees of black belts in Korean Ta Kwon Do. He had practiced with two other Masters before he found Master Choi, a ninth degree black belt who was revered for his teaching skills. Under Master Choi, Howard undertook a near religious devotion to this particular martial art. He worked tirelessly to hone his skills. He received his first degree black belt in less than two years, with more degrees to follow soon after.

I helped him.

I was tasked (actually it was Mrs. Ross's job) to have a clean supply of ghee's ready at all times.

We enrolled the boys to study under Master Choi.

I began to yearn for a little of that kind of power.

"Mrs. Choi practices, too." Master Choi winked at me one day when I inquired about studying with him.

I saw how Master Choi's two daughters practiced. There were several other females, of all ages, in the school. And so I began.

"My hair never sweated this much from the gym!' I lobbied a soft complaint. But I kept going. Twice a week. Practice at home. Coaching the boys.

I never thought I'd get used to the sheer exhaustion at the end of each session, but the recovery period was quick, and the results were fabulous: I was lean, with rock- hard muscles, and a sharpened awareness of everything around me.

My course of study lasted a little under one year when I developed a set of skills to defend myself; I earned a blue belt. And, I could break a board or two, myself.

But, by far, the greatest benefit was I strengthened my mental fortitude.

Eventually, Kito earned a brown belt, and Issa got his Orange belt, but then their interests turned to other sports.

For a brief period of time, we were a kick-ass family of brick and board-beakers.

We added Master Choi, his wife, and their three children to our extended family.

At one particular dinner party in their home, we sat down to enjoy an appetizer of snapper sushi, freshly caught that morning by one of Choi's neighbors. Mrs. Choi had prepared a typical Korean dinner to follow. I had not had eaten raw fish before. I decided to repeat every move Master Choi made. Following his lead, I scooped a wad of wasabi into my mouth before taking a slice of the fish. Within seconds, I felt the top of my head 'explode' and my heart race outside my chest. I thought I was going to die.

"I wondered why you would do that," Howard said as I gasped, choking.

I almost fell out of my seat.

"I was trying to be a good guest and do what our host did." I sputtered, several glasses of water later. We all laughed once I appeared to return to normal.

"You are supposed to mix the wasabi with soy sauce. You can't eat it like Master Choi."

When did Howard learn so much about eating sushi? He and I had never had sushi together. Oh yes. I almost forgot about the time he was running with Ray.

Unfortunately, I could not enjoy my beautifully prepared authentic Korean food. My tongue, throat, and stomach burned for two days. But I have come to love eating raw fish now since I know how to mix the condiments.

One day while sparing and practicing his forms, Howard suffered a leg injury. It was not broken, but the sprain was severe enough to require hospitalization. Much to my regret, he gave up his devotion to the martial art. I wished he had returned. The discipline of the practice had such a tranquilizing effect on him; it helped smooth his unravelling edges.

His ensuing choices and substitutions were never as wholesome.

The daily tensions mounted, with seemingly no outlet. I stayed out of his way.

⚘

EVEN BEFORE HE WAS APPOINTED AS MANAGER, I STARTED getting invitations to join various groups of 'ladies who lunch'. I liked the attention. I changed my image. I shopped a lot but I was still buying at discount prices; constantly looking for that $2.00 dress.

Oftentimes, total strangers felt free to give me advice about how I should look and behave, in public. My hair and wardrobe became the object of their concern since I had, by extension, become a public entity.

"You need a stylist. The City will pay for it." Someone offered.

I refused. *I don't need or warrant so much attention, or notoriety.*

A few women approached me with their advice.

"There are women who want to be with your man because of his position", a well-respected professional woman, told me one day over lunch.

"You need to be aware of it," she said, "and, I also want you to know, I'm not one of them."

This was a new phenomenon for me: power as an aphrodisiac. I was not unaware of the equation; I had seen it portrayed in the movies, and I read many books where it worked both ways; between men and women. But I had not computed how it fit in my life. Yet.

I had simply not appreciated Howard as such a powerfully attractive figure. He was a lot of things to me: my husband; my babies' daddy; and, my tormentor- for years.

When I was just a young girl, my mom used to tell me about women who just want to see if they can sleep with another woman's husband.

Could that be what's keeping me? Is there really so much attraction from power?

Here was another factor I had to figure how to incorporate into my relationship; it was overwhelming.

Then Jackie Bell, another friend, told me more about the flip side to the power/attraction phenomenon.

Jackie Bell is best known for her very vocal and aggressive advocacy of civil rights for blacks. She was fond of reminding me I would not always be so young and pretty, and how I should capitalize on my current standing. Jackie encouraged me to dress up, wear more makeup, and to keep my hair styled. She also told me to be prepared for predators.

"Women who are attached to important men attract other men," she told me one day.

"Some men are attracted to these women as a means of getting to, i.e., fucking over, their powerful husbands."

Jackie would know. She prided herself on being involved only with powerful men, from the halls of Congress to the corporate board rooms of Miami. Jackie bragged about her conquests.

The revelation sent chills up my spine, and I would never forget her words of wisdom.

In the meantime, I must have done alright with my new image, by my own hand, because I soon gained a reputation for putting together a great 'look'. I strived to always be appropriate, sometimes a little edgy, but tasteful. I maintained myself in the same dress size for years. Exercise was a calendared event for me; three times a week.

I was often at a loss with some of the attention I got. Was it because I was attractive, and/or because I was attached to Howard, like Jackie told me? Sometimes, I knew.

⚯

PROFILES OF ME AND HOWARD WERE PUBLISHED DURING HIS early tenure as Manager. The public relations stories were heartwarming and uplifting. Most drew a sketch of the hometown boy who grew up on the 'wrong' side of the tracks, got an education, went away to hone his professional skills, and returned home with his wife and family to better his community.

I was usually profiled as the supportive wife; loving, and behind the scenes.

But the stories usually missed the context and texture of Howard's early beginnings; the stuff at his core which gave him the cojones *grande* (the large balls) to fire the police chief at 2:47 AM.

Those would be published after he grew the really big ones; after he fired Harms.

Actually, after the Harms' firing, there were so many articles, profiles, reviews, and editorials on Howard, and at one point, someone asked, "Do you and Howard own stock in the Miami Herald?"

In the meantime, I continued to build my professional skills. I started out working for Miami-Dade County as a community organizer and planner. I apprenticed in the infamous Liberty City/Model City and learned from some of the best grass- roots advocates known at the time: Bernie Dyer and Annie Love, both widely respected and hailed for their acumen and knowledge of the needs of the black community.

"Just follow my lead," Bernie told me one night at a particularly difficult community meeting.

"Forget about who your husband is. He can't help you out here." I had grown frustrated because I wasn't getting folks to listen to my presentation about how the grant funds I was administering were going to 'help' them. There was a lingering air of protest, and the louder voices were prevailing.

"You just need to toughen up and learn to stand on your own two feet," Annie Love told me. She was a large woman, who was legendary for her strong demands for services to the area, and she took me under her wing. She was recognized years later with a large community service center named for her.

In my job, I was constantly out and about representing the department at various organizations, e.g., The Greater Miami Chamber of Commerce, Small Business Administration, etc. I was establishing my profile as a professional, with some degree of importance and weight.

It was all relative; I was behaving as if.

Not only was I enjoying my job, I felt like I was making a difference.

I was pregnant again; this one I'd keep.

❦

LONG BEFORE HOWARD STARTED TO RIDE HIS MOTORCYCLE on weekends, we would, as a family, visit with relatives, usually his, where he parked me and the boys for hours.

He had become less and less present in my house, and we usually only appeared out together in public at official functions. We co-parented our sons with little effort, but it was becoming more evident I was merely only his legitimate wife.

"I'll be back soon," he'd announce after only a short stay at some aunts' or cousins' house.

He would return several hours later. No questions asked.

This was our pattern for years; before he began his weekend rides.

"Why does Howard always leave you here?" My Aunt Doris was a meddler. "I'd be the one leaving him," she harrumphed in total disgust at what I tolerated.

I could never satisfy her, no matter what I said, and I would have stopped hanging out there on weekends, except the boys loved going in her pool, and she and uncle Ozzie loved having them around.

"Howard, have you played this one?" Uncle Ozzie knew a wide variety of billiards games and he managed to lure him into playing a few games before Howard announced he had to go somewhere.

"I'll be back later, Ozzie. Then we can play some more Keely."

I let Howard get away with his growing neglect, partly because his family kept me entertained, especially his cousin Laurestine and her husband Walter. Plus, I knew I wasn't going anywhere, and I had convinced myself, neither was he. So, it was easier to just go along with the charade.

After a few years of this pattern, I began to balk at our practice of going in just one car to visit relatives on the weekends.

"I'll meet you there." I was lucky to have several built-in babysitters on both sides of our family, so it was easy when I finally decided to take off by myself and leave the boys with one of them. I tried not to abuse the privilege.

I added Akua to my roster of weekend outlets.

Howard grew to rely on her, too. It was not spoken about so such, but he knew she kept me company while he was away, or otherwise engaged. Once, Howard implored Akua to accompany me to the long-anticipated Prince concert. He had two tickets, prime seating in the Orange Bowl, for the Purple Rain tour; privilege of the office. I had a purple outfit, which I dressed in from head to toe: a jumpsuit, scarf, shoes, and socks. Howard was still at the house when Akua arrived.

"I see why Howard doesn't not want to go to the concert with you." she screamed in shock at my costume.

"What's wrong?" *I felt fabulous.*

"I don't know if I want to be seen with you either."

I tied my purple scarf around my neck- sailor style and pranced out the door. The two of them were getting a big laugh at my fanatical devotion to the purple one.

Whatever.

Akua and I had a great time. Prince was fantastic, and I didn't miss Howard not being there.

I came to rely on Akua to help me through many weekends when Howard left me, alone; she was always available, except during the football season, when her team, the Washington Redskins were playing.

Life's pattern of high-highs and low-lows continued; it was still manageable. Except my mind began to betray me.

I've got to get out of here. But how can I leave the boys' daddy?

✠

"Look what I got." Late one night, Howard came home and joined me upstairs in our bedroom. He proceeded to unceremoniously dump money out of a rumpled paper bag on top of our bed. The bag was small.

He had only been manager for a few months. He was shaking.

We counted out $7,000 in very used bills.

"You can't keep this," I said.

"Shit, I know," his voice was just above a whisper, as if someone else was in our bedroom, listening.

"Where did it come from?"

"I found it just sitting in the middle of my fucking chair. Must be the Cubans"

"That's crazy. Was there a note or anything?"

"No, just the bag," he slumped at the realization of what this might mean.

"Whoever left the money wants something from you. They probably figure if you keep it, there'd be more to come."

I know what happened in Newark, but this was too close to criminal bribery. You're not going for it, I hope. Not for $7,000!

"Baby, don't worry, I am not going to jail for some god damn measly $7,000!"

What is your price? How much did you get in Newark? Is there an acceptable amount you'd consider risking jail time for?

I sighed in relief at his declaration. But the Newark thing nagged around the edges of my memory.

"You have to return it in the same bag tomorrow."

"But I don't know who left it. There were so many people in my office this afternoon."

I was excited to share this moment with him. We were making decisions. We.

There are so many possibilities.....

"I know." I was eager to help him figure this out. It was a unique challenge, and I was leaning into my role as Howard's helpmate.

"I know. Why don't you have Lilly block out a period of

time for you to be away from your office tomorrow. Have her call everyone who visited you yesterday to come back, one by one, and have her tell each one she thinks they may have left something by mistake."

"You think it'll work?"

"You got a better idea?"

"But what if someone takes the bag back and more people still have to come in."

"No problem. The only person who knows about the bag is the one who left it. Just tell Lilly not to go into the office until after everyone who was there today has a chance to go in and out."

He tried it. It worked!

As far as I know, this was the first and last time money was presented in a brown paper bag. Other offers, much higher amounts, became part of doing business with the City.

Did he take any?

He never told me if he did.

It bothered me: Howard thought it was a Cuban who had left the money.

The Cubans.

In Miami, everyone was learning how to live with the Cubans- they were the majority.

Howard and I had both immersed ourselves in the Cuban culture when we first returned. First, there was the Corona family, and then there was Jack Alfonso, a Cuban's Cuban. Jack Alfonso, we always called him by both his names, owned an investigation agency. He was also actively involved in Cuban politics. He gave Howard a passport into the political minefield of the Cuban exile community.

Jack carried a gun on his hip- at all times. It was the first thing I noticed about him. His gun was as big as he was round. Jack, and his wife, Margaret loved to cook and eat, and they loved to entertain.

"I have eaten a lot of pig in my life, but this is the best I've ever had," my daddy told Jack at one of their annual Christmas Eve traditions: Noche Buenas.

Jack offered my dad a choice piece from the back of the pig while it was still roasting in the ground. It was my dad's first taste of whole Cuban-style roasted pig which had been marinated in the ubiquitous mojo sauce; heavy with garlic.

In just a short period of time, my entire family would grow to love the typical Cuban-styled roasted pork, and we would look forward to the holiday season for the traditional Noche Buena, the night before Christmas.

It didn't take long, either, before we cultivated our taste for Café Cubano. Two o'clock in Miami signaled the universal time for everything to stop, take a shot of the thick, syrupy sweet coffee, in lieu of the old world siesta. Instead of a nap, the café helped people continue, in the American ways of doing business.

We happily adopted this new way of living in Miami, an American City, but in more ways than not, a Cuban city.

And so our routine now included having a daily dose of café Cubano, lots of pork and flan or Diplomatic pudding.

ANOTHER ONE OF OUR ROUTINES INCLUDED A NEAR-NIGHTLY phone call from Ricky Thomas, community activist, radio talk show host, and City of Miami liaison to the black community.

Ricky's calls served as a direct pipeline from the little man to Howard. The black man's plight was filled with frustration, but Ricky' reporting was filled with mirth; gossip mostly.

His nightly news helped leverage some of the burden Howard brought home from the office, so I laughed along, discerning what I could from listening to Howard's responses to Ricky, and his laughter.

Howard's laughter was infectious. It carried me through my tears.

And so it seemed Howard and me, the helpmate, were all set to take the City to another level. Howard had his trusted staff from Newark; he had picked up a few other loyal supporters along the way represented by Kennedy, Jack Alfonso, Rickey; others; and he had gotten a tenuous grasp on how to get his three votes from the five seated commissioners. He was slugging his way into local history.

And I was his partner. It felt ok.

Lillie helped me manage my life with Howard: she kept his calendar up-to-date on his family obligations, and he never missed a milestone: birthdays, anniversaries, etc. There was always a gift or flowers delivered, on time.

I could get used to this. Maybe things aren't so bad, after all.

There were additional perks derived from being married to the City Manager.

When I was about five months pregnant with Issa, we paid my way to travel with Howard and a group of representatives from the City of Miami, to visit one of our sister cities: Mexico City. The entourage included Mayor Maurice Ferre, his wife Mercedes; Jeb Bush, then a private businessman, his wife Columba; David and Dorothy Weaver, developers; and, maybe a half dozen others. Everything was first class and the hospitality was unparalleled.

"Buenas dias, Doctor Gary."

As it turned out, in Mexico City every professional is given an honorific title.

There was much pomp and we were treated like royalty-American royalty.

"Howard, the police chief has his own race track at his house," I remarked on our tour of the Police Chief's estate.

"Yeah, I hope Harms doesn't hear about that." We laughed.

Harms had already begun to flex his muscles with the City Manager.

I experienced altitude sickness and could not enjoy all the planned events (night clubbing was definitely out of the question), but the balance of the itinerary was superb.

The Mexico City trip remains symbolic of the peak experiences I had while Howard was City Manager.

In 1983, Howard's reach and impact was being felt, nationally. He and six other municipal managers from around the country lead a successful effort to establish a new professional organization: National Forum for Black Public Administrators. It is still active.

"Aren't you proud of Howard?" Several of his fellow graduate students from Michigan attended the kick-off in Ft

Lauderdale, Florida. Several of them held positions as Manager or Assistant City Manager of small municipalities.

"Yes. I'm proud of him, and all of you."

The Ann Arbor group held their own small reunion. I was happy to see them and to reminisce about those graduate student days, and to speculate about the whereabouts of the few who did not 'make it'.

"Whatever happened to so-and- so? You know the white woman in y'all's study group?"

No one could tell me.

Maybe, no one would tell me.

15

I'M A MOTHER...ADDITIONAL REFLECTIONS

1976-1983

Once Kito was born, I put it out of mind that Howard had once urged me to abort him. I stuffed it down to where I had buried all the other slings and slights; where I kept the other sludge of my life.

Kito was simply precious from the moment he arrived. We found a name which literally translated into the same meaning. It's a word from the Swahili language I had found in one of the baby name books we'd bought. Kito: Precious jewel. Perfect.

Kito would be Howard's mother's first grandchild. At least, I thought so at the time. She acted beyond excited. My mother already had two other grandchildren- from my brother Gerald. I am my mother's only daughter, so my child was especially anticipated by her, and her sisters. They said they knew Kito would be part of their family: "Momma's baby, daddy's maybe" was the rule they lived by.

The pregnancy was text book perfect, and I wish I could say Kito's was an easy delivery. But it was not so.

I had asked my mother to be my coach. She was an experienced nurse.

"Toni, I'm honored, but you don't want Howard in there with you?"

"He says he wouldn't be able to handle it."

I had prepared for a 'natural' birth and Howard didn't think he could withstand the rigors of watching me give birth.

He voted correctly. Kito struggled to be born.

"Push."

"I'm pushing"

I pushed for a long time, but no baby.

While I was thankful for my mom's experience as an obstetrical nurse, I wanted her in the delivery room to help me breathe, and to take photos with the small, automatic camera I had given her.

"Mom, take the pictures," I urged her in between pushes.

"Damn those pictures," mom dropped the camera on a side table. "I got to watch this doctor."

Why does she have to watch the doctor? She needs to take pictures.

Gerald Relkin, MD, was chosen because of his sterling reputation. Mom had gotten to know him well, too. During one of our last office visits, the doctor and my mom conspired to calm me down when I learned he was planning a trip on my due date.

"Don't worry," he said, "I'm sure your mother will agree with me the baby will probably not be born until the full moon."

"You're right Dr.," my mother agreed. "That has been my experience. Baby's usually come during the full moon." I thought they had both lost their minds. The full moon was another ten days away. I knew from the exchange my mother liked and trusted him.

It seemed like it was taking forever. I had already been laboring for six hours. Now, here I was with my legs open up on the delivery table; I couldn't see or feel anything by this time since I had been numbed against any sensation, except pressure.

"Stop pushing."

Great, the baby must be here.

I was oblivious to the drama playing out down below. All I could see was mom looking at the doctor, not at me. I was annoyed with her. I had pushed and pushed. No baby. No pictures.

Finally, I heard the doctor talking to the nurses about cleaning the baby up and taking care of me.

Mom disappeared from the delivery room.

"Oh my God, oh my God," my friend Fay Williams reported how my mother broke through the doors, sobbing, and declaring thanks to God, and was near collapse.

"I thought you or the baby had died when I saw your mother crying." Howard had been waiting with Fay outside the delivery room. While waiting, he had tried to pay bills. Later, I found many 'voided' checks he had written during the hour.

Several minutes passed before he got word all was well. He had his son. I was ok, too.

He entered my recovery room dressed for work; suited and tied up in his role as Director, Management and Budget, City of Miami.

Days later, my mother told me in detail what had happened during the delivery

When I found out about her ordeal, I felt badly about how I pressured her to take pictures.

"Antonia, I'm so sorry. I tried so hard to take pictures, but when I realized how much distress the baby was experiencing, I couldn't think of anything else. I had to watch that doctor."

"I was paralyzed. I couldn't do anything but watch his hands."

"Mom, I couldn't feel a thing. All I know is you just abandoned me and the pictures. And y'all weren't saying anything to let me know anything was wrong."

"Toni, you were killing the baby with his own cord. Every time you pushed, the cord tightened more around the baby's head and neck."

She must have really suffered, standing by and keeping silent.

"The doctor gave you the biggest episiotomy I've ever seen. He had to go up inside and unwrap the cord. You're lucky. Your doctor has good hands."

Thank God for Dr. Gerald Relkin. He was recognized at the time as one of the best in the business, and he brought many years of experience to the emergency procedure.

Any photos of Kito's birth would not have been very pretty.

His was a face only a mother could love.

My precious baby boy had black bruises all over his face, head, and upper torso, but he was breathing and he scored high on all his newborn tests. He was beautiful to me. The bruises faded after a few weeks.

I had specified I wanted a 'natural' birth, but I was given Demerol for anxiety during my six hour labor. I didn't like how woozy it made me feel. On hindsight, I think my mother and Dr. Relkin might have needed to be drugged more than me.

I took a shower the day after Kito was born. When my aunts and grandmother heard what I had done, they pounced. Their wrath felt like all the gods from above, along with the demons from below.

"Don't you know you're not supposed to expose yourself to water so soon after having a baby? Aunt Lorrain had never had a baby, but she was all knowing.

I'm glad for them I did not also wash my hair. I wore it long and red. I'd thought about it, but I didn't bring my rollers or my hairdryer to the hospital. I think if I had, I would have been responsible for a few heart attacks and/or near death of my relatives; Aunt Lorraine and my grandmother for sure. To say they were 'old school' would be a gross understatement.

Yet, I took Kito into their loving arms when he was five weeks old. I had a job to return to, and an on-going point to be make: *qualified black woman gets hired at seven months pregnant; returns to work five weeks after delivery; excels on the job in every other respect.*

Except, I didn't feel good about going back to work so soon after delivery.

朶

I MISSED KITO TERRIBLY EVERY DAY. OUR BONDING TIME WAS so abbreviated. I felt secure knowing he was being cared for by aunt in her home. My grandmother rocked him on her bosom throughout the day. I did not want to nurse this baby. I was busy being important, and Howard was also not in favor of me nursing. We were both ignorant about the benefits of nursing, which was out of fashion then. But I heard plenty from various relatives about how I had deprived 'this' baby by not nursing him.

But something inside me felt empty. I tried to make up for not nursing in many other ways.

"How is your experimental child?" Howard would sarcastically ask.

I must admit raising children was not something I had given much thought to before, so I never had any qualms about taking 'outside' advice, or giving up what a lot of people thought was my authority over my children. I relished in having so many mature relatives around who had successfully raised their own families.

"I'll never let anyone tell me how to raise my child" was a common refrain I heard repeated by many of my peers. Not in my case. I welcomed sound and tested guidance. I had read many recommended books on child raising, yet, I constantly sought advice from all the experts I could identify.

During much of Kito's infancy, one of my most trusted sources was Muriel Solomon, who was part of my special work unit. She was the County's resident expert on early childhood, and was responsible for drafting the policy for licensing child care centers.

"I don't know why you take so much advice from some old white woman," Howard castigated me.

"White or not, she's getting paid big bucks for her knowledge, and I have access to her for free."

My dad was another reliable source for me. His philosophy for child rearing was simple: if crying, change the diaper, feed, burp, and then put the baby down to sleep. He was given the opportunity to demonstrate how it worked on many occasions with Kito and, five years later, after Issa came.

Howard reacted to any little distress or discomfort he perceived Kito felt. He would often cry, himself, if he thought Kito was hurt, or in any pain. At times, he demonstrated the most tender touch. For instance, he extracted splinters from Kito's fingers as if he was performing brain surgery.

Once, Kito lost his balance while scooting on a small bike in the house. He was taking a turn, keeled over, fell, and split his lip. He was just over one year. There was very little blood.

At the time, several of our combined relatives were visiting us, including Howard's mother.

Howard came home shortly after the incident, saw Kito's bloody lip and screamed at me: "Where were you?"

Howard grabbed up the baby before I could answer.

"Oh, Kito. Oh, Kito. Oh, Kito," He started pacing in circles. He was squeezing him tightly and moaning over the minor injury.

Kito looked frightened. He began to cry. He squirmed, trying to get down from his father's arms.

"Howard, he's ok." "The baby is ok." "You're holding him too tight." A chorus of various relatives' voices rang out, trailing behind Howard's steps.

Howard could not be easily consoled.

"Where were y'all?" He gestured to the room. Kito, clearly in distress, cried louder.

"I was right there looking at him," I was totally put off-guard by Howard's overreaction.

"We were all looking at him," someone from the visiting family group offered.

"It happened so fast," I continued, "I could not catch him."

"Next time," Howard screamed at us all as he stormed upstairs, "don't let him fall at all."

Everyone clucked on about his bizarre reaction. I took notes and filed this incident away for future reference.

Have I short-changed him? I thought he would be an inadequate parent. I never imagined he'd be overprotective. I need to rethink a few things.

Kito may have been raised by committee, but Howard and I kept our veto power.

Kito remained our only child for almost five years. He was cherished. He thrived, and he was fulfilling all my maternal needs. So much so, my joy from having him made me want to have another child. I liked being pregnant, and my recessed memory of delivering Kito had become more pleasant. I was ready to try it again.

I brilliantly thought having a second child would cement me and Howard even further into the death do us part status, I began to plot and plan for the eventuality. But I was proven wrong in my thinking, again.

I easily got pregnant again when Kito was around three. But the timing was awful. My marriage was on firmer grounds, we had made renewed commitments to one another and the baby- but Howard's career trajectory was really taking off, and he was not around much. I was awash in conflicted feelings. The worm was turning, but I could only put my finger on any single source of my discomfort: his job. I quickly realized another baby did not fit in, and this time I did not hesitate to have the pregnancy terminated. I concentrated on Kito, my career, and my mental health.

Things continued to change with us. It was gradual and subtle. On the surface, an outsider looking in would be hard pressed not to say, "What a great family" or, "They certainly make a beautiful couple," or some such uttering.

It may have been my hormones, PMS, or some other chemical imbalance taking place in me, but I began, again, to suffer from signs of stress. This time it took the form of a severe acne breakout on my back, chest, and neck. I began paying closer attention: Howard's old pattern of prolonged absences returned. As before, it was not always his job keeping him away. I didn't want to hear any lies, so I asked no questions. The mortgage was being paid. I had titles. I had credit cards. I had all the food I could eat. I had Kito. But he was no longer an infant and required less of my time. I grew restless.

It was a perfect storm brewing for the death of intimacy. Howard's level of responsibility at City Hall was increasing; the baby was becoming more independent; I was building my own career; numerous distractions were coming in from outside sources; I began to falter once more in my increasing self-confidence. I needed a bolster.

In the meantime, only the best would do for my first born.

❧

THE CARE AND FEEDING OF KITO BECAME A GREAT distraction from my marital stressors.

My first selection for Kito's formal education was a Montessori center when he turned two years old. He remained in the Montessori school until he was almost five, when he was selected from a waiting list to attend West Laboratory Elementary School.

About a year after he was enrolled at the Montessori school, Howard began taking Kito to school most mornings. Commuter traffic was always terrible, and I had an increasingly more important role as a Division Director at the County's Office of Community and Economic Development; stressful. So, I welcomed the relief from my daily grind.

Besides, Howard's office at City Hall in Coconut Grove was located nearby the school.

One of the instructors greeted the children every morning. She was a very friendly, beautiful, blond woman from an English-speaking Caribbean Island. I always enjoyed talking with her; she was very affectionate with Kito.

During this time period, I had begun to collect reggae music. I especially liked Bunny Wailer/The Wailers, featuring

Bob Marley. The influence of the Jamaican culture was rising; it was not long after when it would become dominant in Miami; second only to the Cuban culture. My collection of cassettes started to disappear, little by little.

"Howard, do you have my CD's?"

"Yeah, I play them in the car."

"Well, I miss my music, so please return them."

I never got them back.

Bastard! You think you're slick. I hope you get caught and she gets fired.

I filed it away. I was getting busier with my own interests, which included having another baby.

I planned to get pregnant, for the third time. Kito was four years old. I was ready.

⚜

MY PRAYER FOR AN ALL-NATURAL CHILDBIRTH WOULD BE answered when I had Issa.

When I awoke one Saturday morning, my contractions were every twenty minutes.

Oh no! Not yet. I have errands to complete.

Howard's mother's birthday was the following day, May 23rd, and I was determined to hold the baby back until then.

It'll be great to give mom another grand on her birthday!

But first, I had to make an early run by Fingertips to make sure everything was ok. I was the day-to-day manager of the hair salons.

I got there around 10:00 AM.

"You better get to the doctor," one of the operators urged me. I laughed it off as several of the salon staff suggested I go straight to the hospital. I'd only had one contraction while in the salon; they knew my due date was eminent.

My next stop was at the mall adjacent to Fingertips. I picked up cards and gifts for mom, and for two children whose birthday parties Kito was scheduled to attend that same afternoon. I had to stop walking at least twice in the mall because the contractions took my breath away. I was moving slowly.

It was a twenty minute drive to Howard's mother's house where Kito had spent the night. I had three contractions while I visited with her.

I need to get Kito home for a nap, and then get him ready for the two parties.

By now it was almost noon.

"Baby, don't you think you need to call your doctor?" mom watched me breathe through the contractions.

"No, I am ok," I calmly responded, in between deep breaths.

I can't have the baby today. There were too many other things on the calendar. Maybe I better change the plans. Better be sure to eat.

I recalled how hungry I was during my labor with Kito, almost five years before. I had gotten to the hospital 'early', got immediately hooked up to a monitor, given Demerol, which I hated, and had to suffer hunger pangs throughout the ordeal. I had taken some fruit with me but the nurses wouldn't let me eat it because of a fear I might choke during labor. I resented them for the next five years.

I'll fix myself some lunch when I get home.

After I left my mother-in-law's house, I made one last stop at the drive through Farm Stores for a gallon of milk. The contractions were coming hard, and fast. I went into overdrive, planning my next moves.

Please don't let his baby come now, I silently prayed.

I put Kito in his bed for a nap as soon as I got home.

Contraction. Breathe.

I wrapped the two children's gifts.

Contraction. Breathe.

I called my aunt Doris to arrange for her to take Kito to the parties.

Contraction. Breathe.

I called my neighbors to cover the house until my aunt arrived. *I'm running out of time.*

Contraction. Breathe.

I prepared my lunch, a peanut butter sandwich on wheat toast, and a cup of coffee.

Contraction. Breathe.

I called my doctor as I was finishing the second half of my sandwich.

"Hello Dr. Relkin, my contractions are every 10 minutes."

Contraction. Breathe.

"I'll meet you at the hospital."

I then proceeded to put on a full face of make-up.

"Can't let them see you without your face on."

Contraction. Breathe.

I awakened Howard from his afternoon nap.

"It's time to go," I gently aroused him from his deep sleep.

Neither of us was getting much rest at night because of the imminence of the delivery. Our nightly dance included my pregnant toss, his turn, my turn, his toss. We were in unison during this intimate time.

Funny. Having a baby drew us closer.

"You ready?" he asked me, sleepily. It didn't take long for him to dress.

"What about Kito?"

"He's asleep. Ellie is coming over and Aunt Doris is on her way."

My bag was waiting by the front door. I had packed it two days before.

Organized.

This time, Howard was prepared to be my coach. He had attended Lamaze classes. I wanted him to remain calm, so I did not tell him how close together my contractions were coming. But any pretense of normal breathing was nearly impossible. I put up a brave front and a fake smile for him.

We pulled out of the driveway and headed south toward the hospital, fifteen minutes away.

"You better stop and get a hamburger. You don't want to be hungry through my labor and delivery."

Wendy's was near the house.

Another four minutes passed while Howard ordered his hamburger.

Two more contractions.

Oh no!

I hung my head out the car window and gulped oxygen.

Just a few more minutes Antonia. Stay in control and hold in this baby!

We arrived at the hospital around 2:50 PM. Howard left the car at the valet. Dr. Relkin and the nurses had gathered in expectation of my arrival. They were all in a jolly mood as they watched me try to raise up from the wheel chair. I couldn't make it out without assistance.

I had done the unthinkable: kept the doctor waiting.

"Look at her, she can't even stand up," Dr. Relkin and the nurses had one good, hard laugh at my 'condition', and then within seconds the team went into their expert, well-rehearsed routines. By then, I could not even hold my head up. I was having my baby right then.

Howard quickly washed up and got into his scrubs. I bypassed the labor room and was hoisted onto the delivery 'table', and except for a few swabs of disinfectant, there was no other preparation. The baby came, quickly.

Issa was delivered at 3:20 PM.

Natural child birth. No drugs. No episiotomy. I was high on adrenalin. I felt like I had enough energy to run a marathon. I was served two dinners, and two desserts. I ate it all with gusto. Every hair was still in place, and my makeup was perfectly intact.

As he entered the world, the pattern for Issa's life was set. Everything was on his timetable. On his terms. And so it was; and so it still is to this day.

❧

LET ME BE CLEAR: I WAS ONLY ABLE TO PERFORM MY demanding job of being "Howard's wife", executive director of GMU, and mommy, because of the daily support I got from Mrs. Leola Ross.

I needed someone who was mature, could speak standard English, was flexible with her work schedule, kind to children, respectful of my rules and regulations, and, who was discreet.

I interviewed several potential employees before I found Mrs. Ross. This African-American woman had raised and educated four beautiful, independent daughters. Her husband's family was well known throughout south Florida as pioneers-and they were also religious leaders.

Jackpot! My prayers were answered.

I hired Mrs. Ross at the end of my six month maternity leave after giving birth to our second son, Issa in 1982. Her list of tasks grew from baby care, to include grocery shopping, cooking (using my recipes), laundry, organizing the after-school cookies and milk brigade for our sons, and their neighborhood friends. She remained on-call during the weekends and evenings when other baby sitters were unavailable.

She managed my household.

When Mrs. Ross came into my life, it freed me up to do, and be, more than I had planned.

Initially she expected us to call her "Leola." She had never worked for a black family before and she was accustomed to being called by her first name by her employers.

No, no, no.

She called me "Mrs. Gary", and she called Howard, "Mr. Gary."

She was always Mrs. Ross to us. It was all about respect. It was mutual.

"Mom, how much do you pay Mrs. Ross?" Issa was about five when he surprised me with the question. Mrs. Ross stood right in front of us waiting for my response.

"Well Issa, I pay her what she earns," I said, all the while looking at Mrs. Ross waiting for her agreement with me.

Not satisfied, Issa rejoined, "Well you should pay her more money because she has to put up with me every day, and you know how bad I am sometimes."

Mrs. Ross did not disagree with Issa, and we all had a good laugh, considering the source. Issa always held a strong opinion of himself. He was strong-willed, from birth, and remains quite formidable. This character trait of his carried over into all his choices; into his adulthood.

Issa and Mrs. Ross formed a very close bond, but I was never jealous. I was glad to see my son had the capacity to love many people. I would always be mom.

I did pay Mrs. Ross at the top end of wages for her valued services, also paying into her unemployment and her social security. I felt it was important to pay a fair wage, and to set an example for all the other households who employed 'domestic' workers. I also knew, like every other matter in our personal lives, Mrs. Ross's salary might, one day, come under scrutiny. It never did, but the eventuality was always lurking.

In fact, for years, and at every chance I got, I'd encourage other working women who were trying to do what I did, i.e., juggle time between parenting, increasing levels of responsibilities at work, and being married to a high profile partner; to get themselves some hired help.

On one of the television interviews I gave about being a working, professional, parent, I told my female counterparts: "Just do the math, ladies. Compare what you get paid hourly, to what you would pay someone to keep your household. You'll see it doesn't pay to do your own housework."

As far as I could calculate, there was no comparison. But many balked. Some of the responses I got, on air and in person were: "I just can't see someone else taking care of my business;" or, "I'd have to clean my house before I could have someone come in and see how messy I am." And even more commonly, "I don't trust people in my house." These were all nonsense to me.

❧

PARENTING IS TWENTY FOUR SEVEN!

"Mom do we go to a private school?" the boys asked me one day.

"No, West Lab is a public school." I wondered where this question came from after all their years in attendance.

I waited for their follow up, curious about the source of their inquiry.

"Well, you know most kids walk to their neighborhood school, but you and dad, or granddaddy have to take us to our school," offered Kito.

"And there are no school buses for West lab," added Issa.

"Well, your school is a laboratory. It's a school of choice.

The University of Miami helped develop the curriculum, but West Lab still has to conform to all the same standards of any other public school."

"So, why do the kids have to be on a waiting list to get in?' Kito knew the most.

"Your school wants to have a mix of students who look more like the real population in Miami."

I hoped their experience at West Lab, and all their other exposure to Miami's diverse groups, would help them develop into persons who tolerated differences; help make them citizens of the world.

Kito and Issa knew how important it was to me for them to adapt in a diverse environment, but what they learned at home was sacred. I did not worry about how many different types of people they interacted with on a daily basis at school, on the playing field, etc.

"The best people in your life are your family members." Whenever my sons and I had any differences of opinion about what was right, wrong or what was the best behavior for then to emulate, I'd refer to their grandparents, their aunts, uncles and legions of cousins.

I don't recall Howard being involved in too many of those teaching moments. I usually told him about them once he got home, you know, during the exchange of how was your day? How was the kids' day?

❧

"JUST PUT A STICK AND A BALL IN THEIR HANDS," MY DAD

used to say about how to raise boys. "That'll keep them busy, and tired by the end of the day." Daddy was so wise.

Kito and Issa spent a large part of their childhood at the Coral Gables Youth center where they participated in almost every sport available: swimming, basketball, soccer, football, baseball, et al.

"Go Kito, go. Run baby," Howard's mom yelled. She was running down the sidelines along with Kito. They reached the goal line together. I remained hidden behind a magazine or newspaper each time Kito ran. I could not bear to see him get hit. Often, my dad had to grab me by my shirt, to hold me back when he began playing in high school.

I never approved of him playing football. I thought it was a brutal sport. I still think so.

Even though my feelings were clear, Howard ignored me and took Kito to register for the Pop Warner program one weekend when I was out of town. He was only seven years old, and up till then had been playing soccer, which I approved of as a good team sport.

Howard's mother loved football, and she was a big supporter of Kito playing, even at such a very young age. She never missed any of his games. My dad was also always at the games; tacitly approving. I was outnumbered. I was somewhat reconciled when I accepted in the little leagues, all the boys were matched by age and size.

I knew it hurt him to be knocked down, and tackled time and again. But Kito ran very fast, and soon became a star player. His position, each time, was to carry the ball. He was always the target.

As a rule, neither Howard nor I missed any of his games. There was one time when Howard came straight from the airport just to see Kito play.

So strange. I wonder where he is coming from, all dressed up in his business suit!

He left immediately after the game and returned to wherever his business meeting was being held.

On hindsight, it was another one of those incidents which raised more questions than answers. But, in the moment, I was caught up in the excitement of Kito's game- not Howard's games.

৩৯৩

KITO WAS SURPRISED WHEN HE WAS NAMED ATHLETE OF THE Year at his high school's annual banquet to honor graduating student athletes. He had set and/or broken many of the school's records for speed, touchdowns, etc. He was recruited by eight Colleges and Universities. I selected Wake Forest University for its outstanding academic standing, and because Wake graduated a high percentage of its athletes. He was awarded a five year scholarship to the prestigious University. I was so proud of him. Wake Forest played in Division 1A, and they recruited their players for scholarship, character, and athleticism.

Once, I went to visit Kito while he was a freshman, I had gone up for one of his football games. He was a running back with a very promising future.

Over lunch, Kito and I began to reminisce about his early childhood.

"Thank you for your wonderful gift, son."

"No. Thank you, mom." We both laughed.

"You know, I really didn't miss out on much during my childhood; you know all the good stuff." We laughed out loud about all my efforts to keep him on a narrow path: to stay out of contact with the police; to make good grades and graduate from high school; to get a good College education; to not have any babies before marriage; etc.

He grew silent for a minute. His voice lowered to almost a whisper.

"You know, daddy made me nervous and I was always scared, but I didn't know why."

"Oh, Kito. I'm so sorry. I tried so hard to keep you sheltered from all the craziness."

"Yean, well I really didn't know what was going on with daddy when he was the City Manager. You, Mrs. Ross, and granddaddy made sure me and Issa stayed busy, and too tired every day. Issa was too young to understand anyway."

I smiled. *That was the plan, son. That was the plan.*

❧

ISSA'S ATHLETIC CAREER TOOK A DIFFERENT PATH FROM HIS brother's. He developed into an across-the-board power player, and he used his tremendous body strength and low center of gravity to his advantage.

"Back up!" "Back Up!" Opposing little league coaches yelled to their outfield whenever Issa came up to bat. When he did connect, the ball was guaranteed to be a home run if it stayed in the diamond. He was fearless, and he excelled as his team's catcher.

It was like that in every sport he played.

"Oh my God, it must really hurt," was all I could say as I watched Issa use his head, elbows, knees, and hips to muscle the basketball into his hands. I felt badly for the smaller boys who were defending against him. He took no prisoners.

"Don't worry son, you'll be able to catch up so you can play football." Issa's age and size were out of sync until he reached the 110 pound category. He was eleven when he started with Pop Warner football program.

By then, he was recognized for his strength and power. His position was set for the rest of his football career. He played the line: offense and defense. His best position was as the Center.

"Another take down by 'Eye-Sah' Gary, mispronounced at every game.

It's pronounced Eesaw!

"Daddy, did you see?" My dad never missed any of Issa's games. He attended his practices too!

"Yes, Toni, I saw it."

"I hope his dad saw it."

By the time Issa played High School football, Howard was on the sidelines of our lives, and where he usually remained during Issa's games. Invariably, I or my dad would spot him, sometimes hovering near the entrance, watching, as 'Eye sah Gary' sacked the quarterback.

Coming or going? I wondered.

I admit I liked to watch Issa play football. He stayed low to the ground and was the aggressor; not being pursued for carrying the ball like Kito. I treasure a photo of him in the Miami Herald showing him dragging down the opposing team's quarterback. His team was on their way to winning the State championship.

"Daddy, I never thought so many people would turn out for a high school football game."

There were over 70,000 in attendance.

"This is big business in Florida. You know, all the Colleges recruit our boys."

"I just hope Howard makes it." I flashed back to how Howard never missed one of Kito's games. By now, he was Issa's custodial parent, but Issa reported his dad had mostly been MIA. I prayed this would not be one of those times.

Daddy signed, "Relax, Toni, he'll be here."

We had driven for nearly five hours from Miami to get to the University stadium in Gainesville. We followed a miles-long procession of fans, boosters, and other parents.

The parking lot was enormous, but we managed to find the other Northwestern supporters, and sure enough, there was Howard. He had travelled up with his other family.

❦

PART OF OUR CHARGE IN RAISING THE BOYS WAS TO TEACH them how to be responsible citizens. Howard and I both took our jobs petty seriously and we seldom, if ever, disagreed on how to do it. When Kito was about age ten, and Issa age five, we showed them how, during Orange Bowl events, to use the pocket lawn out front to earn them extra money. It was a community-wide tradition which had been going on since the 1930s.

We enjoyed those times when we got to bond with our neighbors. Many of them, too, 'sold' spaces on their lawns. The area was just a short two block walk from the Orange Bowl, where the patrons felt safe in our residential community. Often, people we knew would call in advance to 'reserve' a space. The arrangement was a win/win for everyone.

Our yard was mapped out to hold up to 20 cars, spaces priced from $10-$20. The boys would hold up a sign which read: "Twenty Dollars No Block" to lure the paying public onto our property.

"Don't forget the house gets 30%," I would remind the boys. A good event, a major concert, for instance, could bring in more than $400, with additional tips and bonuses, for street-front parking.

"But mom, you didn't do anything to help," they'd whine after they learned how to manage the job without my assistance.

"That's true, but I have to pay for the water for the grass, pay taxes on the property, and pay for repairs and general maintenance, so the house takes thirty percent."

There was only one time the arrangement 'went south'. It was during a very popular event at the Orange Bowl. There was an overflow of people looking for parking. Someone quickly parked, paid the boys and left. The offending patron ignored my sons and blocked the driveway; the spot reserved for their dad.

When Howard returned home, since he did not have a spot to park his own car, he blocked the violator.

"Kito, what happened to my spot?"

"Daddy, I told the guy not to park there, but he did it anyway and walked away real fast."

"Howard, what are you going to do?"

"I'm going to teach the mother fucker a lesson."

We waited.

I sure hope the guy is polite.

Several hours later, the driver returned and rudely demanded Howard unblock his car to let him leave.

Oh oh. Wrong move. He's young. Fool!

"You think you can get away with this because you are a white boy," Howard shouted at the guy. "But, you're just a dumb ass," he continued. The boys were looking and listening. I could not shield them, this time.

Stupidly, the driver exchanged words with Howard about blocking his car and how he had paid, blah, blah, blah.

Why can't he just eat a little crow, and apologize so Howard would move his car and let him leave?

Instead, the heated exchange escalated. The driver was still in his twenties, and while he was clearly wrong, he did not know how to admit it.

Howard was harsh.

"Mother fucking, sorry ass bastard. I will put my foot up your white ass if you say another fucking word with your punk ass self. You just took advantage of my son 'cause you thought you could get away with it."

"Well I paid him twenty dollars for the spot."

"Fuck you and your twenty dollars", Howard yelled and threw a $20 bill at the guy. "Kito, go get my briefcase."

Oh no, that's where he has his gun! Kito knew. Issa Knew. We all knew.

I tried to get Howard to back down, but he had not finished proving his point. *What was his point? This young guy had no idea at all who he was dealing with.*

"My dad is an attorney and he'll take you to court for threatening me with a gun."

"Bring him on," Howard shouted, waving his gun. He relished the thought of having a more worthy adversary.

"I'll kick his ass too. As a matter of fact, give me his goddamn name and number so I can tell him what a fucking prick of a son he has."

Seemingly satisfied he'd soon have an equally formidable opponent, Howard made the guy give him his dad's contact information before finally letting him leave our driveway. Howard called the guy's father. We waited for the blowback.

Once the guy's father realized who Howard was, he called to apologize for his son's disrespectful behavior. But not before calling the press. The matter made the paper.

Howard Gary threatens man with a gun for blocking his car.

It was a small item, but Howard did not look good in the telling. He has already been fired, and he was starting a new career: investment banker.

Wrong image!

I never knew what lesson the boys were supposed to have learned from that incident; it was such a minor infraction to have to bring out a gun.

"Mom, I was always nervous around daddy," Kito revealed to me as a young adult. "I never knew what he might do."

He had remained mostly quiet about his feelings.

Not so, Issa. As he got older, Issa would, get in his dad's face, too many times for my comfort.

"Issa, please don't do anything which will give your dad a reason to do something he'll regret for the rest of his life," I'd plead. They both survived the confrontations. Issa was strong. Issa is strong.

I often felt helpless in trying to protect my sons from an image of their dad, the maniac. It seemed the harder I tried to cover him over, the more Howard fanned out his tail feathers.

BOOK FIVE

GRIN AND BEAR IT

16

UNRAVELING THREADS

1982-1991

"Have some fish Joyce," I offered.

"No thank you. You know I'm watching my weight." She was on a very strict diet at the time. My fried fish was one of the best. I had learned how to make it perfectly crispy on the outside, without burning, and remaining moist on the inside. The secret was to season the fish, apply a heavy coating of yellow mustard all over the top, and heavily dredge it through flour before placing the fish in a large pan of very hot oil. I cooked it uncovered. Few could resist.

I admired her discipline.

Joyce Hanks Knox, my good friend and business partner, was running for the Dade County School Board. She would stop by my house on a regular basis, ostensibly to use the restroom, even though her own house was less than two miles away. I enjoyed her excuse for a bathroom break or any other reasons she might have to visit me.

On this particular Saturday morning, she had completed a run of campaign appearances, and had stopped by the house to make her 'restroom break'. Howard and I were still eating breakfast. Fresh fried fish, head and tail on, and grits was a favorite of ours. Kito and Issa had spent the night at one of the relatives. It was precious time for just the two of us, and we were enjoying the moment.

Joyce was clearly agitated when she came out of the powder room.

"I want to let you know I just ran into an accusation that Howard and I are having an affair. The rumor is I fit the description: a light skinned woman, named Joyce."

She chuckled as she dropped the bomb.

Oh no, here we go again.

More than a year into his tenure as City Manager, sometime around 1983, rumors of Howard having another woman kicked up again; they simply would not go away.

My first inclination was to go into my self- protective mode: to deny the rumor as untrue, or, at best, old news. But Howard was right there. And now here was a name and a description being offered for my consideration.

Wow, so Howard was, in fact, having an affair; the woman was light skinned; and, her name was Joyce. More information than I ever had brought directly to me.

"I assure you it is not me," she declared and turned to my face.

Her statement exploded. It fell over the breakfast room, leaving a speechless gap. It just lay there like a dumb biscuit; heavy from too much lard.

Awkward.

A split second after Joyce's denouncement, Howard burst out in laughter, breaking the blanket of silence at this notion of him and our Joyce being lovers. Howard had an infectious belly laugh. It drew people into him, and it also served to deflect from matters at hand.

Joyce and I joined him in laughter. The three of us hugged our sides, holding in the pain while laughing out loud.

Well. She did fit the description. Except she really didn't.

Joyce Knox was a force. She was an attorney with the Legal Aid Society, where she was a champion for the poor and dispossessed. She was, at the time, married to the Miami City Attorney, George Knox. They were another black power couple in town.

George was Howard's peer, not his employee. We became close social friends, and eventually business partners.

Joyce Knox was well known for her matter-of-fact manner; she struck a fearful respect in everyone she encountered. She was the leader of Dek Cartel, the group of ten women, including myself, who, in 1982, opened the Fingertips hair salons.

And, she most certainly was not Howard's type!

After we were all spent from our belly laugh, Joyce left us, alone.

I was stunned into silence. Follow up questions remained unasked and unanswered for a long time. And on this Saturday, I was too exhausted from playing my role as Mrs. Howard Gary to say anything.

☙❧

IN APRIL, 1984, I, THE BOYS, AND HOWARD TOOK A MUCH needed family vacation during the school spring break. By then, Howard had completed a full two years in office, and we were all tired and stressed out. Issa was a little under two years old; Kito was a little over six. It was the boys' first airplane flight. We went to Wilmington, NC where my good friend and former college big sister, Fanny, had a house on the beach at Top Sail Island. We were scheduled to spend nearly a week. I had a tough time falling asleep from the sound of the Atlantic Ocean crashing onto the beach. With such a thunderous roar, on some nights it felt as if the house might get carried away in the sweep of just one of those waves.

We went to town. We toured. We went bowling. The boys loved visiting an old, WW II battleship, the SS Wilmington. And of course, we shopped.

I was placing some packages in the trunk of our car after one shopping trip, when I spotted a few items in a bag clearly meant for a female.

There goes Howard, buying me gifts, again.

There was a scarf and a card. The card read: "I miss you, and I can't wait to see you again." It was unsigned.

My blood ran cold. *These are not for me.*

My whole body started to tremble. I broke out in a sweat.

Quickly, close the trunk; don't let him see you looking in the bag.

That night, those ocean waves weren't the only noises keeping me awake. A loud voice rang in my head, screaming: *"Why are you staying with this man?"* My file was thick with recriminations. *If only I'd act on them. Confront him. Why? I wasn't leaving, and neither was he.*

But, I didn't speak on it. Ever.

Shortly after we returned from vacation, the press began an unprecedented and unrelenting scrutiny and examination of all things Howard Gary. This close scrutiny bordered on an invasion of my privacy, seeping into our personal life which was, supposedly beyond the scope of public purview.

This is unfair. Howard was not an elected official, and his responsibility was to the Commission of five, not to the entire readership of the local newspaper chain.

I felt naked. Exposed. Vulnerable. I tightened up my mask. It was the beginning of his end as Manager. I felt compelled to come to his defense.

I've got a lot at stake too!

❦

DURING THOSE TIMES OF GROWING TURBULENCE, MY DAD began to make daily appearances at my house. He seemed to intuitively know I needed the cloak of his care and watchful eye. I was relieved to have him around.

"Daddy, here is a key to the front door. Make yourself at home."

This feels like when I was a little girl. I felt protected.

Daddy came and went at his leisure when Mrs. Ross wasn't there to let him inside. While there, he tightened every screw in the house and he kept my knives sharpened. He also helped himself to my favorite liquor. I couldn't keep enough Jack Daniels for the two of us.

Howard always behaved better with my dad around. They had a mutual respect and some unspoken man-code which continued over the rest of their lives.

"A.G., I got some more suits and shoes for you."

"Well thank you. I have someplace to wear them."

Because of Howard's gifts, my dad didn't ever have to buy many new clothes. Howard even gave him a tuxedo, which came in handy after my divorce, when daddy was my principal escort for three years following the end of my marriage.

After Howard was fired, daddy practically took up residence. I needed him. The boys needed him. He was there.

❦

HOWARD HAD GAINED A REPUTATION FOR NOT TAKING ANY prisoners. To this day, it was not unusual to hear someone say about him, "Howard Gary was a "mother fucker". And, depending on what side of the argument you are on, it could either be interpreted as a curse, or a compliment. In fact, in his funeral remarks about Howard, the first word our friend George Knox uttered was "Warrior!"

"You know we loved Howard because he had big cojones (balls). He did and said what we couldn't get away with." I would often hear something similar from various folk in the black community.

The first failed attempt to fire Howard was at a Commission meeting at City Hall in 1983. Advocates and organizers had three buses loaded with black people brought in to sit in protest against the action. The attempt to fire Howard was led by his nemesis, Commissioner Joe Carollo, who had begun his relentless scrutiny and campaign shortly after Howard was appointed. The irony is it was Joe's nomination of Howard that set up his confirmation. He clearly was not expecting the two additional votes to actually seal his appointment.

He must have never gotten over how he was tricked!

Joe's crusade knew no boundaries. One night, during Howard's second year, Joe approached me at a charitable event, and cornered me.

"So, how is Howard's nose? I heard he had a bad drip." Joe simulated sniffling, alluding to Howard's alleged cocaine use. I almost wet my pants. His breech of respect was typical of how Carollo behaved toward anyone he felt got in his way.

I was terrified of him. I was not the only one terrified by Joe Carollo. One instance of his unpredictability was at a political campaign event, where Carollo was expected to pledge his support of Maurice Ferre for another term as Mayor. He reversed his anticipated endorsement and declared, on television, he would never support Ferre. Typical.

Joe orchestrated Howard's actual firing. It took place months later at a middle school in the predominantly Puerto Rican neighborhood of Wynwood. The change in venue for the Commission meeting took the street organizers by surprise. The area was considered foreign to most City residents: black, white, and Cuban.

The meeting had one item on the agenda: firing the City

Manager. It was over in a matter of minutes.

Howard came straight home, but was not home for long before the phone started to ring.

"Howard, its Barbara."

"Motherfuckers changed the location at the last minute. Nobody knew about it. Went to some fucking middle school nobody ever heard of." They got their three votes."

"Yes, come on over."

Barbara Carey, Chairman of the County Commissioner and Athalee Range, civic servant and, an acknowledged king-maker, were two of the most powerful women in the Miami-Dade County/South Florida. In fact, their might stretched to Washington. They arrived together within a half hour.

The phone was blowing up. "No, he is not available right now." I fielded the calls over the next two hours while Howard, Barbara and Athalee strategized about what recourse Howard could take.

"Toni, I'm not going to fight it. But I'm going to make them wait for my acceptance. The community needs to be calm so I'll let them know, I'm not going to fight."

No riot took place, but there were fears of a street level reprisal.

Howard wanted to carefully shape his departure message. He wanted to go out on a high note, and to especially leave the black community feeling vindicated by his/their achievement. He cautiously let his supporters know he was not going to 'fight' the firing.

The ordeal was prolonged for an additional three weeks, before Howard actually took his leave from the City. There were last minute negotiations to conduct: non-disclosures; severances; and a statement of his accomplishments.

Again, I helped edit his formal response. It was brilliant.

Amongst many other accomplishments he read into the record of his last City Commission meeting was he left the City with a budget surplus and an AAA+ bond rating. Enough said.

Nearly thirty years after the firing event, I talked with an old friend who was part of the Justice Department team organized to quell any outrage after Howard was fired, and he told me about one of the last strategy sessions called by Mayor Ferre on the 'eve' of Howard's firing. There was no question about if he'd be fired. But when. And where.

"The bottom line proposition was about how to fire Howard and prevent a riot by black folk. Also, the white power structure wanted to guarantee Howard a safety net."

"Is that how he got to go to Florida Memorial University?" I could never understand why Howard's agreement included his appointment to work as an adjunct professor. There was no money in it.

"Yes. Well, Alvah took care of the arrangement. It backfired. The University didn't have the money to pay Howard the salary initially negotiated."

The agreement with Florida Memorial College turned out to be a sham, and Howard quit teaching after just one semester. He delivered a course in Public Finance, his expertise.

In the meantime, Howard and I, along with four other people, including George and Joyce Knox, opened Chicken George, a fast food franchise.

At first, we were skeptical to go into the venture as equal partners. I was still participating in most of our household financial decisions and I felt good about being at this business table.

"Toni, do you really think it's such a good idea? We will be double dipping in our finances if we are both co-investors in this deal."

"Maybe, but over the long term, the potential of making a lot of money is great since we have the franchise for all of Florida and the Caribbean."

It was an intoxicating notion. We were both excited.

It took four months to build out a converted corner store to meet the specifications of the Chicken George franchise. It was located on a busy intersection in the heart of Liberty City. Of course it made the news. The Miami Herald ran a feature story and a photo of Howard with his arms covered in floor, preparing the chicken to be cooked, and serving 'mean greens'. It was a great public relations piece, and free advertising! Nobody need worry about him/us anymore. We were doing well after his firing.

But just a few months after our grand opening, we learned the franchise was not healthy. We quickly cut our losses and closed the business. It was an eye opening, and money-losing experience. Howard and I had restaurant equipment stored on our property for years before we finally liquidated it.

What to do next?

"Toni, I have an opportunity to go into the investment banking business, but I'll need to use my severance money to open the office."

"How do you do that?"

"I have to study for a series of licenses. I already know most of the requirements, so it won't take me long, and Raul Masvidal is selling me M Bank."

"Of course you can. Do it," I insisted. I was making enough salary to cover the burden of our day-to-day expenses to fill in any financial gaps until Howard started making money from the business. I felt good, for once, about being the steady, reliable partner,

I'm the bread winner. This is a no brainer. It was about time Howard cashed in on his nearly twenty years of experience and extensive knowledge of municipal finance.

"Howard, you have my full support," I cheered him on. I saw a wonderful opportunity to increase our wealth; of course I would benefit from the business.

In very short order, he purchased M Bank, studied for, and got all the licenses and certifications required to run his company, and was then off to the rat race as an investment banker!

I had no idea. After only a few months, his conversation was about hundreds of millions of dollars.

Out of my league? You bet!

And I never caught up, or caught on.

My life with Howard turned, again.

The number of blacks in the investment banking industry in the 1980s were few; less than a dozen around the country were doing any business, of note. The environment in Miami-Dade County was perfect for Howard's success. Barbara Carey made minority participation in all of the County's business, and especially participation in the County's bond issues, the centerpiece of her administration. A well drafted set of guidelines for minority participation in the County's bond issues was firmly in place, thanks to the keen legal mind and steady hand of Dianne Saulney Smith, bond counsel for Miami-Dade County.

These women were our friends, so he had the right combination of supporting players to be successful in his bids. He could not fail.

"Toni, can you help me pick put some furniture for the office?" At first, it was fun, and I felt a growing excitement about his new venture. I enjoyed giving him advice, and being part of the grand design for our future- seemingly now financially secured.

"Don't start counting the money yet, Toni. I have some loans to pay off, and the staff expenses are high." There was no real profit, the first year.

Two years later, he told me, "Toni, I don't need you coming by the office. You'd only be in the way."

Deja Vu. Shut out, again.

But, by then, we were divorced.

Are you going to walk away from all that money? Yes. No. Have another drink. You'll feel better.

I cared, less and less. I had more than enough on my own plate than to chase after Howard's day-to-day machinations. I had a title: Associate Dean/Executive Director. It was a lofty position of authority. I was serving on several nonprofit Boards. I was an important civic volunteer; and, I had an overinflated ego boost propping me up. The College maintained a very healthy public relations staff, and suddenly, I began to be in the news, all the time. I enjoyed it, and I never met a camera I didn't like.

Only once did I have a problem with the growing publicity and exposure. The Miami Herald published an experimental magazine insert featuring me and several other notable women. The photographer had won a Pulitzer, and I was excited to participate. He shot down from the second floor. I was posed in a very provocative position- laying on the floor of the new College outreach center. It was an unusual angle. I liked it.

The magazine was targeted for distribution in the wealthier zip codes. I found this out after I agreed to the interview and the photo shoot.

"I didn't agree to be part of this elite distribution. The target audience doesn't fit me very well, and I'm really uncomfortable about being in it." I called the publisher to file my protest. Too late.

I felt duped. I thought the magazine insert was scheduled for all of the Herald's subscribers. Up until then, I had safeguarded my image, and I was careful to not be perceived or portrayed as elitist. After all, I had cut my teeth as a community organizer, and I had run Greater Miami United for three years getting folk to unite, regardless of race, ethnicity, language, or economic status. I carried my democratic outlook into my personal life, as well as throughout my professional career. I did not purchase the Magazine. There was only that one edition. The Herald said there were not enough advertisers to publish another.

Good.

෴

IT WAS 1987 AND WE WERE ENTERING INTO OUR TWENTIETH year of marriage.

I had long before ceased fighting him, having replaced the God of my youth with Howard. It was tough to admit to myself: any moral compass I had ever had was irretrievably broken. I was no longer getting 'good' readings.

"What's this I hear about Howard and a baby?" daddy asked me one day. I had not visited the question since Joyce Knox dropped her bomb four years before.

Daddy and I only discussed the outside child rumor once.

"Daddy, that's old news left over from when Howard was in Newark." I dismissed it since I had already been reconciled with knowing he had the girl child from New Jersey. It's about all I could handle.

"Hrump", daddy uttered. He didn't press me on it anymore. He knew when to stand down from an argument he could not win. Daddy and I could not sustain a fight with one another; we loved each another too much. I was his 'only daughter'; his 'one Toni', and I knew he would not let any irreversible harm come to me. He also knew Howard. The silent code between me and my dad was confirmed by his constant presence around me and my sons. It was a simple and profound showing-up-presence. It was comforting

Howard had a most peculiar idea about children, his children. I had become pregnant with him four times. Two were planned and fully assented to. I had two abortions: one in between the birth of Kito (1976) and Issa (1982), and another almost five years after Issa was born. Both are painful to recall.

"That was a mighty big pregnancy", Dr. Lozeman said at the end of the procedure. I had already met him once before for a termination of pregnancy. I was not planning on seeing him ever again after this time.

I was only about ten weeks pregnant, so I could not understand his comment. I was still groggy from the surgery. I had also insisted on having a tubal ligation because I wanted to end any possibility of another pregnancy. I was finished! I have since had the haunting thought about the "big pregnancy". They were twins! In fact, I dreamed they were girls. My daughters. While the memory of the experience remains vivid to this day, I have forgiven myself countless times for giving in to Howard's plea to terminate the pregnancy, mostly for his convenience. He had me convinced, and I agreed, it was not a good time for us to have another baby.

The last abortion was under duress. I thought we were doing well. His investment banking business was taking off, but he was also becoming more and more erratic. I had lived with all kinds of rumors and reports of another woman and another 'outside' child, but I was unprepared to confront Howard about any more extramarital affairs. There were just too many other stressors in our life at the time, and our own two children's lives consumed me. My career had taken off, and Mrs. Ross had my household under control. It was enough for me to get up and get through each day with a degree of decorum and dignity, than to have to deal with another outside woman and her child. It was too much for me to rise to, until later.

I'm Howard's nigger bitch now, for sure.

Spring break, April 1987 came with a surprise offer from Howard to take another family vacation. I had completely recovered from the abortion, and I was ready to go skiing.

He made all the arrangements for me and the boys to go with him to Vail, Colorado, for a full week. I knew he had taken up skiing as a hobby; I was happy he found a replacement for Karate with another physically demanding outlet. I was not jealous of his interest. I had my own.

Lee Damus, a good friend and one of my partners in Fingertips, and her husband Al, had a house in Vail they shared with two other families. Lee, Al, and their son, Aaron, were expert skiers.

Over the years, she had accumulated a great wardrobe.

"Lee, I need you to help me put together a wardrobe for my ski trip."

"Toni, don't buy anything. Come on over and try on some stuff. I have more coats and other pants in Vail you can use. I even have silk underwear for you."

Howard had his own ski paraphernalia.

The Damuses were going out at the same time, so I'd have the company of folk I knew. I enrolled in ski classes to learn how to start and stop; I spent most of my time snow plowing down the blue (bunny) slopes.

Kito, age ten and a half, became expert after following Aaron around the double diamonds. All the skiers met at the intersections at the end of our respective runs. It was great fun for everyone, except for Issa.

He was just under five and he never got to a slope. Poor

baby, he remained in ski school the entire week. It was an unusually warm spring, and the snow had turned to slush where he was taking his lessons.

"I went water skiing," Issa softly cried.

I felt badly for him, especially after I learned how over his teenage years, when he lived with his dad, Issa turned down offers to go skiing with his other family.

"Mom, that was for Joyce and Jordan to do with daddy. I did not want to participate in their family vacation."

On our second day, Howard fell while he was hot-dogging down a difficult slope. He sprained his shoulder so badly, he had to be taken to the ER by ambulance. Loaded up with pain killers, and with his arm in a harness sling, Howard returned to the slopes on the second day after his accident.

We spent the week in a fabulous chalet owed by Monty Trainor, owner of a popular eponymous restaurant in Miami, and CATS, the club. Monty shared ownership in the beautiful house with a few other business partners. Shortly after our ski vacation at his chalet, Monty was arrested and subsequently convicted to six months in federal prison, plus 2500 community service hours, on tax evasion charges.

What a week.

Overall, it was a first class experience, but it was marred by an incident I could never make sense of, until years later.

One morning, we were preparing for our daily run. Just before dropping Issa off at ski school, we went shopping for some last minute supplies at the ski shop. It was less than half way through the trip, when to my horror, I watched Howard steal a knit ski cap. He picked up the cap, pulled the price tag off, and stuffed it in the pocket of his ski jacket. In broad daylight; right in front of my eyes! The price tag? Five dollars. I could not speak. I was beyond shocked.

We were spending thousands for this vacation, and he steals a five dollar hat! Is this what having so much money does? What else is wrong with him?

I wanted to run away; to put as much distance as I could between me, him, and his newfound money. But, I couldn't run fast enough or far enough. We still had two more days to go.

When we returned to Miami, I became depressed; despondent. Howard was a tycoon, but he was unravelling, fast. I was struggling to hold my own. My private parties with myself sustained me at nights when, often left alone, I'd play music, sing, dance, and drink.

Drinking became a nightly ritual. While I never got into any real trouble- no arrests for driving under the influence; no public disturbances; no loss of property, or other bad things- it was growing progressively worse.

Truth be told, I had become dependent on alcohol to keep me propped up.

After the skiing incident, another few years passed with increasing episodes of Howard's ever-darkening moods and manic behavior. We tried therapy as a couple, again. It didn't work.

"Tigers don't change their stripes," one psychiatrist told me after a few futile sessions.

I encouraged Howard to get help on his own. He was reluctant at first. When he finally acquiesced, we devised a plan together; in support of him getting 'better'.

At the time, I chose to continue to ignore the gathering influences and outside forces which were beginning to play a heavier role than mine, as his wife and help-mate. I simply attributed most of his mounting troubles and woes to the pressures of running a growing and very successful investment bank. I gave him a lot of room.

Then one day, in 1991, after twenty three years of marriage, Howard presented me with a proposal for a divorce. It was the first time the subject had ever been seriously discussed, despite all we had experienced together.

Why now?

⚜

1991

"Hello, Mrs. Gary, this is Joan Fleishman calling."

It was around 6:00 PM when I got a call from Joan, gossip columnist for the Miami Herald. I'm sure she had another title, but it's what most people in polite company called her. I was preparing dinner when she called, and as was my habit, I had already had a few glasses of wine. I was in a mellow mood despite the circumstances of my life and all of the uncertainties surrounding Howard's mental health condition. I was making it one day at a time.

"Yes?" Howard is not here."

I could not imagine she wanted to talk with me. He had always been the newspaper's target.

No, this time she was calling to talk with me.

"Mrs. Gary, I need to verify some facts for my column

which is scheduled to run tomorrow."

She began to summarize her account of our trip to the Dominican Republic, where me and Howard had gone for a quickie divorce. I saw red.

How did she know? We had been quietly divorced for about three months, but nobody knew. We had not even told the boys.

My breathing stopped as I listened to her spot on recitation of the entire trip.

"Joan, please don't print your article." I softly uttered. I fought back my tears. "Putting that stuff in the paper would damage me and my sons." Empty pleas.

"Well, you and your family are not the target here," she offered, lamely. "But I do have this information I need to verify. I'm only giving you a courtesy call to give you a heads up, and to make sure I have the facts right."

"Where did you get this information?"

"Well, when you filed a law suit against your husband, it became public record, so I called your attorneys. I saw your lawyers having drinks, so I interviewed them."

Oh my God! Our Attorneys had drinks together? Were they laughing at me? They, or no one could imagine how painful the DR episode had been.

Howard and I had walked around the Capital city as if we were ordinary tourists. We shopped, dined, and stayed in the same Hotel room, looking and behaving as if we were still a couple: friends/ lovers; not two people getting a divorce. The divorce itself was a perfunctory procedure; it lasted less than an hour. It was all conduced in Spanish. Hector Montes was our interpreter. I understood only a few of the spoken words.

Who was listening?

The bottom line was we only needed to establish domicile in the DR, and after two days, we received a decree of a legal divorce as citizens of the DR.

We flew back to Miami just as we had flown to the DR, in first class. Our flight class, was the headline of Joan's article. She was intrigued by the status of our travel!

So trivial.

What she, or anyone else, did not know was how Howard's mental health had deteriorated to such a low point, and that he spent the entire return flight curled up, in a fetal position, in my lap whimpering like a wounded puppy.

What did Joan know about our suffering? Didn't she realize I was saving his life? All she wanted was the facts, not the truth of the matter.

"Joan, what's your point?" It was pretty well established by now that Howard was a least favored person with The Herald, which continued to profit from his peccadilloes.

Almost seven years had passed since he had left the City employ as manager, yet Howard's exploits were still selling newspapers.

People love a train wreck.

What Joan's article could not have captured was the abject pain I had endured.

"Please don't publish this", I screamed. *I'm going to look like an idiot.*

The more I begged her, the harder her line was regarding the facts.

"Can you just confirm the facts, Mrs. Gary?"

"I cannot deny the facts. But why is it necessary to write all those details?"

I tried to appeal to her softer side.

"Joan, I am a mother and I need to protect my children. Don't you understand?" "Do you have children"? I cried to no avail.

Alas, she was unmarried with no children, and my arguments were to no avail.

"Bitch", I yelled.

The alcohol was kicking in.

"You can go to hell with your fucking facts." I felt some small satisfaction from cursing her. I slammed the phone down and disconnected her.

I had another glass of wine.

I called her editor, but he too, just wanted the facts. By then it was after 8:00 PM.

Howard called me shortly after I hung up from speaking to the Herald's editor.

"Toni, I just talked with Joan Fleishman. Did she call you?"

"Yes, I tried to get her to back off."

"That's what you get for suing me," he snarled. "You're too stupid to realize all law suits are public." He screamed. "And your attorney is a bitch. She's dumb, and she talks too fucking much."

"Your Attorney talked to Joan too."

"Yeah bitch, but you're the one going to look really bad in the morning," He chuckled.

He never mentioned any concern he might have for our children.

I was desperate, and made one last effort to get the story from running.

I called Dave Lawrence, publisher of the Miami Herald. Dave was relatively new to the community; he had been in Miami for less than a year. But he knew me; primarily, as a community servant and as the executive director of the Miami-Dade College outreach center in Liberty City. I had his cell number.

"Hello Dave, this is Toni Gary. Sorry to bother you but this is really important."

"Toni, I'll call you back when I finish dinner." It was almost nine o'clock by this time.

Dave, a man of his word, called me 45 minutes later. After hearing my plea, he said he'd call his editor. He called back more than an hour later.

"I'm sorry, but there is nothing I can do. I just talked with the editor, and unfortunately, it's after ten. The presses have already run. I checked to verify the facts; I agree Joan's column might be considered damaging to you and the boys."

I was crying softly as he tried to console me with some small talk.

"How old are the boys now? How are they doing in school?"

I tried to tune him out. I did not care if he cared. Interestingly, I continued to have the same conversation with Dave over the next twenty years.

"How are the boys?" He'd sincerely ask. *As if he was somehow responsible for them being okay.* I continued to assure him they were fine, relieving him of any responsibility. I did not want to feel tied to his sense of largess; his expressions of some small interest in them were just small. He had a job to do, and it was all I expected of him, ever.

I had another glass of wine and went to bed, defeated.

The gossip column appeared in the next day's paper. My phone started to ring early that morning.

"Joan should be ashamed of herself. Her story went beyond the boundaries, even for her." One friend was astounded.

"It was totally unnecessary to print all those details. Why did she need to put all those details in the paper? It was nobody's business what you and Howard did in the Dominican Republic." Another friend commiserated.

"Joan is vicious. I'm going to write a letter in protest." A sympathetic friend offered in support.

Joan Fleishman was a popular gossip columnist for many years; she remains one of only a handful of persons I've ever hated, a strong feeling and word for me.

Why did I sue Howard?

Let me count the reasons: For one, he was trying to get away with living a double life, at my expense.

Then, he was no longer attempting to hide his relationship with his Joyce.

And on top of that, he was keeping house with her and their son, and living between two and half places: my house, her house and 'our' condo.

His 'breakdown' was in large measure the result of him finally losing control. He became delusional.

"YOU SPEAK SPANISH DON'T YOU, MRS. GARY?" RICHARD Burton (yes, his real name), Howard's Attorney asked me.

The question came from out of nowhere. I was being deposed as part of my law suit against Howard. I had been unsuccessful in my attempts to negotiate a settlement. It was now four years after our quickie divorce in the Dominican Republic.

"Yes, I speak a little Spanish," I admitted.

"And isn't it true you can also read Spanish?"

My Attorney's raised eyebrow signaled trouble.

"Well, my speaking is better than my reading," I allowed.

Richard leaned across the conference table, shrinking the small space between us. "In fact, you studied Spanish in High School and College, right?" I began to sweat. I swallowed hard and a familiar fear rose around my heart, squeezing my breath into a thin exhalation.

Oh shit! This is a trap! Not feeling so clever about my old habits, anymore.

Howard had 'one-upped' again.

Yes, I knew a little Spanish. Just like my aunt, my grandmother, and her mother before her. I knew enough to survive. Enough to get along with the ever increasing number of Cubans in Miami. Enough to hold polite cocktail conversation and chatter about small matters.

But not enough to read and understand a divorce decree.

Richard's badgering sent me back to the immediate circumstances surrounding my agreement to go along with Howard's request for a divorce.

I had only agreed to take the first class flight to the Dominican

Republic, and to sign the agreement Howard pushed on me because it was supposed to be temporary!

Yes, there were those thirteen items on his list: some division of property, visitation rights; some cash, etc.

I simply did not have time to read, let alone understand the divorce documents. Nor did I get my own interpreter. It was an urgent matter to get accomplished as soon as practicable.

Howard needed me to help him get better. I was being a good wife!

Besides, we had Hector.

Hector, as well as his wife and two children were our friends. He was Puerto Rican by birth, and fluent in Spanish. Hector was Howard's number two in his investment banking firm. *He was a trusted ally. Wasn't he?*

Hector joined us in the DR for our quickie divorce. He served as our interpreter through customs at the airport; helped us check into the hotel, ordered our meals, and squired us around town.

He stood with us both, and made sure we understood what the judge was saying.

I had an interpreter. We had an interpreter.

Alas, shortly after our divorce, Hector was jailed for stealing more than a half million dollars from Howard Gary and Company and, for performing other illegal transactions.

Later, I wondered, just what was Hector translating?

No, mine wasn't just a dissolution of marriage. My divorce couldn't be so simple. That would never do, for me.

My motives? I was on a rescue mission! A mission of mercy to save Howard's life.

Before we flew to the DR, Howard approached me one day

with what sounded like an earnest plea:

"Baby", he still called me baby, "my doctor told me I can't get better if I stayed in the house with you and the boys, and I need to live alone for a while."

I would not argue with 'the doctor'. I was desperate for my husband and the children's father to get healthy again. I would have agreed to anything he proposed at this point.

"I'm going to move into the condo, and visit you and the boys. It will be temporary; no more than six months."

Howard and I had purchased a two bedroom, two bath condo, at auction, at a great price. It was on Biscayne Bay, near downtown. We talked about using it as our in-town 'get-away'. I had so looked forward to saying there, but it would be another three years before I even set foot in the place.

No one knew it, but he had suffered a complete breakdown two months before the divorce. He had also had a short hospitalization in a psychiatric facility.

As part of his treatment, Howard proposed we divorce, and then remarry after six months. His psychiatric treatment included daily visits to the doctor. I was prohibited from asking his doctor about the recommended course of treatment. The plan sounded reasonable to me.

Truthfully, I needed a break from him too.

So what if I could read, speak and write a little Spanish?

Snapped back to the cold reality of the deposition, as Richard Burton continued to lean in to me, I felt my mind slip into another gear: I was entering into the final days of Toni Gary. But then again, Antonia didn't come back for still a little while longer.

❧ 17 ❧

WHEN MADNESS COMES HOME

TONI, JUST READ AND SIGN THIS." HOWARD'S HANDS WERE shaking as he handed me a carefully typed list of about thirteen items. There was some property distribution; I got the family home, a monthly stipend of cash, and other conditions for our separation.

"What do I need this for?" I looked it over, but I did not study the list.

"It's just temporary, but just in case something happens to me while I'm in treatment, you'll be covered. And when I'm better, we will remarry."

Howard and I made a verbal agreement to remarry in six (6) months); he would have free access to the boys, and, he would have an open door to the family home, etc.

That was all fine with me, and thus, I freely accepted the temporary conditions of my quickie divorce for the sake of his sanity. I signed the agreement without hesitation, and needless to say, no legal representation. This took place in November 1991.

Saving Howard's life.

He was very depressed. He cried all the time. He was nervous and agitated to the point of becoming incapable of performing his daily routines, either at home, or at work. Medication was prescribed and he indulged himself with daily psychotherapy sessions, a luxury he could not afford to miss. I was supportive and much relieved when he became amenable to getting help.

I was also relieved I would not have to talk him down from threatening suicide, for a second time.

The first time it happened was at the end of a most bizarre day. We were newly divorced; Howard had moved out of our home. He was living in our condo. He had come over to visit the boys, then fourteen and nine, and to collect a few additional personal items and some furnishings, pieces of art, and objects from the house I agreed he could have.

"I want the condo to feel more like home, and I want to surprise you when you come over to see how I decorated it."

Something was terribly wrong. I followed him out to his car which was loaded with items for the condo.

"How is your therapy going? Did your doctor given you a date when you can move back in yet?" He had only been 'gone' for a few weeks, but it felt much longer. The boys were beginning to ask about when their dad was coming back.

How long before we 'remarried?

Howard reached into the glove box and took out his gun.

Oh no! Why did I have to open up that can of worms? I didn't mean to upset him. He's still so fragile.

He stood in front of the car door. He began to cry, quietly. He waved the gun and started blabbing.

"You and the boys will be better off if I was dead."

I have always performed well under pressure, so I immediately went into my 'reasonable self' mode.

"Howard that's not true. The boys need you to be alive. I need you to stay alive, and to get better."

Damn!

I did not have a cell phone, and I was afraid to leave him alone to go inside to call 911. The scene was quiet; we were whispering, so it did not attract the attention of any neighbors. It looked rather ordinary. Just the two of us talking outside the house.

We remained standing outside his car door for what felt like eternity. I continued to beg and plead for him to give me the gun, to please stop his threats.

How I could raise an alarm to get someone else to intervene. But who?

The boys were inside playing video games and I did not want them to see what was happening.

Where is Bob now when I needed him?

God bless Bob Worsham, my beloved neighbor and friend. He had helped me in so many ways before. He was a retired motorcycle police officer; a self- described good old white boy, from Georgia, who, years before, took his time to help me understand what Howard was up against when he took on Chief Harms and the 'motors'.

"Toni," he had explained, "you have to understand there has always been a long-standing, and deeply embedded culture in the 'motors'. It's considered an elite group within police departments, but there are lost in their old ways."

Bob was a wise man, and on several occasions, he helped counsel my boys.

After what felt like hours, Howard finally quieted down and assured me he would call his psychiatrist as soon as he arrived back at the condo. He slowly drove off, and I ran into the house to call his doctor. Thankfully, the psychiatrist took my call.

"He's got a gun and he threatened to kill himself." I relayed what had just happened. I silently prayed for Howard to make it to the condo, alive.

A few minutes later, the phone rang. I jumped on it, thinking it was the doctor calling with a report.

It was Howard.

"I made it home. I talked with my doctor. I'm ok." Howard assured me. All I wanted was for him to be okay, to return back to us. Back to our crazy normal.

Within a few weeks of this episode, Howard's doctor and I worked in tandem to convince him he needed hospitalization. It was a tough decision. His insurance would have covered an extended stay, but he only remained at Larkins Hospital, South Miami for just a week. It was a very private facility. I took him photos of the children and myself, and a few other comforts from home which were allowed by the Hospital. I visited every day.

Yes, we were divorced, but it was only an inconvenient,

temporary, way-station. We still behaved as if we were in a committed relationship. As far as I was concerned, we were.

On hindsight, I wish he had stayed hospitalized longer than one week.

I admit I was more than a little crazy myself. What was my motivation? Partly I was glad for his diminished mental capacity. I sincerely thought once he was 'fixed'; after the psychiatric cure put him back together, we would be able to start over. I was a confirmed believer and practitioner of the art and science of mental health, and I had long harbored a wish for Howard to get 'help'. I was finally getting my wish.

So, I went along with all his proposals: to live separately, to date, to remarry in six months, to visit the boys, etc. I even agreed to have sex with him, feeling at the time it was in his best interest to get well first, and to deal with the relationship issue second. I fully expected everything would return to 'normal' in six months, per our agreement.

We even went shopping for a recommitment ring. This time, I wanted a big stone. I found the perfect one and Howard did not flinch at seeing the price tag: $40,000.

I had read about his profits. Within two years after opening his business, Howard's company was listed in Black Enterprise. It was featured in the annual listing of the magazine's top black-owned businesses: Howard Gary and Company.at number *twelve* of twelve. The next year: number six of twelve, then, number three!

He had opened seven different offices around the country. I saw them listed on his business card.

I never got the ring. Actually, I refused to accept his

proposal. Instead, I filed a suit against Howard a few months after the quickie divorce when I woke up one morning and realized it was all a ruse, and his marriage proposals had nothing to do with his recovery.

※

"TONI, LISTEN TO THIS."

Howard established a pattern of appearing at our home at about the same time every afternoon to get his mail. He still had free access to the boys, and we were still sharing some business matters, and a lot of his mail was still being delivered to our house.

He proceeded to read out loud from a letter addressed to him:

Dear Friend,

Please be careful about sleeping with your wife because she sleeps with other men and probably has a STD." Use protection if you have sex with her."

Signed,

Your secret Friend

I felt as if cold water had been injected into my veins! First, the accusations were not true: *Who was this secret friend who was so concerned about Howard? The letter was perfectly typed. The envelope showed it had been mailed from a nearby post office. There's no return address.*

"Howard, do you know who sent this?

"No, I thought you might know."

"None of my friends would send this. Do you think it was Joyce?"

Silence.

Yes, he was crazy alright; like a fox.

I had already filed the suit against him.

Two or three additional letters with similar messages came over the next three weeks. Same scenario. He would show me the letter which was addressed to him, and then he would read it out loud. Each contained an ominous message about some 'misbehavior' of mine and then give him some advice to take precautions against me.

One of the letters included a long list of the names of men with whom I presumably had had affairs. None were true; some were laughable.

By the fourth letter, I decided to focus on the tone, the neat typing, and the post office stamp from a facility located in Howard's office zip code. I nearly fainted when, in clear recognition, I realized Howard had written the letters to himself, and he wanted me to hear him read them out loud.

What kind of new madness was this? What is he doing?

It suddenly dawned on me. Howard was fighting back against my legal action against him. I had demanded full financial disclosure. He was making a lot of money as an investment banker, and he was trying to short change me.

His new trick to intimidate me won't work this time.

The final straw was when his secret friend sent a letter addressed to me. There was no note inside, only a copy of the news account of the murder-suicide of a recently retired black police major who had killed his girlfriend, then himself, because she had tried to leave him. I made copies of the letter and sent one to my attorney.

Howard just made a direct threat against me.

I called his psychiatrist.

"Dr. Cohen, you better talk to your patient and have him stop this craziness. And, you may want to consider tweaking his medications, 'cause what you're giving him isn't working anymore. Tell him if he doesn't stop, I'm filing a police report."

The letters stopped coming, but the fight ratcheted up. Howard had thrown the gauntlet.

Suing Howard took its toll.

"I have already paid you all over $40k, and you need another $30 thousand to finalize the settlement?

"Don't worry, Mrs. Gary. When you win, Howard will have to pay all the settlement costs, including our fees."

I didn't feel like a winner.

Also, it was intolerable knowing mine and Howard's attorneys had shared drinks, and maybe a laugh or two over our case, and one of them may have called the gossip columnist Joan Fleishman. It is still disputed about which one, even though Howard accused my attorney of making the call.

I decided to change attorneys after a very expensive, nearly three year protracted battle left me exhausted, and broke. I was at one of the lowest points in my life.

I drank at the mess. A lot.

The year 1994: more than ten years after my former business partner, Joyce Knox's fateful Saturday morning pit stop telling me she was not the one. I was finally ready to learn all I could about Howard and his Joyce.

I thought I could face the messy truth, all at once. Here are the facts: Howard and Joyce had a son, Jordan, who was nearly four years old by the time of our quickie divorce in 1991.

Wow, they have spent all those years having an affair? Since 1983? Longer?

I did some math. He had taken my family skiing during the spring break in April, 1987; I had had my last abortion the preceding January, just four months before Jordan was born; the same April. And oh yeah, that first-class ski resort had been Howard and Joyce's annual excursion. For how long? Long.

Who was this woman? The bitch not only wanted my man, she wanted my life. Where should I begin? I know. I'll ask Francena. She will tell me everything I wanted to know about this Joyce!

I had grown to trust Francena Culmer with my most intimate secrets. I thought first of her if I ever needed help to plan a loved one's funeral. She had gone to work for the City of Miami before Howard was fired.

When we first met in 1976, Francena was the 'director' of her division. She was always beautifully coifed, manicured, pedicured, dressed in sophisticated business attire, and perfectly made up. At the time, I was seven months pregnant with Kito, and I had gotten fat. She was my role model for what I wanted to look like, and be like, after I delivered my baby. We remained close friends for the rest of her life. I could share anything with her.

It broke my heart to see her suffer from a bad marriage, and to lose her health in the aftermath. She died at a young age of 50; I still mourn her passing.

One of my fondest memories of Francena is from one

occasion, when I was five months pregnant with Issa, and Kito was nearly five.

Francena was attending a business meeting of about a dozen other women at my house when my neighbor rang the front door bell.

"You need to come with me. Bullet bit Kito." Ellie Worhsam whispered very softly.

Ellie and Bob Worsham, and their two daughters lived across the street. They were babysitting Kito during my meeting. They were always good neighbors. Bullet was their German shepherd puppy.

"I'm so sorry I have to leave, but Francena, can you take over the meeting for me? I'll return as soon as possible."

It was raining. I put on my raincoat and hurried out the door with Ellie.

I returned three hours later. Francena had remained at the house.

"How did the meeting go?"

"How could you be so calm and leave me here to conduct a meeting when a bullet hit Kito?" She screamed.

Perplexed, she looked at me, then at Kito who came in with me.

"There was no discussion after you left," she continued. "Everybody thought you were crazy to think we could do anything after hearing something like that." Apparently, all the women heard the same thing.

"Oh, no. No, Francena," I shook my head and soothingly said to her. "Bullet is a dog. Bullet bit Kito."

I was exhausted, and thankful the razor-like cut on Kito's

lip was precisely stitched by a pediatric plastic surgeon who just happened to be on call in the emergency room when we came it.

Kito's face appeared to be split in half when I first saw him sitting on Ellie and Bob's kitchen counter. By the time I got across the street, they had wiped up all the blood and had stripped off his shirt in an attempt to minimize the shock for me. Bullet was just a puppy, but he had thin, razor-sharp teeth. He and Kito had been playing, kissing one another. Kito's four year old flesh was so tender. I nearly fainted when I saw him.

Francena and I continued talking about the incident for a few more minutes when we realized the house had grown quiet. Kito was missing! We found him leaning over the toilet in the powder room, looking into the bowl. Horrified, I saw he had pulled out four to five stitches. I screamed in alarm and called the ER. The doctor immediately returned my call.

"Don't worry, Mrs. Gary. I'm trained to put extra stitches in children for the same reason-they pull them out. Kito's lip would be fine."

Relieved, I put Kito to bed. He was still traumatized, but he fell to sleep right away.

"I don't' know how you do it," Francena was engaged to be married and she wanted a family.

"I don't think I can have children and go through anything like this."

We laughed. This incident brought us even closer.

I was comforted by my friendship with Francena, and I felt safe turning to her to tell me all of the truth she knew about Howard and Joyce.

I chose a Friday evening. Francena lived in the southern suburbs of Miami; a twenty minute drive from my house. I took a bottle of Jack Daniels with me. I needed to drink as much as I could to get through the ordeal.

Immediately after arriving, I poured a stiff drink; on the rocks.

"Francena, tell me everything," I demanded. I don't know why, but I thought if I drank the whiskey, I could use my impairment to motivate her to tell me more about what was already common knowledge at City Hall. Insane.

"Have you met her? What does she look like?"

"Well, she does look like you, only a little lighter. I see her all the time. She doesn't work at City Hall, but she comes all the time. You've met her too, you just didn't know who she was."

"Where would I have met her?"

"She would go to all the concerts and other events where you and Howard went."

"Everyone at City Hall thinks she's crazy. She didn't try to hide her pregnancy, and she even brought the baby to Howard's office."

"You must think I'm really pitiful," I cried in my drink.

"No." She was so kind. "Everybody knows you loved Howard."

Hearing what she said, I cried even harder.

"Are you sure you are ok to drive home?" "You know you can sleep here."

"I'm fine," I insisted. I knew her marriage was not going so well. "I'm so sorry I worried you."

I picked up my bottle.

More than half gone. I know I was carried home on the wings of angels that night. I drove in my first blackout. Not my last.

While I was at her home, Francena also confirmed what I had recently heard: Howard's other woman was a member of the Junior League, and we had very likely attended some of the same meetings. We had not.

I searched for her photo in the League handbook: *There she is. Not much to tell from the handbook photo. Does she really look like me? Not from the picture. How did she get into my club, anyway? Wasn't it enough she and I were sharing my husband? What else does she want?*

I was mad.

I had been invited to join the Junior League in 1986 when it was mostly white, Anglo Saxon, protestant; albeit, there were a few Jewish women, and some Hispanics, but it was overwhelmingly WASP. That profile was way behind other parts of the country where Leagues had black members.

My candidacy was part of a well-planned strategy to open the membership of the Miami Junior League to women of color.

Two other black women were voted in with me: Irma Claxton- Scruggs, and Marcia Hope.

"Toni, I hope you realize how difficult this has been for us to get enough members to sign on so you all can have a sponsor and co-sponsor." Claudia Kitchens, who led the initiative told me it required thirty members to get three of us approved.

Marcia moved to Orlando shortly after induction, and Irma did not complete her provisional requirements. Which left me, the one and only black member. I took full advantage. One of the privileges of membership was I got greater access to the power structure in Miami. I was ego-tripping for sure. I was very active, even serving as an officer for two years.

And here comes this Joyce Nunez Bell woman. The nerve! The balls! The #$%&@! And, she had gotten around the system!

Admittedly, The League was not for everyone. It required a tremendous amount of service hours, and black women had their sororities, church groups, The Links, Inc., Jack and Jill, and other well-established service organizations, which historically, were far more appealing to them than the Junior League. Several years after joining the League, I was asked to lead an initiative to expand the number of black members. This second cohort of black women were recruited at a reception I hosted in my home. More than thirty woman accepted my invitation, and at least a dozen became members after hearing about the mission of the League, and the requirements for membership.

So, how did Joyce, another black woman, get into 'my' club? How did she get around me, the pioneer, and an officer?

I came out of my mind: *After twenty three years of marriage; two children; two abortions; coming to terms about Howard's first outside child; now a second; several STD's, including Herpes II-the one which keeps on giving; constant public humiliation; estrangement from my own family, etc., and now this insult.*

For years, I had been riding on a pretty high horse.

I don't have time for such a petty consideration as another woman. She's of no consequence to me. She is certainly not of my ilk; not a member of any of my clubs, or civic/social societies, so certainly, she doesn't matter.

I felt justified in my mounting seething anger. I felt so alone.

Someone had invited her to join the League as a Hispanic! I laughed when I heard that because when I first confronted him about her, Howard told me Joyce Nunez Bell was just another 'nigger' to him.

Joyce Nunez Bell was from Honduras, a small Spanish-speaking, Central American country. Mr. Bell, her first husband, was a black man, and she looked like me!

I set out to learn more, and the more I found out about her, the angrier I got. I still wasn't sure how or where to direct my anger: I did not return to cutting myself; my skin flare ups were arrested; but, a bottle of Jack Daniels sure helped.

I was determined to get additional information about Joyce, but I didn't have to wait too long. She presented herself to me at, of all places, the Junior League headquarters.

On this particular evening, I had arrived too early for a committee meeting, so I went to the kitchen to help set up for coffee, etc.

When I came back into meeting space, I saw her. Unmistakable: the other woman.

Oh my God, she does look like me.

I pivoted and went back into the kitchen. I needed to compose myself.

What should I do? I can't leave. I'm a veteran Leaguer, and a leader. The others will be looking at me for direction during the meeting. After five years, I know how the League does business. I thought I had read all the members named on the committee. I usually do my homework. What happened?

I sat down at the seat where I had already placed my bag and notebook. Joyce Nunez Bell took a seat right next to me.

This is much too close.

Her long hair fell beyond her shoulders. Mine was a little shorter. Her make-up was nicely done; my lips were redder. Her dress was tasteful, but no match for my style. Was she wearing perfume? I didn't notice. Why is she smiling at me?

"Hello." She looked me straight in my eyes.

"Hello." I put on my best poker face.

What now? What is she doing here? This is supposed to be a very select group of members appointed by the League President to work on a special project. This must be some kind of conspiracy. Did the League President deliberately put her on this committee?

I couldn't quiet the riot going on in my head. Paranoid, my internal screams of doubt and suspicion collided.

"What do you think Antonia?" The committee chair interrupted my momentary flight from reality.

Antonia, just keep your eyes on the committee chair and the other members. Do not look at Joyce Nunez Bell.

I don't remember what I said, but it must have made sense. I was on auto-speak.

"I agree with Antonia", or "I think what Antonia said is the way we should go," Joyce Nunez Bell repeated throughout the meeting.

I felt like I was hovering above the scene; watching her looking at me. The League members were unaware of the dance Joyce Nunez Bell and I were performing. I wasn't sure to what tune I was supposed to move.

This feels like a slow drag with the worst dancer.

"We need to talk," I said to her face after the meeting adjourned.

"Yes, we do," she continued in agreement. She gazed straight back into my face.

Gosh. We're still speaking in our Junior League voices!

I gathered my bag and League folder and left the room.

Unwavering, she followed me.

Outside, we stood next to our cars which were parked close together on the street.

"I have always admired you and wanted to be like you," Joyce Nunez Bell pronounced without any hesitation.

I was speechless. My playbook was empty. I flashbacked to when I was still a newlywed, and Howard told me I couldn't fight my way out of a paper bag. He was right. I yearned for a comeback, but there was nothing in my background, or any of my experiences, to have prepared me for this moment.

I finally blathered something about how Howard had hurt me. She agreed. She was hurt too.

Whoa! Who is the offended party here?

"I have to get home to the boys," I lamely excused myself, to which she retorted, "Yes, my son is waiting for me too."

Oh my God! Did she just say that? My silent scream pounded inside my head.

I had left Howard 'babysitting' at my house. He still had the privilege of seeing our sons at any time. His visit had been pre-arranged.

I bet he knew about her going to the League meeting. Did he know how she planned to get in my face?

꧁꧂

I STOPPED ON MY WAY HOME AND BOUGHT SOME LIQUID courage and I immediately started drinking from my six pack. Driving under the influence would become a regular habit for the next five years, but I never got a DUI.

By the time I arrived at home, I had consumed half the cans of beer.

For the next two hours, I acted out on all my accumulated anger and bewilderment, and the multitude of resentments I'd built up against Howard, and now Joyce Nunez Bell, and this sorry situation I was in.

Pop! The can was nice and cold.

What next, Antonia?

Then I spotted the hated object. It was a cocktail table I had grown to loathe. I simply had kept it too long. *Like this lousy, sick relationship.*

The table had three glass panels. I took my time carefully removing them, one by one. I set them aside. I looked around. I was breathing heavily. I grew more anxious to do something. Howard sat still and watched me pace the room.

I need something. What? There it is. The perfect instrument for damage and destruction: Issa's Louisville slugger.

It was standing in the umbrella stand by the door. Aunt Lorraine's husband, Uncle Walter, had given it to him for his ninth birthday.

I raised the bat and swung. Hard.

Whack!

"How could you let that bitch come up in my face?" I screamed at Howard. He sat frozen in place on the sofa.

Whack!

"You had better keep her away from me."

Whack!

"She is stalking me."

Whack!

"The bitch had the nerve to tell me she wanted to be like me. Does that include taking everything that's mine?"

"I told you she's just another nigger", Howard uttered, weakly. "She can't touch you", he resorted to his default compliment. It had worked for years, but now I was deaf to his empty utterances.

I continued to beat the table until it, and the bat were left in splinters. My strikes were so forceful my hand got very badly contused. The rush of adrenalin began to mix with the beer, and I looked around for more things to wreck.

Howard hadn't moved.

Pop!

Another beer. I went into the kitchen and surveyed the cabinets.

I proceeded to pull out precisely twenty three plates and saucers. Each one was badly chipped, mix-matched, or of no other value since they had outlived their usefulness-like our marriage. Until tonight.

I went out the back door. It faced the alley which ran between mine and my neighbor's house. Howard followed me, but he stayed inside. By now it was nearly eleven in the evening; still early in my mounting rage. I was just gearing up.

Smash!

"One two, three," I counted out as I smashed the plates, one by one. Howard watched through the screen on the door.

I had gotten up to number eighteen.

"Stop making that noise," Meri shouted from her upstairs window next door. Meri, a Persian-born aristocrat, always wore an air of superiority, but she had been a good neighbor.

"Don't worry Meri," I apologized for disturbing her rest, "I only have five more to go."

"Nineteen." "Twenty." "Twenty one." "Twenty two." "Twenty three fucking years of marriage," I shouted and then calmly headed back inside.

Howard had not uttered a sound during my tirade, except when he tried to assuage my feelings by calling Joyce a nigger.

Too little, much too late. Besides, my being a nigger wasn't so bad on a night like this.

Sated, I demanded Howard help me take the table, beaten into splinters, across the street to the curb for the trash collection.

I had not felt such a level of rage since the first time my mom forcibly gave me an enema when I was three, or that time in boarding school when I cursed the nuns.

All these years later, I found how easy it was to release my anger from the contents of a bottle of wine, whiskey and/or beer.

I had crossed the line.

Pop!

While I was drinking my last beer, Howard quietly left me in my own stew.

The next morning, the boys spotted the table out on the curb as we were leaving to drive to their respective schools.

"You know, some poor person could have used that table", Issa's words slid out softly from under his breath.

"Humph", Kito grunted in agreement.

I smiled. I always liked Issa's line of thinking.

"Baby, I'm so sorry I broke your bat. Maybe Uncle Walter can get you a new one," I was ashamed. Issa didn't answer. He was young. He was fragile. The divorce proceedings and aftermath was beginning to take its toll on all of us.

It would take years before I would win back his trust.

"Why didn't you whack Howard with the bat, instead of the table?" Aunt Doris asked. It was a few days later and I couldn't hide the terrible black and blue bruising on my hand. Actually, I could not use my hand for over a week.

"Aunt Doris, I couldn't bear the thought of killing my babies' daddy in their own home."

We chuckled, but I knew she was dead serious. So was I.

Just how crazy is crazy? Howard and I both have had our respective crises and subsequent diagnoses.

For a long time, I always maintained I had to be a little crazy to stay married to Howard. I constantly fell in and out of love with him. Hell, I was in love with love. I bought into the whole thing, and I became addicted to the love/loss cycle. It took half my lifetime to get cured. I was also becoming addicted to alcohol. How could I enjoy one without the other?

The conditions mixed well together: love, lost, drown the sorrow; repeat until.

I had it bad. One day, before Howard became City Manager, I was walking down the main street in downtown Miami on my lunch hour, when I spotted a very attractive man coming toward me. The attraction was in his walk, in the tilt of his head, in the cut of his suit. There was a magnetism emanating from his entire body. I felt flush with excitement and embarrassment at my open smile and obvious flirtation. He smiled back at me. When we finally met up, face to face, he scooped me into his arms.

"You act like you didn't know it was me." He half lifted me off my feet in a full body hug.

"I don't have my glasses on, so I didn't recognize you until a few feet ago." I was grinning like a school girl.

"Who did you think you were smiling at?"

"A really good looking man, and I'm so glad I'm married to him."

We both laughed.

It was like that off and on, for years. I'd look at Howard and fall in love all over again, and again. He demonstrated varying degrees of affection toward me too. We became equally adept at holding one another hostage. Over the years, we made a regular practice of surveying one another about any interest in divorcing, and we both said "no" each time the question came up. Neither of us took the first step until outside influences began to take on greater impact. For me, I had established my firm commitment to stay put in the marriage until death parted us, and I had voted with my feet time and again.

The year before the actual divorce was the first time I made a move to physically separate from Howard. I had begun to look around for places, and a very good friend, Rev. Linnea Pearson, offered me the use of her condo on the ocean, in South Beach.

"I'll be travelling the whole summer, so you can have it for three months." Linnea knew I was preparing to leave my husband, but I wasn't yet ready to file for a divorce.

When I went to get settled in, Linnea had a bottle of wine, a piece of cheese, some fruit, and a wonderful note of welcome. I cried at the beauty of the surroundings, and the possibilities. But when I thought about my boys, a dark curtain of loneliness spread over the sun and surf. I went home. I had paid for the entire summer, but I never spent one night in the place. I did, however, enjoy the feeling of having a choice.

I played with those keys all summer.

18

MADDER THAN A JUNK YARD DOG

HERE I AM, IN THERAPY AGAIN.

It was in the mid-seventies when we were living in Newark, New Jersey.

"So tell me Mrs. Gary, about why you spent so much time in the kitchen?

I used to like to experiment with recipes, and I had collected a pretty interesting assortment of cook books. I called on everyone whose specialty I had tasted, and which I wanted to duplicate. I was chastened and humbled by my chocolate cake debacle in Bermuda; it took me years before I attempted to bake another cake. Everything else was on my agenda.

I was ambitious.

First up: lemon chiffon pie.

For that, I called Mrs. Minnis, the best dessert maker I knew. She was a seasonal boarder at my dad's Aunt Aurelia and her daughter Mena in their New York apartment. On my weekend visits from Marymount, she would always have some scrumptious dessert waiting for me. Her pies were outrageously delicious.

We were living in New Jersey when, I called Mrs. Minnis for her expert guidance on making a lemon chiffon pie. It was five years into the marriage. I was trying, again, to surprise Howard with a pleasing treat. I was eager to add more desserts to my repertoire, and so far only included banana pudding. Hint to the wise: only use Nabisco Nilla Vanilla wafers.

Mrs. Minnis was well into her 80s, but still sharp. She walked me through her recipe. I first had to go buy the ingredients from her list. Back home, items at the ready, I called her on the phone and followed her instructions, step-by-step. After nearly an hour of blending, mixing, and whipping, she said, "Now fold the filling into the crust."

"What crust?" I swallowed hard.

I don't have a pie crust! Wait. I don't know how to make a pie crust. I had fixated on the filling.

She chuckled. "Baby you never made a crust?"

"No."

All this work and I'm going to have to trash it. It had taken me a whole hour on the phone with Mrs. Minnis.

She laughed. "Don't panic."

"Right." I said, in a panic.

"No, baby, a crust is simple and quick." She was so patient and kind. I believed her.

I had all the ingredients: flour, shortening, etc.

"Mrs. Minnis, I don't have a rolling pin", I began to laugh through my tears.

Story of my life. If only I had the right amount of everything I needed.

Once we both recovered from another spasm of laughter, Mrs. Minnis and I agreed a large Pepsi bottle would work, and that's what I used to roll out the crust. The dough fell into an ugly group of pieces I molded and mashed together in the bottom of the pie pan. I pinched the outer edges. I flashed back to the chocolate cake nightmare: *at least this one will look gorgeous.*

I poured the filling into the pan lined with those jagged pieces of crust.

So far, so good. Out of sight; out of mind. A lot like this marriage.

I placed the pie in the middle of the pre-heated oven.

Howard arrived home before the pie had finished baking. "You can smell that from the elevator," he shouted in gleeful anticipation. The aroma was good, at once signaling the merits and promise of the final product. He had grown used to my experimentations by now: some were good, some great, and a few, not so good.

"Is it done yet?"

"No, Howard, it'll take another twenty to thirty minutes."

Almost thirty minutes later, the timer indicated the baking time was complete. I looked and saw the crust had started to brown. Done! We had diner while the pie cooled. I cut the first slice.

It's not done in the middle!

I cut a second serving. Since a large portion in the deepest part of the dish never cooked, and portions around the edges had already browned, I avoided the middle and carved out a serving close to the edges. It was not pretty.

The problem? The oven, like me, was untested.

I cried, again.

I did a lot of crying during those dark days in Newark, but Howard seemed pleased with what he ate.

After that disaster, I abandoned pie baking. Years later, after we moved to Miami, I added other delicacies to my dessert portfolio, where my baked goods were featured at my annual champagne and dessert 'not quite New Year's Eve parties. Howard missed most of those.

While in Newark, some of my disastrous experiments went beyond any laughing matter.

One day, I found a recipe for Hawaiian-style London broil; always one of our favorite cut of meats. I labored over the recipe for hours: slicing, dicing, marinating, and basting before cooking. *Perfect.* Or so I thought.

"I don't like sweet meat." Howard threw the plate against the wall after he took his first bite. He had come home late from the office.

I was still in the forgiving and forgetting stage of our relationship, but I must admit, I was scared Howard really wanted to hit me with the plate. It gave me pause.

I wonder how folks who work around him get treated when he becomes outraged.

But I knew the answer.

One thrown plate, up-close and personal, was enough forewarning for me. I vowed from that day on to avoid putting myself within arm's reach of his outbursts.

It was the first and only outburst toward me for a very long time to come. I managed well. But I paid a very high price, dodging all his anger.

I changed my behavior. I became cautious, emboldening myself only when I felt safe: either in a group of people, usually always in public, and later surrounded with his family members. I knew violent outbursts were part of his MO. He had told me about some of them, and I had actually witnessed a few, but they were always outer directed. The first one I witnessed, nearly a year before we married, was toward his estranged father. It was pure bottled up anger.

His father had been believed dead; there had been no contact for almost twenty years. Howard's brother discovered him alive and well, and living in Coatesville, Pennsylvania, where Harold worked. Harold was eager for Howard, to meet their 'old man'.

"I want you to come with me," Howard implored. He seemed so vulnerable. I could not imagine what it must have felt like to meet your 'dead' father after almost twenty years.

"I think you should have private time without me." I was not eager to be there. I felt tension mounting between the two brothers over the weeks leading up to the trip.

"But I need you with me," Howard insisted. I relented, wondering how I could be helpful. I had no way of knowing or understanding the complexity of this proposed meeting. I was still working out my strained relationship with my own mother.

We scheduled a trip to meet Mr. William Harold Gary, Sr. during one of Howard's infrequent trips to visit me at

Marymount. We were seniors, and unofficially engaged; there was no ring.

"I really don't want to meet the motherfucker, but I want to see what Harold sees in him."

Harold had told their mother about Mr. Gary, Sr. Years later she told me she was never interested in seeing him again, but was pleased how her sons had found their dad.

I went to Pennsylvania to meet up with Howard and his brother. Harold had been working for almost a year at Johnson and Johnson where, for years, their dad had been doing some occasional maintenance work. One day, shortly after starting the job, one of Harold's co-workers pointed out the resemblance between the two men named William Harold Gary.

Howard brooded the entire length of the drive across town in Harold's brand new car.

We were a somber bunch on arrival to Mr. Gary's house. Nancy, Harold's fiancé, was with us.

"Nice to see you son", William Harold, Sr. offered a hug, but Howard pushed him away.

Awkward.

The 'old man' was still quite handsome, but obviously beaten by his drinking career. His home was small, modest, and clean.

"Look, I take care of myself." He cheerfully showed off his freezer full of meat and vegetables.

"Your brother has been good to me, visiting me some." He paid homage to Harold and thanked him for looking out after him.

He offered each of us a quart of beer. We engaged in small talk. Very small.

Howard and I were seated close together on the sofa. The room suddenly started to feel claustrophobic. Howard took only a few sips of his beer. For the duration of the meeting, he held onto one of my hands, and tightly clinched his beer bottle with his other hand. We stayed for less than half hour. No one had time to finish even half their beers. Wasting all that beer was a sore spot for me, even back then.

"Goddamn motherfucker!" Howard shouted to no one in particular. He trembled in fury and flung his beer bottle to the curb with all his might. Harold, Nancy, and I jumped away simultaneously to avoid the flying glass.

The ride back to Harold's apartment was long. Howard cursed his dad (for years of abandonment); his mom (for lying to him about his dad's death); his brother (for taking him to see him), and everything else not holy. We had been dating for nearly four years, and this was the first glimpse I had into that part of Howard's character. I was sympathetic at first.

His anger at his dad was palpable.

I sure hoped he addressed some of his early childhood traumas during his therapy, including 'losing' his dad.

Howard Gary died from lung cancer in 2009, but I think it was all the stuffed down anger that really killed Howard. And the lies. And the subterfuge.

But, I grew angry, too.

AROUND MIDNIGHT, EARLY 1985

I was having a few cocktails and listening to my music. It was probably a recording of <u>Lady in Red,</u> who kept me dancing. My end-of-the day ritual no longer included a cigarette; I had quit my twenty year, two packs a day smoking habit. Just the drink would suffice; alone inside myself, always by myself.

Howard was, once again, out of town.

Boom! It was louder than any thunder clap I'd ever heard.

The boys had been in bed and soundly asleep for several hours when I heard the explosion. The force of the sound had me immobilized. It had me pinned down for a few seconds before I bolted out the chair. I sprinted across the room to get up the stairs to rescue my sons from what I knew must have been a bomb. After all the police escorts and swat team presence in the preceding years, I was prepared for almost anything to happen, anytime. But not this.

I covered the mere 20 feet distance in split seconds. I quickly realized the house was not on fire, but there was a gaping hole where the front door had once stood.

Planks from the original old door, from 1936, with many cracks all over it from its decades of use, were spread across the floor in my path. Bizarrely, the entire bottom half of the door was gone while the top half was still on its hinges. I stood there for a few moments before I started to panic.

Whoever did this just might return to harm me and the boys, this time, for sure?

I ran across the street to get Bob. Good, good old boy, Bob, along with his wife Ellie, had been faithful, true friends, and they were always ready and able to come to my rescue. I knew

Bob would know what to do about the door, and he did. He plied his handy man skills and put up a make-shift, but safe temporary covering to get me through the rest of the night into early morning. Once my door was secured, I tried to rest a little. Amazingly, the boys slept through the entire incident. They were both actively involved in after-school sports teams, and by the end of each day, they literally passed out for 8-9 hours of deep sleep.

I had a new door installed the next day.

"Screech".

A car stopped short in front of my house. It was another late hour. I was home alone, again. I could hear a car motor running, but it was dark. Next, I heard footsteps on the three front steps.

"Thump." A forceful kick to the front door.

It only took a few seconds; too fast for me to see anything.

The new door was a solid piece of unstained wood; it did not budge.

The assailant left a boot print. It made the distinctive pattern of a well-executed side kick. I was, once again, immobilized by a familiar fear and terror.

Nearly a year had passed since the infamous 2:47AM call had been made. I thought the threats and the police gang activities, were over and done. But, apparently, the offended parties were not yet appeased.

I was way beyond the point of anger or resentment against any outsider. These acts of terror made my anger against Howard grow. I left the boot print in plain sight for a long time before I had the door stained. It served as a reminder of how much I resented Howard for leaving me and our sons exposed to the wreckage he created, and all the other mess he left behind for me to paint over.

Coward(s) trying to keep me off balance. Won't work this time.

I had another drink before going to bed.

❧

JANUARY 2:47 AM, 1985

One year to the date after Howard fired Police Chief Kenneth Harms, my home phone rang at precisely 2:47AM. Home alone, again. For a terrifying few seconds, I could only hear the sound of breathing at the other end of the line. I immediately called the new Police Chief, Clarence Dickson.

"Do you want to press charges?" Clarence was the first black police chief and he not only answered my call at that un-Godly hour, but he extended himself to me to call him at any time I needed his support. I was so grateful for his courtesy.

"Press charges? Against whom?" I was resigned to just ride it out.

What else could be done? The target, presumably Howard, was not at home at the time, and he was no longer a City employee.

Chief Dickson had a police detail make regular passes by the house for a few days, but it was nothing like when I had my babysitters.

I seethed at the notion that Howard was off doing whatever, and with whomever he pleased. I had long given up any soft feelings of love or affection for him. I just wanted him to continue doing right by our sons and me. I was demanding only the minimum obligatory motions, which were okay for me at the time. I was still his legal wife, burdened down from tons of expectations, and other detritus from our near twenty year marriage.

I had gotten dulled by the patterns of familiarity, and I had mastered a set of mechanical responses. I had grown numb from being over-exposed to real acts of threat and danger. I was somewhat reconciled knowing I was not the target, but frustrated the target was seldom there.

I grew angrier.

⚜

1991

"Antonia, you were abused," Angela declared. I had read one of Howard's "Dear Secret Friend" letters to her. Angela was a college classmate and one of my best friends while I was at Marymount. She held a Masters in Social Work, specializing in abused women. When she heard the letter, she instantly recognized it as a form of control.

I broke into a cold sweat; my palms got wet.

That stung: an abused woman.

I began to research the subject, and there it was, in black and white: the classic cycle of abuse. I had already lived my whole life with other labels. I had accepted my psychiatric diagnoses and used the 'insanity' defense to help justify so many of my behaviors, but this one was special. Harder to accept. On closer examination, it fit perfectly.

After I recovered from the shock of the truth, and awakened to my new reality, I felt reconciled with my decision to end the relationship, for good.

So there I was, forty-two years old, and I had spent half my life in a marriage mostly of my own making, or unmaking. My stubborn streak and my inflated ego would not let me leave within the first five years as I had once planned. Nor did I leave nine years in, before I started having children. After all the traumas; debasing name-calling; abortions; STDs; multiple betrayals; out-of-wedlock children; risky gamesmanship, and outright mutual contempt, what kept me in this tender trap with Howard? I was constantly falling in and out of love with him, or at least the idea of love. Admittedly, we had both consistently demonstrated a genuine commitment and dedication to the boys, and I did receive many tangible benefits from being Mrs. Howard Gary, which I cannot deny.

Who had I become? Who was I anyway?

I truly believed that over those twenty-three years, and throughout all those adventures, no one could have loved him more. Only God knows how many tried. I never kept count.

Right up to the end, he still came home to me, even though it grew less and less frequent.

I know him; his childhood secrets. We shared something: our minds had almost become like one. But that's not good for me. I'm becoming more like him: calculating, evil, vindictive.

He had become, well, less good.

I (had) loved him 'in a place where there's no space or time'. But, so much reality had been suspended and/or sandwiched in between some awful truths.

EPILOGUE

"No person is your enemy, no person is your friend, everyone is your teacher". Frances Scoval Shinn

It was pretty typical of me to find lyrics from a song to play out my life with Howard Gary. You'll Never Get to Heaven (if you break my heart) became a recurring theme song in my head whenever I chose to forgive him for yet, another slight. So was The Great Pretender sung by The Platters, and whose chorus, "pretending that I'm doing well", often kept my spirit bolstered. And then there was also I've Never Been to Me, styled by the great Nancy Wilson, which gave me hope to move on. Barbra Streisand's rendering of Gotta Move became a long-time favorite when I felt strength I continually failed to act on. There is one line, "gotta find a place, a new place....." which became one of my favorite repeated refrains.

I danced alone with myself on many nights to Lady in Red, once even dressing the part one night in a drunken rage against the world, railing against Howard, and castigating myself for staying too long. The song actually gave me hope I would one day be someone's lady in red. I still keep a red dress or two in my wardrobe at the ready, just in case.

These soul-rescuing lyrics helped me get over, to get along, and to stay in my marriage; on its face, successful, but most times, just painful. By the end, I had perfected the art of living by the dictum: You can get used to anything, including hanging.

I am haunted by a recent revelation of yet another son Howard sired outside our marriage. This information was discovered after Howard died, while our sons were sorting through their father's papers

After calculating his age, this child was probably conceived during our time in Michigan. *Was this the study partner's?* What I know for sure is the baby's mother is white and the child was placed for adoption. I'm not looking for any more verification. Some dogs should remain asleep.

I have never met Nakia's mother, but a few months before Howard died in 2009, I received a note in the mail from her. It was written on pink stationary inside a matching pink envelope. It was addressed to Ms. Antonia Williams-Gary.

In a very nice handwriting, she apologized to me for her role in her affair with Howard. By this time, Howard was on death's door, and we had been divorced for almost 20 years. In her note, Nakia's mother thanked me for being kind to her daughter. *Why not? I liked her, and Nakia had formed a close bond with my sons, her brothers.* I accepted the apology in a returned, hand-written note.

"Mom, you dodged a bullet by not staying married to

daddy," Issa told me shortly after Howard's death. "Don't stress Joyce, or Nakia's mom, or anyone else," he lovingly assured me.

In the end, I know I killed the babies I did in order to keep the babies I had from being killed. Their souls, that is. I felt I had to keep their tender spirits alive amidst so much turmoil. I protected them for as long as I could. I shielded them from revelations about me and their dad I knew would come into sharper light as they became young adults.

Sometimes I didn't get to them in time.

We had only been divorced for a very short time when Howard chose to tell Issa about Jordan and Nakia. He waited until I was out of town on business. Issa was only nine years old.

"Mom, why didn't you tell me I had a little brother and a big sister?" Issa sobbed into the telephone, blaming me for keeping this information from him.

I was in Saratoga, New York, over a thousand miles away. There was no fast or easy flight to get me back to Miami-to rescue my child. Kito was out of town on a trip with the Jack and Jill club.

My anger toward Howard was seething; I was heartbroken for Issa.

How could Howard expose our son to such ugliness without me being there?

Issa's innocence was crushed, and worse, he now doubted me, and questioned my loyalty to him.

"Does Kito know?"

"No, Issa, I have not told Kito."

I continued to try and console him, but no matter what I said to him, Issa could not understand.

How could I hug him through the telephone?

"Mommy, you kept it a secret." Issa cried harder.

This information is his dad's business. He can't possibly understand I was only trying to protect him.

Just when I thought Howard could no longer hurt me, this new affront caused me a pain unlike any other I had suffered, up until then. I had always been determined to protect my sons from any and all harm I could.

My baby was suffering, and I was so far away and now, in this instance, Howard had taken away my privilege, to protect him.

The insult served as a notice to me. *As long as Howard is still on this earth, I cannot afford to lower my vigilant protection of my sons; not until they reached adulthood.* Only time will tell how well I've done in that regard.

Once Kito did find out about Jordan and Nakia, he didn't register much interest in getting to know them, or to bond with them. On the other hand, Issa, embraced them. He had photos of Nakia and Jordan displayed with his other family members in his dorm room during his freshman year at college.

I was divorced, yet still not free. I got a second divorce from the State of Florida in 1994 which set aside the 1991 quickie from the Dominican Republic. I walked away from a protracted fight over money and property. The fight was making me become too much like Howard, and losing any more of myself was not part of any bargain I wanted to make. I calculated my losses. In the end, I'm the one still standing.

Howard was always full of shit of one kind or another. His was a long, hard, and painful battle with colon cancer.

Howard and I had grown at ease with one another by the time of his death. We shared two grandchildren, and were often in the same venue sharing their affections; birthday parties, etc.

Now that both of my sons are parents themselves, they will have many opportunities to write their own stories on the souls of their own children.

৩৯৩

IN THE END, HOWARD LEFT A FAIR AMOUNT OF MONEY AND property to our sons through the distribution of his estate, and for that I'm grateful.

I'm also grateful for the journey I took as Howard's wife. The road we took was filled with holes, detours, no-passing lanes, and many blind spots, but it evened out for me after a long, terrifying, and event-filled ride. I was forced to grow along the way. The alternative was not pretty.

During most of the years of my marriage to Howard, a large part of my salvation and daily acts of rescue came from an assortment of girlfriends. In addition to Casey and Marsha, my lifelines before I returned to Miami, there were so many others.

Decades after we both got our graduate degrees from Rutgers, Marsha painfully revealed how before she even arrived in New Jersey, she had been told some very disparaging things about me and about my marriage by some woman in her home town, Washington, DC, who had advised her to not befriend me, because of Howard.

"But you were just the opposite of what I had been told, and I feel guilty for keeping that information from you for so long."

"Oh, Marsha. It's okay. I feel so badly for you having to live with your secret for all those years."

She did not tell me name of the other woman. I am not interested in knowing.

Once, I almost jeopardized my friendship with Bobby Klein, when I asked her to cover for me one night.

"Bobby, I told Howard I was visiting you, so if he calls, please let him know I had been there."

"Of course, darling. But you better be careful."

I was having a tryst at my club with some man who was flirting with me. I had joined the very toney, private Oak Room while Howard was still the City Manager.

I was curious about men who flirted with me.

Why? I was studying how to play Howard's game; being married and, yet still dallying with others. My 'affairs' were primarily just heavy flirtations. I would not cross the line, again, for a while.

Howard actually called Bobby; looking for me, and she lied to him. I felt badly about putting her into a compromised position. I would never do that again to another friend.

I did, however, learn a few things through these experimental flirtations.

There were a few men who targeted Howard. They started circling around me once it became apparent his days were numbered as City Manager. Like animals in the wild who smelled opportunity, these men showed me their manes and plumage. I liked the attention and had fun, enjoying the attention for a minute, until it became dangerous.

Howard roared back and made sure I was not 'taken' by any of the predators. In fact, only a very few were real. Most were imagined by him, but I have to admit I wanted him to be jealous of whatever he imagined I was doing. I flirted with danger. I did get burned once again. It was another loveless 'sexual' encounter, but this time, once was enough. It was not good. It was another hard lesson I learned late in life.

I hid that side of me from most of my friends. I was not proud of my behavior; I was ashamed of how far down the scale I'd gone, trying to fight Howard by using some of his tactics.

I'd never get to be as good as him, being bad.

Akua was one of a group of girlfriends who helped me celebrate my fortieth birthday. They threw me a surprise party. A few days before the event, she demanded Howard give me a diamond ring in recognition of the milestone. We were still married, but not for much longer. He bought me a ring; a good stone, but a small carat weight. Initially, I wore it as a ring, but after the marriage ended, I had it redesigned into a necklace which I sold a few years later.

And then there is Dianne. Dianne and I were like long-lost sisters who met for the first time late in our lives. Our friendship was immediate; we bonded quickly, and closely. We were both divorcing at about the same time, but under very different circumstances. Hers seemed so much cleaner than mine. She was an attorney, which might have mitigated some of the interminable hearings I had, but I also know she was, and remains, a very private bearer of grief.

Dianne taught me how to stand up under pressure, with grace and beauty.

Dianne enhanced my life in so many ways; she showed me how to endure with dignity. Most importantly, she led me back to the Catholic Church which, for a little while, became a great source of comfort for me during the divorce. I began to read the bible again, and eventually I found a passage which helped me feel at peace about being a divorced Catholic: 1 Corinthians 7:15: I was no longer bound, or bonded. I had abandoned the church in the very early years of my marriage, when I substituted my worship of the God of my childhood and adolescence to worshiping Howard.

I have since increased my religious and spiritual practices beyond the strictures of any church. It is better.

I don't know if Howard ever personally thanked Dianne. It was under her steady hand and professional expertise as the County's bond counsel, that policies for minority inclusion became transparent, and were so well developed, his small, but fast-growing investment banking firm was able to secure several major deals. Howard became wealthy, in part, because of his strong relationships in the ranks of city and county halls across the country, but also because there was a clearly defined road map laid out for firms like his.

Dianne, on behalf of Howard, please accept a belated "thank you."

There were many others about whom I could write volumes; about how they helped save my life.

One day, I tried to do it in person.

The invitation read:

"Yes, there were "footsteps along every step, but God also sent you, precious friend, to help me during my most difficult times. I want to thank you and toast our friendship, Friday, June 27, 1997, in my home at (Miami) The fete will begin at 3:00, but plan to stay and watch the sunset if you'd like."

And they came: my mother; my Aunt Doris; Fanny Chestnut-Hairston, my big sister at Marymount; Marsha Henderson, my graduate school study partner; Regina Jollivette-Frazier, one of my earliest role models; Kaaren Johnson-Street, entrepreneur extraordinaire; Evalina Bestman, my therapist; Bobby Klein, my most 'senior' friend; Jeannie de Quinne, early co-worker; Francena Culmer-Brooks, confidant; Mrs. Leola Ross, my homemaker; Rene Beal, sister/friend; Akua Scott, sister/friend; Dottie Stewart, my banker; Connie Higgins, sister/friend; Lee Damus, one of my business partners; Monique Hunter, my youngest friend; Carolyn Clark, one of my 'babysitters; and, Robbie Bell, my road dog.

Others sent their regrets: Dianne Saulney-Gaines; Brenda Shapiro, my last attorney; Donna Ginn, sister/friend; Arlene Love, my assistant at the college; and Gwen Armstrong Johnson, my earliest childhood friend.

My beloved Aunt Lorraine had died earlier in the year, but she was there, in spirit.

The love and support of all these women is woven throughout these pages.

Another word about Robbie, who, literally, once saved my life.

I had moved to Palm Beach County, where I worked from 2000-2003. Over those three years, Robbie often drove the 150 mile round trip from Miami to West Palm Beach, ostensibly to join me for some social function, but primarily to make sure I was doing okay. Sometimes she would bring Donna Ginn and/or Rene Beal. As if that wasn't enough, she petitioned a prayer posse at her church to pray with and for me over a two-year period. I thought, "she had me under control, and all was right with me'.

Not.

One night during a telephone conversation, Robbie didn't like the way I sounded. She called Dr. Evalina Bestman and urged her to make the 75 mile drive up to Palm Beach to see me, face-to-face. The two of them had conjoined in a life-saving conspiracy. "Thank you," Robbie. "Thank you," Evalina.

There was no way I could lose in my struggle out of the cycle of doubt and despair with this supportive network of loving and caring women.

By all measures, I remained young, and in and out of love, way past the prime of my life, and far beyond the peak of our marriage arc. I pray not to be judged too harshly by my character flaw. I still love 'love', and I'm still 'young at heart'. I now understand that what I was calling love was an attachment to a malignant set of ideas and behaviors which kept me bound by a silk knot, only to have it turn into a leaded weight pulled tightly around my heart. The knot grew hard and heavy before becoming unraveled.

"Congratulations! You've lost 235 pounds, and you look

great," a good friend laughed with me shortly after my divorce. It took me a long time to be able to laugh at my predicament.

The scar tissue has nearly all faded away, softening over time, and I have to search really hard to find the myriad entry points; time heals all wounds, no matter how deep the cuts.

I wrote this story in hopes that it resounds with the "grace of a woman, and not the grief of a child," to quote a line from Comes the Dawn, a poem by Veronica Shoffstall. I cannot claim that that was always the case. I sat on a pity pot for so long, that when I could finally got off, I was handicapped by decades of wasted time and mired down in self-pity. I almost missed my music, and for far too long I had been drowning in pools of fear and doubt, never to die, just to suffer. I was mad as hell because I felt cheated on, cheated out of, or just plain cheated. But I had only cheated myself.

I found another song, Choices, by George Jones with one line in particular to sum up my life, to date:

I've had choices, since the day that I was born
There were voices that told me right from wrong
If I had listened, no I wouldn't be here today
Living and dying with the choices I've made.

Then something wonderful happened to me on my way to the crying bar and the complaint table.

I decided to write a new song for myself.

My name, Antonia, has many meanings: fortress and defender (of her right to just be). Antonia, strong: fortified, and yet vulnerable. "**A**ntonia, **B**raver than a **C**ave bear" as described by Issa in his first grade ABC book. Antonia, standing as her Greek name-sake; standing even after the mounting destructions of life's battles. Still standing as a monument to this, her blues song; a peon to grace; a hymnal of gratitude; a gospel truth of forgiveness and acceptance.

Oh, and I got sober on July 18, 2001.

I got back to a new beginning. I got back to me.

Appendix A

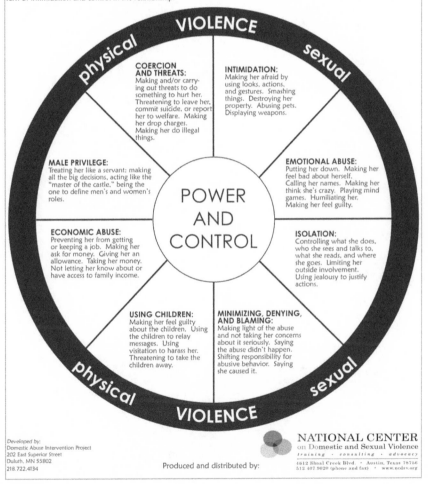

POWER AND CONTROL WHEEL

Physical and sexual assaults, or threats to commit them, are the most apparent forms of domestic violence and are usually the actions that allow others to become aware of the problem. However, regular use of other abusive behaviors by the batterer, when reinforced by one or more acts of physical violence, make up a larger system of abuse. Although physical assaults may occur only once or occasionally, they instill threat of future violent attacks and allow the abuser to take control of the woman's life and circumstances.

The Power & Control diagram is a particularly helpful tool in understanding the overall pattern of abusive and violent behaviors, which are used by a batterer to establish and maintain control over his partner. Very often, one or more violent incidents are accompanied by an array of these other types of abuse. They are less easily identified, yet firmly establish a pattern of intimidation and control in the relationship.

VIOLENCE physical sexual

COERCION AND THREATS: Making and/or carrying out threats to do something to hurt her. Threatening to leave her, commit suicide, or report her to welfare. Making her drop charges. Making her do illegal things.

INTIMIDATION: Making her afraid by using looks, actions, and gestures. Smashing things. Destroying her property. Abusing pets. Displaying weapons.

MALE PRIVILEGE: Treating her like a servant; making all the big decisions, acting like the "master of the castle," being the one to define men's and women's roles.

EMOTIONAL ABUSE: Putting her down. Making her feel bad about herself. Calling her names. Making her think she's crazy. Playing mind games. Humiliating her. Making her feel guilty.

POWER AND CONTROL

ECONOMIC ABUSE: Preventing her from getting or keeping a job. Making her ask for money. Giving her an allowance. Taking her money. Not letting her know about or have access to family income.

ISOLATION: Controlling what she does, who she sees and talks to, what she reads, and where she goes. Limiting her outside involvement. Using jealousy to justify actions.

USING CHILDREN: Making her feel guilty about the children. Using the children to relay messages. Using visitation to harass her. Threatening to take the children away.

MINIMIZING, DENYING, AND BLAMING: Making light of the abuse and not taking her concerns about it seriously. Saying the abuse didn't happen. Shifting responsibility for abusive behavior. Saying she caused it.

physical sexual **VIOLENCE**

Developed by:
Domestic Abuse Intervention Project
202 East Superior Street
Duluth, MN 55802
218.722.4134

Produced and distributed by:

NATIONAL CENTER
on Domestic and Sexual Violence
training · consulting · advocacy
4612 Shoal Creek Blvd. · Austin, Texas 78756
512.407.9020 (phone and fax) · www.ncdsv.org

Used by permission

Appendix B

SERVICE FOR COUNSELING AND HUMAN DEVELOPMENT

A PASTORAL COUNSELING SERVICE • TOM WARD, DIRECTOR

at West Side Presbyterian Church • 201-447-2070
6 South Monroe Street, Ridgewood, New Jersey 07450

at Fifth Avenue Presbyterian Church • 212-757-1843
7 West 55th St at 5th Ave , N Y , N Y 10019

November 3, 1995

TO WHOM IT MAY CONCERN:

This is to confirm that I worked in therapeutic relationship with Toni Gary in April, 1991 during an extended trip from Florida to New Jersey, having established a therapeutic relationship with her in 1975 at the Palisades Counseling Center in Rutherford, N.J.

During the nine hours in April, 1991 Toni related many abusive details of her married life, her anxiety about maintaining the high expectations of her family, and her fear that she would not live up to the perfectionistic requirements of her public image. At that time I diagnosed her with Acute Stress Disorder (A.P.A. DSM IV 308.3) and recommended she see a therapist in Florida on her return. Her stress was the result of the recurring and chronic traumas of her marital relationship that began in the early 1970's and included two abortions, the births of two out-of-wedlock children fathered by her husband Howard, suicide threats by Howard and a persisting fear regarding his emotional stability. She experienced an ongoing helplessness in regard to assisting Howard in his own recovery, and described dissociative symptoms of detachment and an absence of emotional reactions within herself. Recent (October, 1995) telephone conversations from Toni indicate that she may continue to dissociate in times of high anxiety, especially in the presence of Howard and around issues and events that pretain to their divorce. Dissociation is an adaptive technique of protection against recurring feelings related to trauma, and is the result of an extended history of emotional, chronic abuse.

Toni's anxiety reactions are the result of deep internal conflicts and painful psychic splits. She holds high expectations of herself to care for other's needs before her own, failing to nurture herself and yet continuing to set very high personal and professional goals. Her naivete about what appears to be an abusive relationship is typical of people whose reason for being is to please, to provide, to generally perform as caretakers, and ultimately subjugate their own needs. She is caught between the public and private woman with perfectionistic demands both internal and external as well as her desire to maintain a stable marirage and home environment for her two children and her own needs of "self".

Tom Ward
Analytic Psychotherapist
Lisc. Marriage Counselor, NJ

TW/ja